WITHDRAWN

If You See the Buddha

Northwestern University Press
Studies in Russian Literature and Theory

Founding Editor
 Gary Saul Morson

General Editor
 Caryl Emerson

Consulting Editors
 Carol Avins
 Robert Belknap
 Robert Louis Jackson
 Elliott Mossman
 Alfred Rieber
 William Mills Todd III
 Alexander Zholkovsky

If You See the Buddha

STUDIES IN THE FICTION OF IVAN BUNIN

Thomas Gaiton Marullo

NORTHWESTERN UNIVERSITY PRESS / EVANSTON, ILLINOIS

Northwestern University Press
Evanston, Illinois 60208-4210

Copyright © 1998 by Northwestern University Press.
Published 1998. All rights reserved.

Printed in the United States of America

ISBN 0-8101-1612-X

Library of Congress Cataloging-in-Publication Data

Marullo, Thomas Gaiton.
    If you see the Buddha : studies in the fiction of
Ivan Bunin / Thomas Gaiton Marullo.
       p. cm. — (Studies in Russian literature and theory)
    Includes bibliographical references and index.
    ISBN 0-8101-1612-X (alk. paper)
    1. Bunin, Ivan Alekseevich, 1870–1953—Criticism and
interpretation. 2. Bunin, Ivan Alekseevich, 1870–1953—
Knowledge—Buddhism. I. Title. II. Series.
PG3453.B9Z7678   1998
891.78'309—dc21   98-40491
                                                                                CIP

The paper used in this publication meets the minimum requirements of the American National Standard for Information Sciences—Permanence of Paper for Printed Library Materials, ANSI Z39.48-1984.

For Gloria

Contents

Preface		ix
Chapter One	Bunin as Buddhist Disciple 3	
Chapter Two	Self as Peasant: *The Village* 33	
Chapter Three	Self as Lord: *Dry Valley* 54	
Chapter Four	Self as Entrepreneur: *The Gentleman from San Francisco* 79	
Chapter Five	Self as Youth: *Mitia's Love* 102	
Chapter Six	Self as Actor: *The Elagin Affair* 127	
Chapter Seven	Self as Author: *The Life of Arsen'ev* 155	
Conclusion		189
Notes		191
Index		203

Preface

Andrew Wachtel, in a 1994 article on Ivan Bunin published in *The American Scholar*, wrote: "Ivan Bunin is undoubtedly the greatest Russian writer whom no one reads."[1] Until about 1985, Wachtel's words were accurate, if tragic. Indeed, the one constant in Bunin studies was the lack of an appreciative readership in either the former Soviet Union or the West.

With the collapse of communism, though, Bunin's works are enjoying a stunning revival in both Russia and the West. In fact, one of the most noteworthy developments in the literary life of Russian glasnost and *perestroika* has been the new national interest in the writer's life and art. Researchers document a "Bunin craze" among Russian youth;[2] and since 1985, publishing houses in the former Soviet Union have been printing Bunin's works at a feverish rate. For instance, two six-volume editions of the writer's works—one published in 1987–88, the other in 1994—are the first comprehensive editions of Bunin issued by the Russians since the 1967 nine-volume collection of his poetry and prose. (Four volumes of a new nine-tome *Collected Works* were also published in 1994.) Also, by 1991 the Russians had published no fewer than fifteen separate editions of *The Cursed Days*, Bunin's scathing account of life in Bolshevik Russia during 1918 and 1919.

New attention to Bunin has been also accorded by the West. Since 1983, publishing houses in the United States alone have printed four anthologies of his short stories in English, a new translation of his last great work, *The Life of Arsen'ev*, and two volumes of a three-volume "diary," containing selections from Bunin's diaries, letters, critical articles, and fictional works, as well as interpolations from the memoirs of his wife, Vera Muromtseva-Bunina, and from the writings of family, friends, colleagues, and critics.

Russian and Western scholarship, however, has not kept pace with the "rediscovery" of Bunin. For instance, since 1985, only three books have been published on Bunin in the former Soviet Union, all containing the same inadequacies as their predecessors in the 1960s, '70s, and '80s. As the Bunin scholar Yury Mal'tsev wrote in 1994, "It is enough to read one [Russian] monograph on Bunin to dispense with the necessity of reading the rest."³

Western investigations of Bunin have also been lacking. The three scholarly studies on Bunin—Serge Kryzytski's *The Works of Ivan Bunin* in 1971, James Woodward's *Ivan Bunin: A Study of His Fiction* in 1980, and Julian Connolly's *Ivan Bunin* in 1982—introduced Bunin to the Western reading public, but more in-depth studies of Bunin have long been needed.

Two problems have plagued scholarship on Bunin since the turn of the century. The first problem is that critics have been confounded by the many contradictions in Bunin's writing. Bunin could be a "realist," a "modern," a "liberal," and a "conservative." Even more frustrating, he exploited a plethora of philosophical, spiritual, and aesthetic systems in his effort to make sense of the world. The second problem is that Bunin's critics have tended to receive his works according to their own values and needs. They have used their studies on the writer to advance their own political and aesthetic agendas and to disclose what they loved or hated about "modern" life. Like the blind men and the elephant, they have seized an ear, trunk, or tail of Bunin's writing and assumed that it stood for the whole. Such fragmentation has generated pointless conflicts and an incoherent picture of his fiction. Woodward, in his 1980 book on Bunin, lamented:

> Western criticism . . . has thus far proved no more successful than Soviet criticism in resolving the fundamental problems posed by Bunin's art—above all, the problem of whether or not his fiction expresses a coherent view of life and the human condition. . . . Until this problem has been convincingly resolved, significant progress in the study of Bunin's fiction is difficult to envisage.⁴

The present volume, *If You See the Buddha: Studies in the Fiction of Ivan Bunin,* provides this coherence. Initially, my goal was a modest one—to establish Bunin as a "modern" writer whose images and ideas were rooted more in the twentieth century than in the nineteenth. Even achieving this goal, however, would not have adequately explained Bunin's writing and, in particular, his long and best-known fiction.

As this work progressed, however, my early contention that Bunin was a modern had to be extended to encompass a second cardinal point: Among all the systems of belief that Bunin adopted and adapted throughout his literary career, it was his abiding interest in Buddhism that best elucidates the dynamics of his writing. Key Buddhistic concepts of self, craving, enlightenment, regression, and rebirth figured prominently in Bunin's work. These ideas enabled him to make sense of his world and served as the catalyst for an *ars poetica* that tempered his philosophical and aesthetic restiveness and contributed a sense of timelessness to works from both his prerevolutionary and émigré periods.

Preface

My study of the Buddhistic influences on Bunin's writing consists of two parts. Chapter 1 discusses Bunin's enduring interest in Buddhism and, in particular, his espousal of such concepts as chain, regression, and rebirth. Chapters 2 through 7 discuss the Buddhistic underpinnings of such works as *The Village, Dry Valley, The Gentleman from San Francisco, Mitya's Love, The Elagin Affair,* and *The Life of Arsen'ev.* These six works have long been regarded as "classics" in Russian literature and as the basis for Bunin's being awarded the Nobel Prize in 1933, yet they have defied in-depth analysis and classification. What seemed to be traces of a scarcely definable eclecticism remained a stumbling block for even those who conceded strength, originality, and lifelong achievement to the work of Russia's first Nobel laureate. It is, therefore, the two-pronged thesis of this volume that the elusive quality of Bunin's greatness is his personal amalgam of fragmented, discolored, and dislocated modernistic images with timeless themes of cycle, regression, rebirth, and chain.

For their invaluable assistance at various stages in the preparation of this study, I wish to thank the following individuals: Linda Gregory and the staffs of the Departments of Reference, Interlibrary Loan, and Microtexts of the Theodore M. Hesburgh Library at the University of Notre Dame for obtaining many of the materials for this study, for researching footnotes, and for photocopying texts, and to Margaret Jasiewicz, Nancy McMahon, Sherry Reichold, and Cheryl Reed for typing correspondence and preparing the manuscript.

Several individuals deserve a special note of gratitude. Truly, this volume would not have come into being without Professor Klaus Lanzinger, chairman of the Department of German and Russian Languages and Literatures; Professor Harry Attridge, dean of the College of Arts and Letters at Notre Dame; Professor Jennifer Warlick, Director of the Institute for Scholarship in the Liberals Arts; and Professor Roger Skurski, Associate Dean of the college, who allowed me to devote a good part of my energy to this project and who provided technical and financial assistance for this study. I am also grateful to Helen Sullivan and Julia Gauchman, who, along with others of the staff of the library of the University of Illinois at Urbana-Champaign, unearthed sources, researched additional footnotes, and answered myriad questions.

I would also like to thank the many readers of this book for their suggestions and advice: Evgeny Dobrenko, George Gibian, Joan Grossman, Gary Hamburg, Serge Kryzytski, Gary Saul Morson, Marc Raeff, Maxim Shrayer, and Edward Wasiolek. A special note of gratitude is due to Andrew Durkin, Andrew Wachtel, and Caryl Emerson for their meticulous reading of the text, as well as for their excellent recommendations on revising the manuscript.

Preface

Above all, I wish to recognize my wife, Gloria Gibbs Marullo, to whom this work is dedicated, and my longstanding colleague and friend, Sister Mary Colleen Dillon, S.N.D., of the Sisters of Notre Dame of Covington, Kentucky, both of whom read the manuscript innumerable times, who kept me physically and spiritually whole during its writing, and who learned more about Ivan Bunin than they really cared to. My cats Margaret Mary, Ignatius, and Augustine provided affection and support when Bunin and I had exhausted the goodwill and cheer of everyone else. Thank you all.

T.G.M.
Notre Dame, Indiana
January 1997

If You See the Buddha

Chapter One

Bunin as Buddhist Disciple

INTRODUCTION

On 12 March 1910, an angry Bunin complained to an interviewer:

> Critics . . . are extremely conservative in their views about a writer. Early in his literary career, a writer is branded by an epithet which may have characterized his fiction then, but which becomes so fixed that it ends further discussion of his work. So it has been with me. It is easier [for critics] to keep old labels than to find new ones.[1]

In his 1915 "Autobiographical Note," Bunin elaborated on his dilemma:

> The critics rushed to brand me with labels, to establish the parameters of my talent once and for all. . . . In their view, there was never a writer who was more quiet and fixed in his views than I. . . . I was the "singer of fall, of sadness, of noblemen's nests." . . . Later they assigned me tags that were diametrically opposed. First I was a "decadent," then a "Parnassian" and a "cold master." . . . I was a symbolist, a mystic, a realist, a neorealist, a god-seeker, a naturalist, and God knows what else. The critics plastered me with so many labels that I felt like a suitcase that had traveled the world. . . . The truth, however, was that I was very far from being fixed in my views, and that I was living a life that was a hundred times more complicated and more penetrating than anything I had yet published.[2]

With hindsight, one can say that Bunin's anger was justified. By 1915, he had completed only one-third of a literary career which was to span almost seven decades, surpassing, in length, even the creative life of Leo Tolstoi. He still had before him the revolutions of 1917, his emigration to France in 1920, and the Nobel Prize for Literature in 1933, the first ever to be awarded to a Russian. Also, by 1915, Bunin had published only three of six major pieces that would ensure his literary reputation: *The Village* (1909–10), *Dry Valley* (1911), and *The Gentleman from San Francisco* (1915). He still had to write *Mitia's Love* (1924), *The Elagin Affair* (1925), and *The Life of Arsen'ev* (1927–53). Clearly, it had been much too early for labels.

Although Bunin searched for a personal philosophy in many world systems and views, there was one label that he willingly affixed to himself—he was a disciple of the Buddha who sought enlightenment for all. Indeed, it was Bunin's enduring fascination with Buddhism that can be seen as a key to unlocking the treasures of his writing. Key Buddhistic concepts of self, craving, enlightenment, regression, and rebirth are seminal motifs of his fiction and elucidate the dynamics of his thought and art.[3]

BUNIN AND BUDDHISM: THE SOURCES

It is difficult to say precisely how Bunin first became acquainted with Buddhism. Doubtless, he was keenly aware of the interest in Buddhism that swept much of the Western world at the *fin de siècle,* and which enjoyed an enthusiastic reception in many parts of Russia. "I love the East and its religions," Bunin told an interviewer in 1910. "India interests me as a cradle of humanity and religion." Three years later, he noted: "I live wherever my soul likes . . . sometimes India."[4]

Bunin was not alone in his views. Vladimir Solov'ev had enthusiastically espoused such Buddhistic beliefs as *karma* and rebirth. Konstantin Bal'mont had translated *The Life of Buddha* by the Indian philosopher and poet Asvaghosa into Russian in 1913. And Sergei Esenin believed that with the exception of Buddha and Christ, human beings were "sinners who had fallen into the abyss of debauchery."[5] Bunin's contemporaries F. Shcherbatskoi, S. Ol'denburg, and O. Rozenberg were among the most famous Russian Buddhologists. Russian bibliographies of the era list numerous editions and translations of Buddhist texts between 1887 and 1911.[6] Many of these were accessible to the general reading public, and some were even published as pulp fiction for as little as six kopecks and enjoyed two or three reprintings.

Bunin was familiar with at least two of these works. The first was entitled *A Record of Buddhistic Kingdoms: The Account by the Chinese Monk Fa-Hien of His Travels in India and Ceylon* (A.D. *399–414*) *in Search of the Buddhist Books of Discipline.* Fa-Hien was the first Chinese pilgrim to tour all of India, including the sacred spots of the Buddha. Using the account of his travels, together with his newly found knowledge, Fa-Hien wished to enlighten China.[7] Bunin also knew a second and more important work: the *Sutta-Nipata,* one of the earliest texts of the Pali canon of Buddhism. The *Sutta-Nipata* is a collection of the Buddha's discourses, thought to have been compiled after the third century before Christ. Essentially, the *Sutta-Nipata* is an anthology, written largely in verse and including stories, dialogues, lyrics, proverbs, and ballads. In it the Buddha urges his listeners to simple ethics and faith. Since the *Sutta-Nipata* contains some of the earliest and most pristine forms of Buddhistic ideas and teachings, it is the source for other Buddhistic writings and for early cultural and religious expressions of

Buddhism. The *Sutta-Nipata* was particularly popular among Russian readers and was often cited and debated by the intelligentsia (Bunin included) in the years immediately prior to the Revolution.[8]

Bunin's interest in Buddhism can also be attributed to his long-standing affection for Leo Tolstoi, whose own life and writings bear the imprint of Buddhistic thought. (Tolstoi himself wrote a small pamphlet entitled "The Buddha" that sold for one kopeck per copy in 1905 and was reprinted in 1908).[9] Expressing his affinity with Tolstoi, Bunin confided to a friend in 1938: "Tolstoi is very close to me not only as an artist . . . but also as a religious soul."[10] Bunin also took to heart the great writer's own ideas on *Nirvana*, or "Enlightenment." For instance, in *The Liberation of Tolstoy*, he cited this excerpt from Tolstoi's writings: "'Are not our constant strivings toward the future a sign that life is the expansion of consciousness? One gradually discerns that there is no such thing as the material or spiritual, but only one's passage across the boundaries of that which is eternal and endless, a place where Everything and Nothing merge: Nirvana'" (9:34).

Beyond his familiarity with several Buddhistic works and love for Tolstoi, Bunin's interest in Buddhism can be traced more concretely to his travels to India and Ceylon in 1907 and to Ceylon again in 1911. For instance, years later he told Irina Odoevtseva: "In India I thoroughly mastered [*osnovatel'no izuchil*] Buddhism. I was very attracted to its system of beliefs . . . its religious patience . . . and its great love for every living thing. . . . There were even times . . . when I very much wanted to become a Buddhist. . . ."[11]

Bunin also loved Ceylon. His imagination was particularly enthralled by the ancient Buddhist shrines at Anaradkhapura, the Valley of the Shadows of Death, the libraries and services in Kandy, the saffron-robed monks and nuns, and the native rites and lore (especially the so-called Dances of the Devil). Bunin was also mesmerized by the Edenic aura of the isle and by the legend that Adam and Eve lived there after having been expelled from Eden. "Dear Aleksei Maksimovich," Bunin wrote to Gor'kii in 1911, "how many marvelous letters I have been wanting to send to you from Ceylon. If I could tell you one-hundredth of all the fascinating and extraordinary things that we have seen and felt here."[12]

In a diary entry dated 7 March 1911, Bunin's wife, Vera Muromtseva-Bunina, elaborated:

> We are now in Kandy, in the mountain locality of Ceylon. . . . We have seen so many new things, that are unlike anything we have known before, and that are so beautiful, that I still cannot take them all in as I should. . . . Legend has it that here was paradise. Here on Ceylon is Adam's peak, i.e., a bridge on which he and Eve fled to India, after they were cast out of the garden. Yes, it is truly paradise here. I was astounded by a Buddhist service. We entered a temple for the first time in the evening. In the half-dusk, there were the din

of tambourines, the pounding of the drums, the playing on flutes, many flowers with their heavy scents, and Buddhist priests in yellow mantillas. I liked it all so much that I brought flowers to the service.[13]

Such impressions remained with the Bunins throughout their lives. Years later, indirectly commenting on the depth of Bunin's penetration into the Buddhistic culture of Ceylon, Galina Kuznetsova wrote in a diary entry, dated 29 September 1932:

> Bunin told me that when he was in Kandy, he saw the Buddhist books in the sacred library: tablets made from palm and inscribed with circular letters. He was shown them by the religious superior, a man "with insane, deep black eyes, and in a yellow robe with his right shoulder exposed." The library was underground, with latticed windows level with the water of a ditch; and, since there was so much greenery around, the room had a greenish light. The walls were very thick with drawings of dragons on them. The priest gave him one of the books as a gift; on it he wrote his name with a stylus dipped in Indian ink with gold.[14]

BUNIN AND BUDDHISM

Key Beliefs

Unquestionably, Bunin internalized key truths and images of Buddhism, its tenets, and its traditions. Both his personal and artistic writings are replete with references, implicit or direct, to Buddhistic doctrine, mythology, and beliefs. (He even wanted to write a play about the "tragedy of the Buddha's life.")[15] Colleagues and contemporaries attest to Bunin's enthusiastic reception of Buddhistic images and ideas. Georgy Alekseev, for instance, recalls that Bunin in 1919 professed that "this Buddhism is a remarkable thing" and that "its teachings . . . contain so much of the sun's blinding eye and soul."[16] Boris Zaitsev summed up the case of Bunin and Buddhism by succinctly noting in 1924 that "Bunin responded to the world with an Asiatic-Buddhist sensitivity. The Buddha was quite close to him."[17]

From his writings and those of others, one can confidently infer some of the reasons why Bunin found Buddhism so attractive and which Buddhistic ideas he took for his own. For instance, Bunin was drawn to a religion that was at once a philosophy of life, a system of ethics, and an informal but practical way to salvation. Bunin also admired the flexible, egalitarian nature of Buddhistic belief—the *dharma*, or "sacred law," that was the province of all. It could be adapted easily to indigenous ideas and conditions,[18] and it espoused a "middle way" between worldliness and asceticism.

Bunin saw that the Buddha's disaffection with life in the fifth and sixth centuries before Christ was not unlike his own in the early twentieth. Siddartha Gautama (the Buddha's family name) had also grown up in times of uncertainty and change involving, for example, national disunity, urban growth, a "capitalist" economy, and religious ferment. Moreover, Bunin identified with the many trials and travails that beset Buddha in his life. Particularly intriguing was Mara, who in Buddhistic mythology was the Tempter and Lord of Passion and Pleasure, and who tried unsuccessfully to thwart the Buddha in his search for truth. Bunin could easily imagine himself, like Gautama, in struggles with demonic hordes, natural disasters, and Mara's three daughters, "Desire," "Pleasure," and "Passion," who tried to seduce with promises of worldly power and glory.

A truth that appealed deeply to Bunin was that once the Buddha achieved enlightenment, he did not keep secret his ecstasy and joy. Instead, as the "Awakened or Illumined One," Gautama began a public ministry that ended only with the "great total extinction," his death in the eightieth year of his life.

Key Concepts

Bunin integrated many key Buddhistic doctrines into his own worldview. For instance, he accepted the doctrines of *anatman,* or "no-self," and of *anitya,* or the "impermanence of all things." Simply put, Gautama had taught that there is no eternal or absolute being. He asserted that phenomenal realities—humankind included—are in constant flux. They exist only as "aggregates" of elements that are subject to decay and are without permanence or enduring selfhood. Stability and predictability are, therefore, only illusions, and things exist not as "being" but as "becoming," in a constant shifting and rearranging of aggregates. Only at brief moments—if ever—can reality be the sum of its parts.

In this system of flux, the individual ego or self is also a delusion. The objects by which ego identifies itself—for example, fortune, power, social position, family, body, even mind—lack substance and only hinder the genuine understanding of life. Most crucially, Bunin wholeheartedly accepted Gautama's idea that existence is subject to the *paticca-samuppada,* or the "chain of causation." This "chain" is difficult to understand, but its value and purpose are clear. Cause and effect operate via "links" of human ignorance, desire, and craving. Acts deriving from these links do not express or achieve freedom; they shackle humankind in *samsara,* in "circular" return to existence. As a result of predominantly flawed—"in chain"—choices, most of humankind is trapped in continuous rounds of births, deaths, and rebirths and of misery, suffering, and pain.[19]

Closely associated with Bunin's use of the chain of causation is another Buddhistic tenet, *karma.* "Karma" means "deed" or "act," and, according to the concept of karma, the present state of individuals results from their past existences. This is so because karma also includes the notion that individuals reap what they sow. Good deeds bring pleasant and happy results and create a tendency toward similar good acts; evil deeds bring on bad results and a tendency toward repeated evil actions. Since karma is cyclic—that is, just one part of a theory of "becoming"—some karma bear fruit within the same life in which they are committed, but others are realized in the immediately succeeding life or in a remote future life.

Karma, being the stimulus that sets in motion the "chain of causation," binds humans to samsara, to endless cycles of rebirth. Each existence takes on a different form, because, at death, karma determines the form of the next birth. Bunin found it particularly intriguing that, because of karma, individuals can be reborn as humans, subhumans, or superhumans. They can become deified, or (and this is the more frequent case in Bunin) they can regress to neanderthals, humanoids, animals, ghosts, or inhabitants of the hells. As Bunin wrote in "The Book of My Life" (1924), "Each in his own life must and will feel that which I also feel: that . . . *karma* is not a philosophy, but a physiology."[20]

Belief in karma, samsara, no-self, the impermanence of all things, and the chain of causation were cornerstones in the Buddha's system of belief. These concepts helped Bunin to understand pain and sorrow in life; through them he sought enlightenment. Notwithstanding Bunin's own problems in life, he readily accepted Gautama's idea that individuals bear the responsibility for their lives and that they have the power to break free from chain and rebirth. The process will be shown to be as simple as it is complicated.

"The Four Noble Truths"

In Buddhism, the individual seeking enlightenment must accept and live by "Four Noble Truths":

1. *The Noble Truth of Suffering:* Suffering is unavoidable in life. It is rooted in the experiences of birth, frustration, sickness, old age, and death. It is concealed in union with the unpleasant and in separation from the pleasant. It is generic to confusion or ignorance about life and to the failure to obtain what one wishes. In short, since clinging to existence causes misery and pain, one must seek to endure suffering nobly and to become detached, free.

2. *The Noble Truth of the Cause of Suffering:* Suffering is brought on by craving, or "thirst." Craving is always rooted in motives of self-interest, self-assertion, and self-aggrandizement—the desire of ego to possess people, ideas, or things.

Yearnings for life, power, security, and death, along with yielding to the demands of ego or self, ignite the cravings that energize chain and rebirth. For this reason, romantic love is condemned by Buddhism, as it is in Bunin's fiction. Such love is rejected not because it is morally inappropriate per se but because it inflates the self and binds the lover to the illusory object of its love.

3. *The Noble Truth of the Cessation of Suffering:* With appropriate discipline, craving can be extinguished, relinquished, or repressed.

4. *The Noble Truth of the Path That Leads to the Cessation of Suffering:* According to the Buddha, there exists an Eightfold Path of Right that is divided into three categories: (1) *morality,* which includes right speech, right conduct, and right livelihood, as well as the virtues of joy, friendship, compassion, gentleness, and equanimity; (2) *discipline,* which includes right effort, right mindfulness, and right concentration, and which distinguishes between the permanent and impermanent, the pleasant and the unpleasant; and (3) *wisdom,* which includes right views and right intentions and which instructs one in such truths as no-self, the impermanence of things, the chain of causation, the cycle of rebirths, and, the destructiveness of craving and desire.

Nirvana

It is clear from both Bunin's personal and fictional writings that he accepted the Four Truths as the precondition for the Buddhist notion of *Nirvana,* or "enlightenment": a blissful heaven-haven state of tranquility, freedom, and insight in which, metaphorically speaking, the individual leaves the land of rebirth, sails over the "restless ocean of suffering," extinguishes the flames of illusion and desire, and reaches "the harbor of refuge," "the cool cave," and "the farther shore" (poetic images that appear in *The Gentleman from San Francisco*).

Individuals seeking Nirvana pass from sensual desire to inner serenity to indifference to everything, and finally to the abandoning of good or bad states of mind. The rewards for such effort defy description because those who attain enlightenment possess supreme purity and consciousness. These souls repose in a condition of spatial infinity, beyond the perception of form or plurality. So long as these "Enlightened Ones" continue to focus on the infinity of consciousness and on the nonexistence of everything else, they remain in a state in which there is neither perception nor nonperception: peace.

Personal Touches: Memory, Enlightenment, and the "Path of Return"

Although Bunin embraced the method and tenets of Buddhism and used them substantively as a basis for his own life and writings, he devised highly personal variations on their themes. Generally speaking, Bunin simplified much of Buddha's thought. He espoused beliefs that were immediate, sensual, and pragmatic and eschewed ideas that were cerebral, celestial, and obscure.[21] The idea of chain readily fired Bunin's imagination, but the concept of Nirvana needed rethinking before he could claim it as his own.

Essentially, Bunin believed that individuals sought enlightenment by abandoning the "Path of Egression" (*Put' Vystupleniia*) in the present and by pursuing the "Path of Return" (*Put' Vozrata*) to the past (9:18–19). In so doing, they relinquished self, extinguished desire, and found a meaningful place in life, history, and the universe. Also, they came to understand life in a way that they could not have otherwise; and the ensuing ecstasy and peace that they achieved helped them to endure and even to love life in a modern, yearning-filled world.

Bunin understood the Path of Return quite literally, for he often sought refuge in the past. Bunin's recollections of "times gone by" were not, as many of his critics claimed, the saccharine or hallucinatory ramblings of a *barin* who yearned for estates, serfs, and the like. Rather, Bunin's reminiscences were an ongoing creative process, an end in itself, through which he foraged in various "pasts" (genuine and mythopoetic) to find enlightenment and to bring warmth and continuity to the present.

If the chain was the chief obstacle to Bunin in his thought and writing, then memory became the chief guide in his quest. Bunin used memory as a *poputchik*, or "fellow traveler," who endowed him with psychosensory awareness, allowing him to live in "joyous union with the eternal and temporal, with the near and far, with all times and countries, with all the past and present."[22]

Such a transcendent power as memory was described by Bunin in "Night" and *The Liberation of Tolstoi:* "Certain people . . . can pass through the Chain of their ancestors . . . and with special force, sense not only their own time, but also another time, the past. They can sense not only their own country and tribe, but also others, alien to them. . . . They can 'reincarnate themselves' by means of a lively, visual, and sensitive 'memory'" (9:33).

Bunin also grasped that, when attended by memory, he could recast the dreaded notions of chain and rebirth in a new and positive light. He came to understand that ontological "cycles" and "links" could actually set him free. They could move him quickly to various destinations in the past; they could even facilitate genuine "meetings of the minds" with the individuals he found there. Guided by memory, Bunin could travel down "the long path of many, many existences . . . and merge with his savage ancestor, with his awareness, with all the imagery of the ancestor's thought and great subconscious" (5:302).

Most engagingly, memory, for Bunin, was the strength and power of the psyche, a Sophia-like "feminine"[23] power that could literally renew the face of the earth. Memory could transcend spatial, temporal, and biological confines.[24] It could serve as a moral imperative, activate good karma, and counter the cravings of self, the temptations of Mara, and the oblivion of death. It could also stir intuition and creativity, as well as champion love, wisdom, and reconciliation. In short, Bunin's memory was the charisma of unified body and soul, a prism that refracted his experiences of surroundings and self, and a support in times of trouble and pain.

"How do I live?" Bunin wrote in his diary in 1917. "I keep remembering and remembering."[25] Eight years later he affirmed in his story "The Rose of Jericho" (1925), "There is neither separation nor loss as long as there live my soul, my Love, my Memory" (5:7).[26]

BUNIN AND THE "PAST"
The Enlightenment of Ancestry, Culture, and Primordial Existence

Bunin's Path of Return—his "past" born of memory—requires clarification. As will be seen in *Dry Valley* and in other works, Bunin cared little for remembering the historical facts of pre-Emancipation Russia, which prefigured the troubles of the present. He wrote in his "Notes" circa 1930:

> Those who died two or three thousand years before us do not share a likeness with those who died and were buried a half-century ago in some repulsive coffin, in a jacket or uniform and in dead-men's shoes. Two, three thousand years—this is already a great expanse, a liberation from time, from earthly corruption, and the sad and noble consciousness of the vanity of all glory and honors. (9:365)

Rather, the times that Bunin, in his search for enlightenment, traced imaginatively in his passage back along the chain were highly selective affairs that traversed three ages: family history, ancient and medieval civilization, and primordial existence.

When Bunin wrote in his "Anonymous Notes" (1921) that his life was "without beginning or end,"[27] he implied that his personal history extended beyond time and space and that, specifically, he communed with ancestors who lived collectively in him.

He elaborated in his sketch "The Book of My Life" (1924):

> My birth was by no means my beginning. My beginning lies in that (completely inscrutable) murk, in which I was conceived before my birth, in my father and mother, in my grandfathers and great-grandfathers, for they are also I, only in another form, but where many things have so repeated themselves that they have become one and the same. . . . More than once, I felt that I was not only an infant, a lad, an adolescent, but also my father, grandfather, great-grandfather, and ancestor.[28]

Such reflections, of course, testify to Bunin's acceptance of the Buddhist idea of rebirth. They also make clear that when he "remembered," he saw yet another way in which chain and samsara could be salvific. When these were joined to memory, they showed that (1) the individual need not be an isolated self who had to outpace death or to bludgeon his or her short-lived way in the world, but that (2) the individual was, in reality, the most recent link in a long chain of human beings who had not died permanently but who continued to share in the joys and sorrows of life of their descendants.

Simply put, when framed by memory, chain and rebirth allowed Bunin—and all souls—to join the immortal family of humankind.

The Memory of Ancient and Medieval Culture

Beyond memories of family and clan, Bunin also traveled down the chain and the Path of Return to reflect upon the cultural monuments of history and the religious testaments of the ancient and medieval world. He marveled at the pyramids of Egypt, the temples of Ceylon, and the churches and monasteries of Germany, Russia, and Provence. His mind revered "the lost kingdoms of the East and South, the regions of dead, forgotten lands, their ruins and cemeteries" (9:365). His soul drank in the liturgical music of Bach and Palestrina, and he became a "wild fanatic" whenever he heard the "Dies irae," the "Stabat Mater," or the chanting of the cantor of the Warsaw synagogue.[29] Such memorials imbued with the lasting influence of enlightenment preserved the presence of good karma and reinstated the triumph of the Eightfold Path of Right.

Restored amid churches and shrines, Bunin came to understand that humankind need not be condemned en masse. Instead, individuals could rise to new values and ideals, and even in modern times, they could affirm faith, love, and hope. As catalysts for culture, human beings could also be "reborn" to higher lives, to levels approaching the gods. It was observable to Bunin that human evil was rarely enshrined; human goodness, on the other hand, had repeatedly been given enduring forms that could enlighten later ages.

Bunin wrote in his story "The Goddess of Reason" (1924):

> What do we know? Only one thing is certain: From the life of man, from the centuries and generations, there remains on this earth only that which is noble, good, and splendid, only these. All that is mean, evil, base, and stupid leaves not a trace in the end. . . . And what has remained? . . . The best pages of the best books; legends about honor, conscience, self-sacrifice, and noble deeds; marvelous statues and songs; great and holy graves; Greek temples; and Gothic cathedrals with their heavenly and wondrous stained glass, and the thundering and wail of their organs.[30]

Given Bunin's interpretation, his ecstasy over even minute historical artifacts is understandable. A collection of Egyptian scarabs, for example, gave him a moment of triumph over his omnipresent enemy: death. He wrote in his story "Scarabs" (1924):

> The entire history of Egypt, all of life for the past five thousand years, yes, five thousand years of life and glory—and the result is this tiny collection of scarabs! But these scarabs are the symbols of resurrection, of eternal life. Should one smile bitterly or rejoice? I say rejoice! Rejoice in everything that is undying; rejoice in all the great marvels of the earth. (5:144)[31]

Indeed, Bunin's love for religious culture was so ardent that after he had seen the spiritual monuments of the ancient and medieval world, he claimed that, were he able, he would "burn all heretics with his own hands."[32]

Pressing Further: Primordial Existence

The deepening peace and optimism that Bunin discovered in his reflections on family and culture enticed him to press further down-chain and the Path of Return to prehistory, to paradise, to Nirvana.

The paradise of Bunin's memory assumed many forms, but invariably it was a place that was enchanting, remote, and unspoiled by modernity. At times, Bunin's Eden was an abandoned estate, a deserted riverbank, or a mountain Shangri-La. The common requirement was that these be places in which he could see himself as a sole Adamic dweller: fresh, spontaneous, free of the solicitations of ego, and living in a pervasive silence broken only by the ancient rhythms of life.

In his search for enlightenment, Bunin particularly yearned for the pre-Fall garden or, more accurately, the post-Flood Arafat in Genesis. As he told Sedykh, he envisioned a world made whole by "a new cosmic spring . . . and bereft of pre-Flood foulness."[33]

Sometimes he got his wish. Having crossed the equator in 1911, he wrote in his diary: "We came upon a timeless bright summer, a completely new world which spoke to me about some long forgotten, heavenly, and blissful life." Three days later, after having journeyed with naked rowers on a river in Ceylon, he wrote to brother Iulii: "My feeling for that which is warm, primordial, and paradisiacal has again become alive and strong . . . a noble and awe-inspiring order."[34] And in the "Book of My Life," he continued: "The Buddha says: 'I remember myself even as a baby goat.' And, being in the land of the Buddha, in the tropics of India, I myself once felt . . . that I had lived in this paradisiacal warmth and richness."[35]

Bunin also found that he also could find "paradise" within the recesses of his mind. When physical travel proved impossible, dreams, creative visions, pictures on walls and in books, even bouts of feverish illness moved him to Nirvana. For instance, in his story "The Unhurried Spring" (1923), he wrote:

> I felt that the tie between me and my world was . . . being torn to pieces . . . and that I was retreating into an "Elysium of the past" . . . a strikingly alive existence in which dead men with sky-blue eyes had once lived, in empty cas-

tles, in Muscovite woods . . . a single source of happiness, a most private abode in my soul. (5:126–27)

Three years later, he added: "I once saw a picture of 'paradise' in a book. . . . In it was the 'tree of knowledge of good and evil,' together with the Tempter wound around a naked, long-haired Eve. And I . . . immediately felt that I once had been in that 'splendid' garden."[36]

Since Bunin could find Eden both without and within, the enlightenment and Nirvana, proffered by his fellow traveler, memory, were literally his for the taking.

RETURNING TO THE PRESENT
The Fruits of Enlightenment

By "remembering" the worlds of his ancestors, of ancient and medieval civilizations, and, finally, of paradise and primordial existence, Bunin viewed modern life with fresh insight. He was literally filled with the wisdom of the ages, a newfound awareness that gave him confidence and strength and that alleviated periods of anger and despair.

Bunin also returned to the here and now with a self that was intuitive, emotive, and open to life. "If the heart believes it is so, then it is so," he explained to Kataev.[37] "*Gefühl ist alles*," he quoted Goethe in his diary in 1923. "Reality is only what I feel. The rest is rubbish."[38]

"Born again," as it were, Bunin always reentered his own time, scornful of "useless philosophizing" (5:300) and, in particular, the alleged primacy of rational, Western thought. Such a worldview, he believed, was, like everything else in Europe, "constricted and confined."[39] Bunin came to understand that the human race should reflect on the world with Eastern (i.e., Buddhist) simplicity and let creation yield its secrets to those who smelled, watched, and listened, not to those who analyzed or polluted the air with self-motivated thoughts and ideas.

"I feel *everything* physically," Bunin wrote in his diary in 1922, "I have always taken in the world through its smells, colors, and light . . . and all so sharply that, good God, it hurts."[40] "The thought that is uttered is a lie," Bunin quoted Tyutchev in his diary a year later, "Three-quarters of any human conversation is also always a lie. . . . It's all boasting and bragging."[41]

On these returns to the present from the past, Bunin also saw life as "sacredly stable."[42] Existence was rhythm and wonderment, not riddle and wrath; it gave awareness, not answers. Akin to Buddhistic teaching, it was made up of *khanavada*—"flashes," "instants," or "pulsations" of intense experience that enshrined the passing moment, kindled aliveness and joy, stemmed the riptides of change, and gave meaning to life. Bunin wrote in his travelogue "The Waters Are Many" (1925–26): "I gaze into the empty expanse of 'many waters' . . . and with the same question in my heart: for what reason and why? . . . But in this divine numbness . . . incomprehensible, but not meaningless—I found a holy calm" (5:327).

Beyond intuitive and emotive rewards, Bunin's "remembering" also caused him to recognize his artistic androgyny. Memory, his Sophia, claimed him as her own, and released the creative "female" within Bunin. He told Kuznetsova in 1933, "The fact of the matter is that with the years, and especially now, I . . . feel in myself . . . the embodiment of all that is wonderful and feminine, something of a oneness within me."[43]

Toward a Selfless Life

The post-paradise enlightened Bunin returned from the past possessing two life truths: there is intrinsic beauty in the world, and humankind is capable of spiritual fellowship. Figuratively speaking, Bunin's sojourns to the past acted like an elixir. After he had traversed the Path of Return, Bunin related to his environs as a disciple of the Buddha and of the "yellow-robed brethren" he so admired. His understanding of Gautama's beliefs may have been highly personalized, but he diligently practiced his version of the Master's Way. For instance, Bunin took to heart Gautama's injunctions that the seeker of truth wander alone, seek out quiet places, and strive to be controlled, collected, and content.

Indeed, Bunin often impressed his friends and colleagues with his Buddhist-like bearing, and his new and reflective way of looking upon the world. Kuznetsova, for instance, wrote in a 1927 diary entry that "Bunin lived his life like Buddhist monks . . . people who embark on a spiritual journey, and who gradually 'purify' themselves."[44] Several years later, she noted that whenever Bunin recalled his youth, "his eyes did not see us . . . and that he would be off somewhere else. Looking at him, I thought about hermits, mystics, and yogis—those who live in the world they summon forth.[45]

Bunin himself often described the interior experience of this change. "What a great joy merely to exist!" he exclaimed to his nephew, Nikolai Pusheshnikov, in 1911. "If I had no arms and legs, I would be content only to sit . . . and to look at the setting of the sun. This would not prevent me from being happy, for only one thing is necessary: to sit and to breathe."[46]

Tellingly, whenever Bunin enjoyed a glimpse into Nirvana, he was so taken by the natural beauty of life that he wished to live as long as possible— even for all time. "People live gloomily," he told an interviewer in 1913. "This seems to me strange and surprising. . . . Life is so interesting. Indeed, if I could find someone who could guarantee me a life of ten thousand years, I would not hesitate to strike up a bargain with him, whatever the conditions."[47]

Just as important to Bunin as his recognition of the innate beauty of the world was his post-paradisal belief in *sobornost'*. This opened his heart to "spiritual affiliation" with the people of this life and, more poignantly, with those of the past.

In direct contrast to much of the thought of his time, Bunin had little use for messianic nationalism and for the political, social, and economic unions that promised heaven on earth. Such coalitions, he reasoned, were self-motivated in that they kept their members from "wandering" and from finding inner peace and solitude. "I laughed at both Marxists and Populists," Bunin's narrator says in "Without Kith or Kin," "and I told them that I could become a socially minded individual only . . . if it could make me the least bit happy personally" (2:169).

In place of emerging "-isms," Bunin advocated spiritual "unions," such as the psychic bonds between himself and the people he had met on the Path of Return. Bonding with such individuals, he believed, nurtured culture, safeguarded Memory, and endowed life with faith, hope, and love. Indeed, for Bunin, it was the people of the past—not the political, social, or economic demagogues of the present—who were the rightful teachers of society. For instance, having recalled a 1911 visit to the remains of Ramses the Great in Egypt, Bunin commented in "The Scarabs": "Just think: Here I was next to the Great Ramses himself, his actual body . . . his very self! . . . My heart is linked to a heart . . . which, in those legendary days, just like in our time, so staunchly refused to believe in death and affirmed only life. All will pass away—only this faith will not pass away!" (5:144–45).

ADDITIONAL LESSONS: COMING TO GRIPS WITH PAST, PRESENT, AND FUTURE

Whenever Bunin came away from the past, and, specifically, whenever his spirit was possessed by a reverence for life and by the *sobornost'* of humankind, he found delight in the very things that had grieved him in the present. After he had remembered, the liberated Bunin could transmute any present sorrow into joy. He could effect a similar metamorphosis of his view of past and future. For Bunin, the magic of memory's wand could soothe and transform the trials of youth, the terror of sickness, and dread of old age. No evil was impervious to the creative power of memory.

For instance, whereas Bunin had often regarded his adolescence and young adulthood in terms of struggle and pain, in the company of memory, he saw them as precious, a godsend. They were times that were marvelous, formative, and replete with the wisdom and strength that he needed for the present.

Bunin elaborated in "Night":

> Many times I have experienced something miraculous. I return to those fields where I was once a child, a youth—and as I look around, I suddenly feel that the many long years that I have lived since then have never existed. In no way

is this a recollection; no, I am simply my former self again. I again have the same relationship with the fields, the air of the meadowlands, the Russian sky, the very same perception of all the world that I had right here, on this country path, in the days of my childhood and youth! In these moments I have often thought: every moment that I have lived, has left . . . its mark on the infinite and most treasured records of my Ego—and now several of them have suddenly come to life. . . . Another second—and they will again fade into the darkness of my being. But let them; I know that they exist. "Nothing perishes—but is only altered." (5:303–4).

Whenever Bunin had roamed the past, he could cast aside the rancor occasioned by the idea that his birth was an accident, a cruel twist of fate—just a new round in the endless cycle of human misery and pain. He could understand that though he was not the center of the universe, he was, nevertheless, a small, integral part. He could grasp that his mortal beginning, like everyone else's, was a joyful defiance of death. Each birth repudiated time and space, perpetuated memory and culture, and ensured Adam's lineage and the promised dominion over the earth.

In "The Book of My Life," Bunin recorded this testimony to his beliefs: "It is no meaningless accident that I have been fated to live neither in the time of Christ or Tiberius, nor in Judea or on the island of Capri, but here in so-called France, in the so-called twentieth century. Throughout my long life with its papers and books, travels and dreams, I have convinced myself . . . that I have always lived everywhere from time immemorial."[48] Sixteen years later, he summarized in *The Liberation of Tolstoi:* "This world and my life is only one of innumerable possibilities of other worlds and other lives . . . it is only one of the innumerable stages which I am passing through" (9:34).

Succored by memory, Bunin could also feel reconciled about whatever his future might hold. In circumstances that threatened him day and night, he could be the supreme optimist. He knew that the "coming of dawn is inevitable,"[49] and he hoped that everyone would know joy and peace. "Let all beings be happy," Bunin paraphrased an aphorism from the *Sutta-Nipata* in 1912, "the weak and the strong, the seen and the unseen, the born and the unborn."[50]

Reentering the present enlightened by the past, Bunin could similarly dismiss physical and psychological decline. For instance, he greeted his forty-ninth birthday with the joy that he was still the man of his youth and that he was alive to experience another day.

He exclaimed in "Night":

Not long ago, having perchance awakened at dawn, I was suddenly staggered by the thought of my age. I had thought that a person who had lived forty or fifty years was some unique, almost awesome being. And now I, too, have finally become such a being. "What then am I," I said to myself, "What exactly have I now become?" And . . . looking at myself as one would a stranger—how marvelous that we can do such things—I . . . felt that I was absolutely the same person I had been at age ten or twenty. I . . . looked into the mirror: yes, my face was now gaunt, my features were rigid, there were silvery patches on my temples, the color of the eyes was somewhat faded. . . . But so what? And with singular spriteliness, I got up and went into the other rooms, still barely brightening, still nocturnally serene, but already taking in the new, slowly dawning day. . . . And suddenly I again experienced that ineffable feeling that I have experienced all my life when I happened to awake at daybreak—a feeling of great happiness, the childlike, trustful, soul-touching sweetness of life, the beginning of something completely new, good, and splendid—a feeling of intimacy, brotherhood, and unity with everyone on earth. (5:304)[51]

Enlightened by the past and convinced both of the beauty of life and of the potential for universal fellowship, Bunin looked calmly to the future. The motifs of dying days, autumns, and winters that most critics deemed the stuff of Bunin's fiction told only the first half of the writer's creative story. Invariably, these were followed by bright tomorrows and "gradual springs" (5:118), by resurrections in which a "mass of dry, prickly stalks" became a "bouquet of pink flowers" (5:7).[52]

Even Bunin's inordinately dreaded enemy, death, no longer frightened him. Returning from the past, Bunin saw death not as personal extinction but rather as a great adventure: a "vital awakening," the "final liberation," and the "pathway to life" (9:11, 15, 33). Death had become a phenomenon without which existence, in its fullest sense, would be trivial, unjustified, and incomplete. "The hour of death is not so terrible as we think," he told the émigré writer and critic Marc Aldanov. "For without it, neither the world, nor man could exist."[53] Indeed, he believed that he had experienced "rebirth" several times in life, and that multiple personalities arose and faded within him. "A man is reborn every seven years," Bunin wrote in his story "Night." "That is, he dies as imperceptibly as he comes back to life. So I, too, have been reborn many times. . . . I was dying but I was also living, I have died over and over again" (5:301).[54]

BUNIN AND BUDDHISM:
THE CASE IN FICTION

A Buddhist ethos overtly figures in Bunin's works for a period of little more than twenty years, beginning in 1914 with "The Brothers" and ending with *The Liberation of Tolstoi* in 1937. These works clearly bear the influence of Buddhist ideas, while they vary widely in emphasis, genre, and form. Some make only cursory or allusive reference to Buddha's life and thought. For instance, in the sketch "On the Night Sea" (1923), Bunin's narrator gives a brief account of Gautama's love for his wife, Yasodhara (5:104). Other stories are veiled allegories drawing from Buddhistic legend and myth. In "Gautami" (1919), a peasant-turned-princess follows the path of her namesake (Gautama), and renounces family and wealth to join a Buddhistic sisterhood. In "The Son" (1916), an early sketch for *The Elagin Affair*, Bunin's heroine, Madame Marot (compare Mara), demands that her young lover, Emile, kill her. Still other pieces, like "The Brothers" or *The Liberation of Tolstoi*, are heavily laced with citations from the *Sutta-Nipata*.

Close analysis of these stories allows one to observe Bunin's additional improvisations on Buddhism, and in particular, Nirvana and enlightenment. For instance, Bunin thought that, in theory, access to Nirvana was an either/or matter. For him, there existed only two types of people: individuals who pursued worldly notions of security and success and a precious few who disavowed societal sham and who sought enlightenment. He wrote in the story "Night" (1925):

> The first, huge category [of people] are those who are fixed in their own definite time, and who are dedicated to worldly building and action. They are people who seem to be almost without a past, without ancestors, faithful links in that Chain about which the wisdom of India speaks (5:306).

Such "men of action" Bunin contrasted with another group, the

> nonbuilders and nondoers . . . actual destroyers, who have recognized the vanity of action and building. These are people who dream and contemplate and wonder at themselves and the world; they are the "philosophers," who have already responded to the ancient call, "Abandon the Chain!" and who crave to dissolve and disappear into the All-One! . . . But these "nonbuilders" also suffer fiercely, grieving as they do for all people, for all their previous incarnations, and especially for each moment of their present existence. They are endowed with a great wealth of perceptions which they have received from their countless ancestors. They sense the infinitely remote links of the Chain, of being; marvelously (and perhaps not for the last time?) they have resurrected in their person the strength and vigor, the bodily essence, of their forefathers in paradise. (5:306)

It was this second category of people, the "philosophers" who saw a purpose and life beyond self, that Bunin pinpointed as the beginning of enlightenment for humankind. He wrote in *The Liberation of Tolstoi* that most people journey the "Path of Egression" because they grasp only temporary, corporeal being and live as an "I" isolated from the "All."[55] These people could, if they so wished, follow the "Path of Return" and live a "spiritual existence." Specifically, they could relinquish the desire to take and develop the will to give back. They could surrender to the urge to fuse with the "one life, the one 'I,'" and reign supreme (9:18–19).

In theory, therefore, Bunin presented individuals with bivalent options. They could lead either a self-centered or a selfless life; they could hate or love existence; they could wreak havoc on life or offer guiding light for humankind.

Working through many variations on these themes, Bunin sometimes sought to present the renunciation of desire and self to be a simple, spontaneous matter. Princess Gautami, for instance, moves quickly to Nirvana, rejecting her life of power and ease without visible effort or regret. "Blessed are the meek at heart, who have broken the Chain" (5:25), the narrator of "Gautami" summarizes.

In other variations, Bunin has characters approach enlightenment with effort that is more physical than spiritual. They climb mountains, roam forests, and brave winds and seas to swear fealty to Gautama and to renounce cravings for life and happiness. For example, the anchorite-monk in Bunin's story "The Night of Renunciation" (1921) first addresses the Buddha in "firm and sonorous tones": "Glory to Thee on High, O Hallowed One, O All-Enlightened One, O Conqueror of Desire." Defying the night chaos as well as the "countless fiery eyes" that peer out from the forest behind him, he then renounces Mara and renews his own profession of faith:

> All in vain, Mara! In vain, O Thousand-Eyed One, dost Thou tempt me, You who soar above the earth in cloudbursts and storms, You who are fecund and fragrant anew with the putrescence of graves, You who give birth to new life out of dust and rot! Get thee hence, Mara! As a drop of rain runneth down and away from the smooth leaf of a lotus tree, so doth Desire run off my soul! (5:39)

Seeking a tie between ideology and practice, Bunin expanded his circle of philosophers to include historical figures: people who had actually stilled craving in their lives. As he wrote in "Night," such individuals belonged to a "regal tribe of geniuses and saints" (5:302). They included Gautama, King Solomon, Francis of Assisi, Mohammed, and Bunin's saint for modern times, Leo Tolstoi.

In this group, Bunin distinguished several features that made them candidates for canonization. They were individuals of great intellect and power who had traveled the Paths of Egression and of Return. They had been "first great sinners, but then great saints; first great accumulators, but then great distributors." They

> had experienced the curse and happiness of . . . especially powerful Egos. They had felt a craving for the greater assertion of the Self; but, at the same time, they possessed a greater awareness (by virtue of the accumulated experience acquired during the time spent in the endless Chain of existences) of the vanity of this craving, as well as of a keen sensation of Universal Life. (5:302)

In their youth, Gautama, Solomon, Mohammed, and Tolstoi had "greedily embraced the world"; they were "gorillas . . . terrifying in their strength, immeasurably sensual . . . and merciless in every satiation of their lust." Later in life, though, these men were "reborn" to a higher stage in life: superhumans. Having discerned a life beyond ego and self, they "cursed [worldly] temptations" (5:303). They became "hesitant, pensive, doleful, and humane . . . [but also seized] by a sensation of the All and of one's inevitable dissolution within It." (5:302–3)[56]

Bunin came to realize, though, that his idealistic variation on the theory of enlightenment did not accord well with the observable practice of it. It was only very exceptional individuals, Bunin gradually understood, who could move sequentially to Nirvana and who could live without desire and without succumbing recurrently to the demands of a permanent ego or self. For ordinary mortals, the complicated and frustrating task of trying to live selflessly had to be played out amidst desires for power, wealth, and other Mara-induced temptations. These temptations, furthermore, assaulted them in forms from larger than life to the embarrassingly small—and in every complicated combination thereof.

If most characters in Bunin's Buddhist-based stories fail to attain Nirvana, the reason is straightforward. They recognize the futility of desire, but they cannot escape its seductive power. "Verily, verily I say onto thee," Gautama tells the anchorite-monk in "The Night of Renunciation," "thou wilt deny me again and again for the sake of Mara, for the sake of that sweet deceit that is mortal life" (5:40).

Another significant variation, of course, is Bunin's characters who rebel outright against Buddhist teachings. Zotov, the hero in Bunin's story "The Compatriot" (1916), feels that Gautama's instruction is "appallingly inapplicable." Gautama's shrines are repugnant; his monks are "insane" (4:402, 404). The captain in the story "The Dreams of Chang" (1916) deplores the Buddha's withdrawal from love and life. He tells his dog Chang:

> All these Buddhas . . . You listen to what they say about this love of the universe and of all things corporeal . . . [about] this Path of all that exists, and which no one can resist. . . . Every minute we want to turn our desire not only to the soul of a beloved woman, but also even to the entire universe as well! . . . I am too fond of happiness, and all too often do I lose my way: dark and evil is this Path. (4:377)

Bunin believed that ordinary mortals, if they ever broke through to Nirvana at all, had to experience liberation and the process of "escape" and "return" over and over again, since they quickly capitulated to bad karma and to crassness, ambition, and ignorance that had shackled them before. The chain of causation that Gautama believed operative in the world thus caused its victims perverse pleasure as well as searing pain. Convinced of this same belief, Bunin envisioned that humankind rushed periodically either to relish the chain's enticements or to escape its shackles. On one hand, when fettered by the chain, individuals enjoyed power and position in life; they took solace in an ego that could exercise some control in the world. On the other hand, human nature knew too well the heaviness of the chain's shackles. Cravings and the desires of self banished inner freedom and peace. Captives of the chain regressed to humanoids and animals, devils and ghosts, and also in Bunin's fiction, to modernist tangles of lines, angles, arcs, circles, and dots. ("Goyaesque visions," the critic Gleb Struve summarily pronounced on Bunin's writing.)[57] Hence the key dilemma of Bunin's fiction, as well as the centering force of his art lies in this: the conflict between "the torment of leaving the Chain, of being separated from it, of being conscious of its vanity—and of its special, awesome charm" (5:306).

DEFINING A PROTOTYPE: BUNIN'S "THE BROTHERS"

Bunin's story "The Brothers," which he wrote almost exactly in midlife, occupies a special place in his fiction. In no other work did Bunin so overtly use and espouse Buddhistic beliefs. In no other work, either, did he expose a precise paradigm of his life, thought, and art. Bunin writes "The Brothers" via a narrator who is a fervent disciple of Gautama, well versed in Buddhistic legend and text. He not only begins "The Brothers" with a citation from the *Sutta-Nipata*—"Behold brethren slaying one another! I would discourse about grief" (4:256)—but he also casts his story as a parable built about the core of Buddhistic belief: chain, rebirth, karma, ego, suffering, and desire. Moreover, the narrator styles himself as a spiritual master who instructs his charges in a simple and engaging manner. The setting he uses is exotic and apt: Ceylon. Also, he structures his work as a classical dichotomy between rich and poor and, in particular, the ways in which haves and have-nots confront ego and enlightenment.

In "The Brothers," the narrator wrathfully targets the European masters of Ceylon, whom he views as "men of action," wayfarers on the Path of Egression. These lords have whetted self to a rapacious degree, and necessarily inflict ego on their surroundings. For them, native islanders are merely beasts of burden: bodies to be numbered, beaten, and harnessed to haul them in rickshaws about the isle.

These Europeans of Ceylon pay dearly for their wrongdoing, though. They lack personhood. The narrator describes them only in the aggregate, as lumpen patricians who are without roots and who exhaust their waking hours in mindless pleasure and escape. They are, in words the narrator quotes from the Buddha, "men who are forever going to feasts, excursions, and diversions . . . victims of desire that entwines them like a creeping plant, green, beautiful, and death-bearing" (266).

The Europeans in "The Brothers" also lack memory and the enlightenment implicit in ancestry, culture, and primordial existence. They thus wander in an endless present that is rife with images of death, execution, and chain. They are "half-dead": their voices are hoarse and deep, their eyes are lifeless, and their foreheads are "clammy and cold" (266, 269). Moreover, they inhabit surroundings that are cryptlike and funereal. Dining rooms, for instance, are dark and airless, and are fitted out with menacing props. Ribbed Chinese mattings (Scythian, chain) sway in wide, samsaric arcs; and, whirling fans gash the air, guillotine-like, just above the merrymaking (269). Indeed, many of the lords in "The Brothers" suggest mummies in that they are often supine, wrapped in white, and covered with helmets and veils.

In addition to these literal details, and crucial to the understanding of much of Bunin's thought and art, the Europeans in "The Brothers" are on the verge of samsara, or rebirth. They are drawn by the narrator as a "modern" profusion of lines, daubed with splashes of color. Torsoes are stilted and stunted, and faces are black, yellow, or red because some lords are flushed by alcohol or rich food, while others are sallow from sickness and heat.

It is even suggested that many of the Europeans in "The Brothers" have actually regressed to lower forms of life. At times, the jumbled lines that sketch these elite are arcs, links, and spheres. Such lines and shapes repeating the contours of the props in the dining room reinforce the signals that one life is ending to bring "circular return" into the next. An elderly gentleman wears his "chains" to dinner, being dressed in a piqué jacket and trousers (265, 266). A grande dame is represented as a nearly sacrilegious parody of the Buddha. She is "of heroic size, in marble, double-chinned, in crown and royal mantle, and seated on a throne of marble" (265). Many of the Europeans are buck-toothed, flashing their shackles in broad smiles. Others wear glasses or use binoculars, thereby intimating their myopia in the present, and the samsara that is their future fate.

At other times, the Europeans in "The Brothers" go backward in personal and historical time. Some appear as children attended by waiter-"wet nurses" (269). More darkly, others suggest cavemen and ghosts: for example, people who appear as "sinewy red-haired men" (268) or individuals who wear "white raiment, speak without moving their lips, and . . . vanish into the half-darkness" (266).

In sum, Bunin's narrator presents these lords as having no chance for enlightenment and escape. For all their bluster, the masters of Ceylon fear life greatly. They live in a perennial state of siege, finding peace of mind only when they sate their senses or when they take refuge in the "Fort": a physical haven that also serves as a metaphor for the barriers that the ego erects against life.

Retreat is the Europeans' overriding response to life. The lords of Ceylon are as unmoved by the Edenic beauty of the isle as they are by the images of chain and rebirth about them. They also disregard repositories of Guatama's wisdom. They treat Buddhist sanctuaries as curiosities and Buddhist monks as mad. They miss the implications, good and bad, in a bust of the spiritual leader: "a giant of sandalwood, with a broad gilded face and elongated slanting eyes of sapphires, with a smile of peaceful sadness upon his thin lips" (259). Such obtuseness is not surprising, for, as Bunin's narrator makes clear, the lords of Ceylon are bound tightly to the things of this world. "Everyone of them—everyone!" the narrator says, "has within his soul that which compels a man to live and to desire the sweet deception of life!" (266).

An Englishman as Ego Exemplar

The narrator in "The Brothers" distills the tragedy of the Europeans in Ceylon through an English colonel. His choice is a strategic one. The Englishman hails from a land whose geopolitical self controls much of the world, and he wears well his country's power and pride. With "habitually firm and soldierly bearing" (274), he steps forth as master of the universe, ready and willing to engage ego with the milieu. The Englishman barks out orders and directions; he beats rickshaw drivers for the slightest wrong.

For all his show of power and might, though, the Englishman is firmly enslaved in chain and rebirth. The Englishman lacks a name and distinguishing features; he is merely an extension of his caste. Like his colleagues, the Englishman also suggests the living dead. His eyes are "almost white"; his voice is "croaking and hoarse" (257). Lines define the Englishman's figure; circles shackle his body; gaudy and drab colors alternately enflame and blacken his being. Bunin's narrator writes:

> The Englishman had gold spectacles, black eyebrows grown together over his nose, a short black mustache, and an olive complexion. . . . Liver trouble had already left its sallow trace upon his face. His helmet was gray. . . . His eyes looked out of the coal-black darkness of his eyebrows and lashes, and from behind the shining lenses of his glasses. . . . The sun had scorched his hands and knees. (261, 263)

Unlike his associates, though, the Englishman does show some potential for enlightenment. He is a well-seasoned traveler, a free-style philosopher, and earnest student of world religion and culture. The Englishman could also have the power, within himself, to break free from samsara; he has become well versed in the wisdom of the Buddha, and, in particular, in Gautama's admonitions about self. For instance, he tells his listeners the Buddhist legend of the elephant and the raven: two animals who, "tortured by desire" (278), drown in the sea. He cites Gautama repeatedly. "Buddha understood the life of Ego in this world of 'being'," the Englishman says, "and he was horrified with a sacred horror. We exalt our Ego above the heavens; we want to be the center of the world" (278).

In the same vein, the Englishman even extends his knowledge of Buddhism to his own lot in life. He intuits that he has been, metaphorically, a keeper of life's chain. He admits to being one of the "new men of iron" (277), who has wrought utmost havoc upon the world. He confesses: "In Africa I slaughtered men by the hundreds; . . . in Japan I bought little girls to be my wives; in China, I beat . . . old men with sticks; in Java and Ceylon, I drove rickshaw-men until I heard the death rattle in their throats" (277).

In these insights and confessions, the Englishman realizes that the victory gained by ego has been Pyrrhic only—self has won skirmishes with reality but has lost the battle with life. Specifically, he grasps that he is lonely, frightened, and dead to the world. The Englishman, though, goes into denial and pontificates on the predicament of his self-absorbed class: "We do not fear anything . . . neither life, nor the sacred mysteries, nor the depths that surround us, nor death. . . . I am a murderer, but I am not going out of my mind. I never even think of the hundreds that I have killed" (276).[58]

Approaching Nirvana

The Englishman is a great sinner, true, but such candor as his can be a first step on the Path of Return, to an awareness of life beyond illusion and craving. The Englishman has glimpses into truth, Nirvana. He derides as "madness" (275) the attempts of anyone to inflict machinelike order on existence. He accepts sickness, suffering, and death in life and recognizes the ego as the root of all evil. The Englishman also sees himself and his fellow Europeans as "degenerating" (275), regressing, and he indicts his caste not only for their mad rush to impose themselves on the world but also for their equally deranged frenzy to ignore the consequences of their actions. "O ye princes, ye men in power," the Englishman quotes from Guatama, "O ye, who have arrayed your covetousness against one another, insatiably pandering to your lusts!" (278).

The Englishman at first travels the Path of Return so quickly that he actually peers into Nirvana. He tells his listeners: "It is on the ocean . . . in storms . . . in India or Ceylon . . . that one feels the individual melting, dissolving in . . . fearful All-Oneness. Only then do we in slight measure grasp our pitiful Ego" (278).

The Englishman, though, does not follow through. He does not renounce self or attune ego to the world about him. Instead, he censures the East as a hell-hole and resumes life as before. Such obduracy has repercussions both for this life and for the next. In this life, the Englishman finds that he is fettered physically and spiritually, as stolid and as impassive as the idols he sees here and there. He fits more snugly into his carriage and clothes, and he becomes increasingly bored, drowsy, and absent-minded. He does not know "how to kill time" (267), or which path to take in Ceylon or in life. Tragically, the Englishman uses tobacco and alcohol to render him senseless. Cluttered surroundings, along with numbing schedules and routines, cause him to roll his eyes, samsara-like, and underscore his increasing loss of freedom and remoteness from release.

When the Englishman looks to the future, he sees only regression and rebirth. Burdened with the cravings of a self that can no longer realize its whims, the Englishman hastens his end. He spends more time in his tomb-like cabin, and he anoints his naked body with water and cologne. The Englishman also moves to "circular return." When he shaves, he finds that he has grown "unpleasantly younger" (267). When he prepares for dinner, he marks his body with new circles and lines; he clips his mustache evenly and combs his perfectly straight hair with a slanting part (273).

Moreover, when the Englishman leaves his cabin, the world seems to be rife with images of chain. Beyond the surging darkness and apocalyptic storms, he see black-tiled roofs, the links of anchors and stepladders, the "black diamonds" of city lights, and the "gleamingly pale-blue quadrangles" of electrified windows and doors (274).

Such images greatly affect the Englishman but not in the way they should. They cause him to retreat from life, to flee from his fate, and to wander the world anew. The Englishman blames Ceylon, not his ego, for his troubles. He leaves the isle much as he had arrived: perturbed, but with eyes behind "gold spectacles, unmoving and seeming to see nothing" (272).

The Other Half

Bunin's narrator in "The Brothers" juxtaposes the tragedy of the Englishman and his caste with the misery of Ceylon's natives and, in particular, of a young rickshaw driver. From the outset, Bunin's narrator makes it clear that "The Brothers" is not a tale of social injustice or an indictment of capitalism. Have-nots are literally brothers of the haves. The former, too, are the prey of ego; they, too, are culpable for self-induced sins.

Bunin's narrator judges the natives of Ceylon even more harshly than he did the Europeans, but understandably so. The islanders, born to an Edenic, Nirvana-like state, readily abjure their legacy. The narrator muses: "Of what need are cities, cents, and rupees, to these direct heirs of the Land of our First Parents, as Ceylon is styled even now? Do not forests, ocean, and sun give them everything?" (256). The citizens of Ceylon do not agree. Like the First Couple, they accede to pride; like the Europeans who rule them, they journey the Path of Egression, tormented by craving and self.

The islanders of Ceylon even outpace their masters in the race to disaster. They are veritable agents of chain and rebirth. They dive for "circular" pearls and take the place of horses and oxen as beasts of burden. They race to assist the Europeans in their search for pleasure and even egg them on when the lords lose heart, become tired, or suspect that there is something more to life. Simply put, the islanders in "The Brothers" are living testimony to "Mara, the God of Life and Death, the God of the 'Thirst for Being'. . . pursuing one another, and rejoicing with a brief joy as they destroy one another" (258).

Because they have rejected their birthright so completely, the natives of Ceylon are more fragmented than the masters they serve. If the Europeans live in "the Fort," the islanders inhabit "Slave Island" and "Black Town." The locals, too, wear white jackets, complemented with symbolically lined or curved accessories: striped shirts, cassocks and gowns, boots with "upturned toes," "conical skull caps worked with gold" (263), and, "an enormous mane of black twining wool about the head" (263, 271).

Such accoutrements, though, do not conceal the bodily decay of the natives. Their eyes are bloodshot, their teeth protrude, and their mouths and mustaches are flecked with bloody froth. Their bodies are, alternately, burned black, brown, or red. They are wrinkled and "spotted" with sweat and bent under their burdens into sharp angles and arcs, and gray hair curls up from stomachs and abdomens.

The natives are also further regressed than their "brothers"—lords. One group compares most closely to "skeletons" (268). A second group has lost sexual identity: Men have "feminine heads" and look like "eunuchs" and "mummies of old women" (261, 263). Members of a third group return to their youth and are "reborn" as cannibals, cavemen, and ghosts. One islander falls between "a stripling and a woman" (257). Others run about naked and eat bananas, which "are like the flesh of children" (261). Still others "blend into the darkness, their loin-cloths showing dimly white" (269). The narrator summarizes the regression that the natives undergo by portraying a local purveyor of young girls. He details: "[The man] was corpulent, with breasts like a woman's; he had hoary hair, carefully combed, and ornamented with an expensive comb of tortoise shell; he walked about barefooted, but under a sunshade . . . his blouse was of piqué" (260).

A Raw Youth

Just as the narrator in "The Brothers" focused on an Englishman as exemplar of the lords of Ceylon, he targets one young rickshaw driver as prototype for the natives of the isle. The young man is even closer to "return" than his fellow islanders. His face and torso are painted black, blue, and cinnamon; both are excessively lined and curved. The young driver has eyelashes that curve outward and nostrils that are distended. His eyes burn like fire, and his hair is blue-black, stretched taut, and thick like horsehair. Also, the youth has a girlish neck, rounded arms, and legs that are "disproportionately long" (259).

There are two reasons for this character's rapid move to new "rounds" of life, one remote, the other immediate. As regards the former, the young rickshaw driver is host to bad karma. His father, also a rickshaw driver, has, in his lifetime, yielded to craving and self. The narrator clarifies the dilemma affecting both father and son by paraphrasing the *Sutta-Nipata:* "'Wherefore, monks,' The Exalted One might have said, 'did this old man desire to multiply his earthy sorrows?' 'Because,' the monks might have answered, 'because, O Exalted One, he was moved by earthly love, by that which from the start of time, summons all creatures into being'" (257).

The earthly love that driver-*père* expresses for his world results in a large family and in expanding cravings for their well-being. "Moved by love" (257), the old man spends his life on the Path of Egression, in a relentless march to samsara. For instance, he offers his services to lords who hasten his entrance to the nether world. He does not have a name but a brass badge with the number "seven"—the number of years that the body is said to assume a new form.[59] The old rickshaw driver also holds rotating shafts in his hands, a symbol of the samsaric chain that, like a drill, bores into his body and soul.

Driver-*père* readily shows the effects of his "shackled" life. His hair is gray and bound in a knot; his chest is narrow and convex; his shoulders hunch upward; his hands are cupped like a monkey's; and his head is bandaged like a mummy's. He creates the illusion of being without feet, "flying like an arrow . . . scarcely touching the ground" (264).

The old rickshaw driver in "The Brothers" also turns his back on opportunities for enlightenment. Like his fellow islanders, he is culpably ignorant of his spiritual heritage and practices a religion of ritual, coercion, and fear. He worships wooden statues and mutters cryptic prayers but makes scant offerings. Although he can acclaim the name of Buddha joyously one moment, he looks with fear upon pictures of hell and torment the next. The old man also worships other gods: "horrible Hindu statues" (263), demons, serpents, the stars, darkness.

When the old driver dies, the narrator expresses anger, not compassion. In his final hours, the old rickshaw driver is a reduced version of what he has been in life: a "little contorted corpse" (258). Racked by cramps and dysentery, he seems to dissolve into the cold mist about him. The narrator predicts that the old man will make "circular return" because he has not striven for and achieved the right living that ends suffering. The narrator says: "The voice of the Exalted One had not reached him when it had summoned him to forsake earthly love; for that beyond the grave a new life of sorrow awaited him, as a consequence of his previous unrighteous one" (259).

The narrator of "The Brothers" drives home the fate of driver-*père* by rendering his widow's grief dispassionately. The woman's sadness at her loss will, he claims, only forge new shackles for her husband and herself. "The Exalted One," the narrator continues, "would have likened her emotion to the copper earring, resembling a little barrel, which hung in her right ear.

The earring was big and heavy; it had so pulled down the slit in the lobe of her ear that a considerable hole had formed" (259).

Like Father, Like Son

The sins of the father in "The Brothers" are visited upon his son: bad karma. Driver-*fils* follows the same egressive path as driver-*père*. He, too, rejects his religious legacy and falls victim to earthly love. This time, though, the object of affection is not his own family but a young woman, and the narrator views this attachment more critically than he had the father's. He likens the young man's passion to the "most potent of poisons," or to a "scorpion creeping into its lair" (259, 264). He also cites Guatama's counsel on romantic love: "'Forget not,' saith the Exalted One, 'forget not, O Youth, longing to enkindle life with life, even as fire is enkindled with fire, that all torments of this universe, where everyone is either slayer or slain, that all its sorrows and plaints, come from love'" (259). This warning falls on deaf ears. Enflamed by desire, the younger driver fails to reflect on his father's life and falls prey to multiple cravings. As with links in a chain, his love for the young woman advances to cravings for sons and property and well-being. Eagerly, he appropriates his dead father's badge, and all that it represents, as his own.

At this point, the young driver's bride-to-be vanishes without a trace. By a follower of Gautama, such an event might be regarded as evidence for *anatman* and *anitya*, for no-self and for the impermanence of all things. To the young rickshaw driver, though, the loss of his bride is an impetus to energize self. He craves to sate its inordinate whims. As Bunin's narrator takes care to note, driver-*fils* does not mourn the loss of his love; in fact, he seems to forget about her altogether. Such nonchalance is not surprising when one realizes that the young hero has made vows not to his bride but to Mara. "Mara snatches out of the hands of man that which man has seized upon," the narrator in "The Brothers" pronounces summarily, "but then, Mara also inflames a man to seize anew that which has been taken away, or something else that is like it" (264).

To fill in the void left by his bride, driver-*fils* avidly pursues business and money, for chain. "It was impossible to understand which he was more in love with," Bunin's narrator observes, "his running or [his wish for] those circles of silver which he gathered for it" (260). Initially, the craving that holds driver-*fils* captive seems unbounded. The young rickshaw driver is remarkably successful in his quests. He handily beats out competitors for choice jobs, since he negotiates crowded streets with "greater speed than is called for" (262) and without showing the slightest strain or effects of "rebirth." Not a single drop of sweat marks his back.

As was the case with his father, though, driver-*fils* can repress his self only temporarily. He becomes unwell. Externally, the young rickshaw driver mirrors his parent's decay. His face is wrapped in a bandage "like a sick man's"; his skin is "ringed darkly with perspiration"; his feet also seem to disappear, since he "flies like a bird" to his destination (264, 267, 270). The young driver's unwell state is also internal. He becomes "fitfully volatile" (263) as he regresses to other life-forms. Hauling the Englishman about the isle, the young rickshaw driver squats like a dog and bares his teeth in caninelike snarls. He becomes ravenous for betel, a dotlike pepper-kernel that bloodies his mouth and, like a fire, stokes his senses and wants.[60]

Even more detrimental to his inner life, the self-crazed young driver conjures up an image of his lost bride that stands as living testimony to Mara, samsara, and chain. The girl looms large, dark, and circular in his imagination. Her head and eyes are round; her forehead is convex. A coral necklace adorns her neck; silver bracelets ring her arms and legs. The young driver, though, does not grasp the symbolic evil implicit in his vision. Rather, he imitates his brother Englishman and uses tobacco, betel, whiskey, and "rice overspiced with [dot]-pepper" to induce a "beatific vision" (266, 270). The latter is a self-promoted pseudo-Nirvana that blots out the world and nature's warnings as to his wrongdoing. The cicadas and toads murmur and moan; the trees stand "interlaced" (270) in chainlike lattices; the lagoons and forests glow with fiery sparks. All give substance and poetic form to the evil that he ignores.

When he attempts his ecstasies, the young driver of "The Brothers" encounters new suffering, not peace. The narrator quotes the moral from Gautama: "'From longing is born the desire for joy,' the Exalted One hath said. 'From happiness is born sorrow; out of joy and sorrow doth fear arise'" (268).

Driven mad by the seductions of a self that he cannot quell, the young rickshaw driver seeks renewed oblivion. He falls victim first to "a coma of ceaseless running" and then, like a "poisoned man" (268), to a host of physical and emotional ills: fear, malice, exhaustion, and sorrow. He crosses the line to rebirth. His lips become white; his face, black; his body, hot. He resembles various animal-like forms: an old horse that is thin and bathed with sweat, and a mad dog that bares his teeth and wishes to gnaw upon his masters. He also smells of crushed ants. Not unexpectedly, the young rickshaw driver in "The Brothers" entertains thoughts of death—specifically, of suicide by snake. He is saved from consummate tragedy, however, in that he has a real-life glimpse of his lost bride, now a kept woman of the lords. He finds that the woman, as the ward of others, has actually entered *samsara*. Dream and reality merge in a round head, in eyes and arms, and in a triple necklace of rubies and broad bracelets of gold: images of the circular return to which she has willingly acquiesced.

Taking the Plunge

The shock of seeing his "reborn" bride goads the young rickshaw driver to leave the Path of Egression and to follow the Path of Return. The trauma does more than bring him to his senses; it "liberates his will" (270) from the cravings of self. For the first time in his life, the young driver claims his Buddhist heritage, the wisdom of his ancestors. The narrator states the moral of "The Brothers" clearly when he says:

> "Awake, awake!" clamored within the thousands of soundless voices of his mournful ancestors, rotting for hundreds of generations in this paradisiacal earth. "Shake off thee the seductions of Mara, the dream of this brief life!" .... A hundredfold doth he suffer who hath that which is a hundredfold dear; all sorrows, all complaints, come from love, from the attachments of the heart—therefore, slay thou them! Not for long shalt thou be in the tranquility of rest; anew and anew, in a thousand incarnations, shalt thou be put forth. ... Thou hast too early run upon the path of life, passionately setting out after happiness; thou hast been wounded by the sharpest of all arrows—by the yearning for love and for new inceptions in this ancient universe, where from time out of mind the conqueror stands with a heavy sole upon the throat of the conquered. (270)

Freed from his earthly shackles, the young hero of "The Brother" wishes ultimate liberation—to quit earthly life altogether. He moves quickly to this end. Without hesitation, he throws down the chainlike shafts of his rickshaw. With high resolve, he takes his place at a beach reserved for lords: a metaphor for the "farther shore" that Gautama had designated the locus of Nirvana. Lulled by the drowsy murmur of the ocean, driver-*fils* acts upon his death wish: he sacrifices self to the snake.

The death agony that the young hero in "The Brothers" undergoes is a stark metaphysical drama, the struggle of a soul perched between being and nonbeing. At first, driver-*fils* seems to have entered rebirth because, in the symbolic level of the text, he turns a cartwheel immediately after being bitten by the snake. On the other hand, and as proof of his newly enlightened state, the young rickshaw driver "plunges repeatedly into nonbeing" (272). The ocean rushes to his head; darkness grips his body. Entering Nirvana, driver-*fils* "breaks into parts" (272)—into aggregates of elements that, he now knows, have been the source of his suffering and pain. He dismembers self into "thought, memory, vision, hearing, pain, grief, joy, hatred—and that ultimate, all-embracing thing which is called love" (272). He is no longer the shackled, obsessed being he formerly was.

CONCLUSION

If Bunin, in his later works, sought variations on any character in "The Brothers," it was not driver-*père*, who capitulates to earthly love and is "born again," nor was it driver-*fils*, who actually enters Nirvana. Rather, if Bunin claimed a character in "The Brothers" for his subsequent fiction, it was the Englishman. In him one finds an ego who sees the error of his ways and even glimpses Nirvana, but who cannot enter into nonbeing and succumbs to samsara and chain. As will be seen in the next chapters, such characters as the Krasovs in *The Village,* the Khrushchevs in *Dry Valley,* the businessman in *The Gentleman from San Francisco,* Mitia and Katia in *Mitia's Love,* Elagin and Sosnovskaia in *The Elagin Affair,* and the young hero in *The Life of Arsen'ev* fail to become enlightened; but their loss is the world's gain: an artistic legacy in which Bunin as a disciple of the Buddha brought the Noble Truths to his "brothers" in real life.

Chapter Two

Self as Peasant: *The Village*

INTRODUCTION

In the wake of 1905, Russians hotly debated the lot of the village in Russian life. Optimists praised the village, for, in their view, the folk had awakened from its centuries-old slumber and was revitalizing national life. "Russia is renewing itself," a critic proclaimed, "The torpor is gone, and hot blood flows. . . . The village has begun to resurrect itself."[1] These enthusiasts particularly applauded the burgeoning *kulachestvo*, or "peasant-entrepreneurs" who, they hoped, would usher peace and prosperity into Russia.

Pessimists, though, dismissed the dream of a village renaissance. Newspapers and journals editorialized: the folk was plagued by debt, dislocation, and disease; kulaks and railroads had destroyed old values and beliefs; and only nihilism and citations from Marx and Nekrasov had filled the void. Class struggles pitted "bourgeois-hawks" against gentry-masters, rich against poor, young against old. The village, these doubtful ones charged, no longer housed "masters" and "men"; rather, it defied protocols and formulas, old and new.

Many Russians, particularly urban intellectuals, sided with the pessimists, seeing the village as a national nightmare, a human hell. In an effort to cope with an unnerving sense of change, they tried to fancy that the peasant was still the stereotype of "classical" Russian fiction. As one critic noted, "We still would like to see Karamzin's Lisa, Grigorovich's Anton Goremyka, Turgenev's Khor and Kalynich";[2] but idealizations such as these only deepened the split between society and the folk. "The village," another critic conceded, "is separated from the city . . . by a genuine abyss in representation, thoughts, and emotions. Russian life is full of contrasts, but the contrast between village and city is the most glaring of them all."[3]

BUNIN AND "VILLAGE" LITERATURE

Bunin's views on the village and the peasants were among the harshest of the time. He had witnessed the peasant revolts near Tula and Orel in 1905 and 1906 and the devastation to his brother Evgenii's estate at Ognevka. These and similar observations decidedly colored Bunin's approach to village fiction. He had come to see the folk as irreversible victims of regression: "zoological entities, and people of ancient times."[4] In addition to such empirical evidence, Bunin detested every form of idealized folk in Russian fiction. He told an interviewer in 1912 that "the time has passed when writers felt compelled to idealize the peasant" or to perpetuate the myth of "Anton Goremyka."[5] To Andreev Bunin raged, "I know the peasants you want . . . just serve you up Platon Karataev, mystical Scythians, and the bearers of religious tidings!"[6]

ENTERING THE FRAY

Driven by a sense of urgency, Bunin began *The Village* in September 1909 and published it the following year. From its incipiency, Bunin saw *The Village* not as peasant fiction per se so much as the starting point for his reflections on the national life and soul. "In *The Village*," Bunin told an interviewer, "I wanted to draw . . . the whole structure . . . of Russian life."[7] A decade later, he reiterated: "*The Village* was the first of a series of works which portrayed the Russian soul . . . its light and dark, but almost always tragic sides" (9:536). Bunin's was the stance of a disciple of Gautama, warning that Russian life is in flux and that both peasant and nation were fettered in the chain, with little hope for enlightenment.[8]

THE KRASOV BROTHERS: THE CURSE OF KARMA

Bunin's narrator opens *The Village* as if it were a peasant family chronicle. With biblical solemnity, he introduces the heroes, Tikhon and Kuz'ma Krasov, as the fourth generation of drifters, ne'er-do-wells, and wanderers. The Krasov history is steeped in bad karma, in rootlessness, violence, and blood. The oldest recorded Krasov is The Gypsy, who strayed into the arms of the estate mistress and was torn apart by the master's borzois.

The Krasovs of the post-Emancipation do not fare any better, though, since they also mistake freedom for license and spurn Russia's soul and soil. Grandfather Krasov tramps about, pillaging churches. His son, Il'ia Mironovich, the father of Tikhon and Kuz'ma, meanders as a peddler of petty wares, a business that he leaves to his offspring.

The sins of the Krasov fathers are visited upon their sons. Tikhon and Kuz'ma enter the novel perched like prisoners atop a cart, roaming the countryside and bartering wares. Bored and frustrated, Tikhon and Kuz'ma quarrel, with daggers drawn, but they spare each other and go their separate ways. The first part of the story features Tikhon the entrepreneur; the second,

Kuz'ma the dreamer; the third, the village itself, the true dramatis personae of the work.

TIKHON KRASOV: ENTREPRENEUR

Bunin's narrator introduces Tikhon Krasov as a model peasant. He is ambitious and steadfast, and he is comparatively successful. He is a journeyman on the Path of Egression, living in isolation from the All, and heedful only of the cravings that warp his life. Tikhon cuts an impressive figure. He is tall, handsome, and lean. His shoulders are broad; his beard is full. Tikhon is also stylishly self-assured, wearing embroidered shirts and smart boots. Appropriately, his speech is brusque and imperious and his movements lithe.

Tikhon feeds ego by taking pride in his accomplishments. By the prevailing way of reckoning things, he has much to be happy about. Like Turgenev's Khor in the 1840s and Chekhov's Lopakhin and Gor'kii's Artamatov in more recent times, Tikhon is a self-made man. He had hailed from serfs, but now he is a successful businessman who buys and sells at will. To the astonishment and pride of the Krasov clan, Tikhon has purchased the estate of Durnovka, or "Foul Land," and has set himself up as the new *barin* of the land.

To the clan's further amazement, Tikhon manages his activities "without going to pieces" [*razorvat'sia*].[9] The secret of his success (that he has not yet devolved into "aggregates") is simple: Tikhon is conservative, cunning, and committed only to self. For example, Tikhon upholds free-market competition, but he is also fiercely protective of his holdings. "We live and let live," he tells his admirers. "All's fair and square, mind you. I'm a Russian person, you see. I don't want anything of yours, but I won't give you anything of mine either, just bear that in mind" (13–14).

Tikhon is also *pro Deo et patria*, but he is either rebel or reactionary, depending on context. Tikhon revels in the collapse of restraints; thus he regards Russia's defeat by Japan and the assassination of homeland officials only as new channels for self-expansion and growth. "Not bad! Give them more, damn them, give them more!" Tikhon says of the Japanese rout of the Russians (25). "The Minister got it right in the guts—just fizzled out!" he giggles scornfully over the assassination (25). As would be expected from one of Tikhon's status and moral fiber, though, rumors of revolution make him moody, defensive, and anxious to find a scapegoat. "It's all the Jews' doing!" he accuses: "It's Jews and those long-haired blokes, the students!" (25).

To Tikhon, belief in a Deity is no better or worse than his concern for his country. Belief is a mere cover by which he strikes up bargains with the Almighty and erects blinds to hide wrongdoing. In his ledger, Tikhon carries God as an asset—with no corresponding liability. He crosses himself before icons, journeys to Zadonsk, and contributes to the upkeep of monks. Tikhon carries out such rituals, though, only so that he may be revered as a Christian and that God may sustain his material well-being.

As rendered by Bunin's narrator, therefore, Tikhon Krasov emerges as archetypal modern man, as ego unbound. Tikhon has severed his ties to the autocracy, nationality, and orthodoxy that have guided the folk for centuries, and, alienated from comradeship and memory, he looks only to himself for strength and support.

Confronting the Void

Despite his success, Tikhon is not at peace. He is distressed that he has no heirs. His wife, Nastasia Petrovna, gives birth to stillborn girls, and his deaf-mute mistress-cook has crushed her child in her sleep. Tikhon's lack of progeny drives him to painful introspection. He sees that he is caught in a dilemma. Estranged from the past and unable to create-procreate a future, he realizes that he is chained to the present. The more Tikhon works and succeeds, the more pointless and enshackling the whole process of material gain is. Increasingly, Tikhon is overwhelmed by the thought "Then who is all this sweat for, damn and blast it all!" (17). Locked in the present, Tikhon confronts an impasse that he cannot surmount and becomes listless and weak. Suddenly beset by other obstacles beyond his control (e.g., rumors of peasant riots and the failure of the wheat crop), Tikhon feels not only that his life in the present is limited but also that it is rapidly closing in on him.

Tikhon responds to his quandary with bitterness and regret. Formerly, he assumed the role of a shrewd businessman who imposed himself on his milieu; now he tries to maintain his swagger to cloak his fears and his muddling through a life he no longer understands. It is the key irony of Tikhon's life that at the pinnacle of his material success, he plummets to the depths of despair and thinks only of his inevitable—and potentially violent—death.

Tikhon's disenchantment with life is a catalyst for enlightenment. He realizes that his life and dreams have been turned inside out, and that the saga of his success has become a cruel joke. In a poignant way, therefore, Tikhon intuits the Buddhist doctrines of chain, no-self, and the impermanence of all things. He begins to understand that ego is a delusion and that his cravings and the objects by which he has identified himself—career, fortune, and social position—are shackles in his life. His childlessness is for him particularly painful since it underscores the emptiness he feels from within. A man without offspring, Tikhon feels, is a mere shell of a man. "With no children of his own, a man is not a man," he tells his friends. "He's just a barren spot or something" (14).

Fear and doubt spoil Tikhon's success. Business, which has been life's blessing, is now Tikhon's jail, a golden cage, a "noose around his neck" (25).

Business is no longer a series of choices or conquests whereby the self can parry, thrust, and cut a wide swath for itself in the world; it is, rather, an endless, enshackling schedule of customers to be charged, peasants to be placated, and barnyard animals to be watered and fed.

Disillusion and Dissolution

Bored with business, Tikhon becomes restless and irate, the victim of morbid thoughts and sleepless nights. The passage of time horrifies him, as does the advent of middle age and a sharp decline of the power of his memory. He is dismayed that "days have slipped past, like water through the fingers," so that "ten years have merged into a couple of days" (48). It occurs to him to write his life story for would-be businessmen, but he realizes that he can recall almost nothing about his climb to wealth and that he also has nothing of value to say to future generations.

These recognitions shock Tikhon, who begins to deteriorate physically. He becomes angular and skewed: "aggregates" appear. It is significant literarily that Tikhon lacks the fleshy roundness of Tolstoi's Platon Karataev. Even in the beginning of the tale, he is cast as a predator who "watches everything like a hawk" (13). Gradually, Tikhon's profile becomes still more "modern"—and regressed. Geometric shapes and bold daubs of paint epitomize his being. Tikhon is red from sunburn, black from dirt, and white from snow. He is also angular and saw-toothed. Tikhon's arms, legs, and shoulders form a rigid perpendicular, and his fingers are unnaturally outstretched. As a cruel note on Tikhon's frustrated manhood, the detail is gratuitously given that his midsection is stretched obscenely by the gun he carries, ready, in his pants.

Tikhon senses that his figure is a caricature, that it betrays his emptiness, sickness, and age. He is an old man who has already died sometime in life. His efforts to look young, though, are misguided and only accent his modern look. For example, Tikhon trims his beard, but it grows back gray, brittle, matted; his shaven face and neck show "triangles of white skin" (21).

Attempting Escape:
Sojourns to the Past

Tikhon tries to escape the entrapment that is overtaking him. He seeks to leave the Path of Egression for the Path of Return, but he is unsuccessful because he does not understand the nature of his distress. Tikhon is the victim of his desires that he deems necessary for survival but that he finds increasingly difficult to fulfill. Indeed, Tikhon becomes almost schizophrenic in his quests. He senses that his present is false and that he must take refuge in the past. Fearing oblivion, though, he shores up self with whatever means he has at hand. His efforts to find solace in memory, in ancestry, culture,

If You See the Buddha

and primordial existence are only hasty, half-hearted, and doomed from the start.

For instance, when Tikhon looks back to his ancestors, he journeys back only to his own beginnings on earth, thereby remaining ignorant of the bad karma that has shackled his family throughout the years. Tikhon finds it so difficult and painful to recall his early years that he does not reconstruct the past so much as he exhumes it. The only images he can uncover are of disorder and decay. For example, Tikhon recalls his home as a mud hut darkened by age and sunk deep into the earth. He also remembers things that are dreary, harsh-sounding, and cruel, or that, like his own samsaric self, spin out of control—for example, rains rasping on iron roofs and a top set whirling by a whip.

Tikhon's recollections of his parents deepen his despair. His father he remembers only as maudlin and drunk, affectionate one moment and cruel the next. His mother he can only recall as a "bent, old woman . . . who dried horse dung for fuel, drank on the sly, grumbled. . . . that's all" (53). Additionally, Tikhon's recollections of his childhood and youth focus on lifelessness, on corpses, living and dead. In solemn proceedings, Tikhon is summoned to bury the dead. Such events, early on, cause him to gaze, mutely and passively, at his own inevitable end. Tikhon's recollection of his father's wake is a case in point. Tikhon cannot remember Il'ia Mironovich alive very well, but he can vividly recall his corpse. It is nondescript, except for the protruding nose, a triangular flourish that emphasizes a geometrically splintered body and recalls the pointed bulge in Tikhon's midsection, his thwarted urge to procreate and to extend his being.

Liturgical details are congruous with Il'ia's tragic state. The chains of the icon-lamp, for instance, cast eerie shadows on the walls and suggest that Tikhon's father and other family members are dead or that they are suspended permanently in rebirth. Il'ia lies unattended, a parable in itself. Worse, villagers, oblivious to the fact that Il'ia has died, carry out a modern service by which they express their sorry state in this world and their damnation in the next. Mourners process by the shack and "bellow ribald songs amid the screech of accordions, sobbings, and wails" (15).

Tikhon's recollections also include living corpses. Of his own journey through life he recalls only one event in detail: his welcoming of the governor to the blessing of a grain elevator. A photograph of the event hangs on the wall in Tikhon's hut, freezing the moment in time. The day is gray, dusty, and dry. Tikhon and his comrades stand like "graven images" (48), joyless and stiff. The governor inspires fear not because of his power but only because he, too, is close to death, a prisoner in the chain. The governor wraps the wraith of himself in manacle-like trappings of power and wealth: gold stripes, sparkling rings, and a gold-braided coat. His efforts are unsuccessful, though, since his voice is hollow, and his gait is painfully slow. The narrator's statement that the governor has died since the time of the picture is ironic for readers aware of the Buddhist ethos of the work.

Having recalled the corpses of his father and the governor, Tikhon sees that his self is more under siege when he recalls the past than when he looks helplessly at the present. Although he deludes himself into thinking that he has shed years by recalling his early days, he is too horrified by the past to continue traveling back through time. Compulsively, therefore, Tikhon makes another tragic mistake. He spurns memory altogether, abruptly reversing direction and rushing to the future.

Looking to the Beyond

Tikhon cannot face things to come with confidence and hope. In fact, as soon as Tikhon begins to look ahead, the first reality he confronts is that very specter, death, from which he is fleeing. Suddenly he is convinced that "everything might perish in one hour" (25), and that in "five or ten years, he would be spoken of as 'the late Tikhon Ilych'" (49).

Haunted by possibilities of fire, of robbings, or even of being murdered by fellow peasants, Tikhon enlists both superstition and religion to procure knowledge of the future, even reassurance. The search is unsuccessful, however. "Circular" entities such as balls of wax and a magic circle convey no comfort, and a book oracle speaks to the fears of his peasant heart. For example, when Tikhon asks the oracle, "How many children will I have?" the oracle answers: "You are fated to die . . . rotten grass must be weeded out" (15).

Tikhon's appeal to Orthodoxy is similarly grim, since his religious beliefs contain within themselves threats of damnation and hell. "We'd like to go to heaven," he says, "But our sins won't let us" (35). Also, in the little spiritual reading that Tikhon does, he finds confirmation of defilement. "I weep and wail when I think about death," he reads, "and I behold our beauty . . . lying in the tomb disfigured, dishonored, bereft of form" (124). Since religion is filled with warnings, when Tikhon prays, his hands shake, his eyes brim with tears, and his voice breaks in mournful sighs. In short, religion cannot connect Tikhon to a faith-filled past or reassure him about some experience of goodness and immortality in the future. Precipitously, Tikhon acts as his own judge and condemns himself even prior to divine judgment.

Return to the Present

Petrified by the specter of death pervading both past and future, Tikhon resumes his present, only to reexperience that the here and now exudes a cosmic nothingness that paralyzes human resolve. At this stage in his life, Tikhon is often so spent that his least effort feels like a battle, Herculean in intensity but Pyrrhic in result. In this exhausted state, though, Tikhon makes one more potentially salvific move. He conceives the desire to rid himself of the things that burden his life and to find release in phenomena that are greater than he.

Tikhon thinks of quitting "home"—Durnovka, his crowning achievement. He subconciously toys with the idea of reattempting the Path of Return in order to have a second look at the realms of ancestry, culture, and primordial existence. Specifically, Tikhon wishes to rebuild ties with family and with Old Russia. He longs for a cozy home, a good woman, and, of course, children. He pines for dawns and groves. He yearns to go to Moscow and even to meditate on the "eternal" questions (47).

Tikhon's dreams—the enlightenment implicit in his desire for "warmth, peace, clarity, and firmness of thought" (47)—lie well within his grasp. The roads he travels regularly feature humid earth, pastoral scenes, and ringing church bells. Other peasants in *The Village* must struggle for survival, but Tikhon has the financial and social freedom to go where his heart and soul may lead. Tikhon does not take advantage of opportunities, however. Even as he contemplates escape, he reverts to the very things that have robbed him of peace and happiness: his desires for stability, for power.

Tikhon's Women

Attempting to escape his chains, Tikhon only shackles himself with new irons. His yearning for a companion is a clear example. Tikhon treats his wife, Nastasia Petrovna, coldly, without achieving "the slightest notion of what sort of person she is, or what she had lived by, thought, and felt all those long years she had lived with him" (52–53). Nastasia, as it happens, is Tikhon's ideal mate. She is as ego-driven as her husband, and her religion is a similarly self-protective meld of hypocrisy and superstition. The two have no illusions about their marriage, and their relationship is as lifeless as the children they bring into the world. "Does my husband love me?" Nastasia mockingly asks the oracle. "Like a dog loves the stick" is its flat reply (15).

The young peasant girl, Youngbride (*Molodaia*), Tikhon treats with even greater rancor and cruelty. Once beautiful, Youngbride becomes duller and more ungainly than Nastasia. In fact, right before the eyes of Tikhon and of the village, she seems to be passing to a lower form of life, to "rebirth" as a dumb animal. Following the village custom for married women, Youngbride wears "horns": braids pinned on top of her head that make her look "something quite hideous and cowlike" (31). Also, immediately prior to her rape by Tikhon, Youngbride is likened by Bunin's narrator to a bitch in heat: squat, flushed, and sweaty. The rape is animal-like in its quickness and intensity. Youngbride's head angles back awkwardly, and her eyes stare blankly into space. That is all. Not surprisingly, Youngbride does not conceive, and

Tikhon remains frustrated in his desire for an heir. Women, to Tikhon, are at best means to ends.

Witness to Chain: Tikhon's Surroundings

Tikhon's ruinous treatment of women scotches the possibility of a healing home and hearth. Turmoil surrounds his every physical and spiritual movement. The rooms in Tikhon's house and pub are cubicles filled with people and junk. His dwellings are cryptlike: damp, airless, and chilly. Each place is dimly lit, and steam "dots" the walls with "perspiration" (43). Tikhon's dwellings are also filled with distressful odors and sharp sounds. At times, sounds focus Tikhon's attention on life's tedium. Clocks tick in loud, even strokes, clappers beat rhythmically against windows, and chicks peck at windowpanes. At other times, noise startles the hero and augurs disaster. These occasions seem to be commensurate with Tikhon's growing distress. For example, rain beats down more loudly and quickly; clappers knock more briskly and smartly. When these sounds are superadded to jingling bells, banging doors, and wailing pipes, they create a modern cacophony that sets Tikhon's nerves on edge and destroys peaceful domesticity.

Smaller items—more tangible than pervasive odors and sounds—can also underscore Tikhon's alienated worldview. Some correspond to his inner turmoil and heighten his premonitions of disaster. For example, a canary, trilling in its cage "like a clockwork bird" (33), recalls to Tikhon his remarks on the binding, regressive power of his golden cage and work schedules. A crack in the stove, "its seam like a silhouette of a skinny, twisted man" (46), replicates his increasingly angular, regressed profile. Common kitchen effects are a daily reminder of Tikhon's sorry state and suggest a Buddhist trepidation of the "arcs," "circles," and "dots" of modern life. For instance, bowls are filled with ringlike biscuits, "braided" breads, and "sucked-out slices of lemon" (76).

Taking to the Outdoors

To free himself from his domestic surroundings, Tikhon seeks release in the outdoors. But travel through Russia does not delight Tikhon, nor do the phenomena that could spark memory or thrill his soul, such as Russia's physical beauty or cultural monuments. He focuses instead only upon his homeland's centuries'-old poverty and its yearnings for a "master" (24).

In truth, the selective viewing is justifiable in Tikhon's case. Bunin's narrator has carefully manipulated the settings of *The Village* to be monochromatic, geometric, and abstract. For instance, the steppe planes where Tikhon wanders are spoiled by rectangles (railway station, grain elevator), dissected with lines (highways and telegraph lines), and displayed against pale, gray, or dark skies. Tikhon's native haunts appear as an endless valley bordered by dying nature on one hand and by menacing machines on the other. For instance, the inertia is rent by the sound of a pistol (yet another image of Tikhon's frustrated manhood), which starts to fire "all by itself" (30), and, regularly, by trains that, as modern symbols of revolution, destruction, and change, move as "chains of flaming eyes" (55).

Blocked on the Path of Return by inordinate desire, women, home, hearth, and even the great Russian outdoors, Tikhon cannot meditate on the "eternal questions" that trouble him. His ideas are outmoded, superficial considerations of the status quo. With all the effort of which he is capable, Tikhon can only vacillate between petty aphorisms and blanket condemnations. In the end, he evades "talk about God and life" (35) and enthrones money. "So long as you've money in your pocket," he says defiantly, "you're on top of the world!" (64).

Again Death

There is one issue, though, that Tikhon cannot simply defy: death. Almost subconsciously, Tikhon attempts to penetrate the mystery of death by seeking out cemeteries. This attraction to graveyards contains within itself Tikhon's greatest potential for liberation, since, when he visits graves, he unwittingly positions himself for a chance to discern the errors of his ways. Walking past crosses and tombstones, Tikhon can reflect upon the vanity of striving, the illusion of self, his destructive urges and desires, and his ties to ancestry, culture, and primordial existence. It is in cemeteries, therefore, that Tikhon brushes most closely with life: enlightenment.

Initially Tikhon makes some headway in his quest. Notwithstanding his consuming fear of death, he finds that cemeteries grant him the peace and quiet that are lacking elsewhere. In graveyards, Tikhon can experience nature's embrace. Flowers bask in sunny stillness, birds sing sweetly, and butterflies lie about in delicious languor. Indeed, when he visits cemeteries, Tikhon is like a "reborn" Adam who returns to Eden in hope of a pre-Fall life.

Tikhon does not profit, though, from all that graveyards afford. Instead, after a few restful moments, his attention wanders to trees that have become sharp and sparse, and whose shadows conjure up shackled spirits who writhe and "ripple" amidst chains of "iron monuments" and "cast-iron slabs" (22).

Tikhon also remains untouched by tombstone inscriptions of love, tenderness, and eternal life. His imagination dwells, instead, on dead and dying things: human bones, rotting flowers, the fresh grave of a child, and the frightful tomb of a millionaire. Conventional symbols of resurrection also drive Tikhon to despair. Graveyard crosses are crude and rotting; tombstone angels are as lifeless and as hollow as those who gaze upon them. Initially,

Tikhon's excursions to burial grounds hold out some hope for new, reflective beginnings; very soon, however, they only heighten his preoccupation with death.

Losing Grip

Tikhon pays dearly for his obstinacy. As his self erodes, he gradually loses his grip on reality. For instance, he loses his business sense. If earlier Tikhon had built an empire that was the envy of his fellow peasants, he now charges such exorbitant prices that he sells nothing and stands alone with his unsold merchandise in the heat and dust. Moreover, Tikhon can no longer control his subordinates. His reactions run the extremes: tense standoffs alternate with frenzied attacks with fists and whips. In civic terms, Tikhon may be the new "master"; but he looks at each "man" with growing fear and contempt. In his paranoia, he says, "Don't give them a chance! Otherwise, they'll take the bit in their teeth and smash us to smithereens!" (26).

Tikhon is less and less able to face the people who become more and more a mob. He is still propelled by violence and rage, but he lacks the physical and mental strength to curb and contain an unruly crowd. When a peasant mutiny occurs at Durnovka, Tikhon regards it as an affront to his dignity, but he hopes to use the uprising as an occasion to regain control of his world. He dashes out, alone, to quell the disturbance. Tikhon brims with anger and energy on this occasion; he feels "extraordinarily strong, audacious, and ready to fight the devil himself" (28). In the confrontation at Durnovka, however, Tikhon fails miserably. Not only does he not disperse the mob, but he engages in a futile shouting match with a harness maker (yet another image of chain), and he is abused by peasants who "roared with laughter, hooting and whistling after him. . ." (30).

Now a victim rather than a master, Tikhon begins to suffer a host of physical ills. Restlessness and angst develop into sickness and pain. Tikhon finds that he is losing "color and flesh" (19). At times, Tikhon's body is weakened by sweats and fever; more often, though, it is wracked by chills and internal cold. "Cracking his fingers one by one" (38), Tikhon acknowledges his frozen state; and, by his frightened sense of fatality, he hastens his fragmentation.

Tikhon's physical form begins to blur. He becomes barely distinguishable from the gray and dreary landscape about him. He also moves to the circuity of samsara. Lines that used to be straight or serrated now curve and undulate; triangles give way to circles and dots. The linear skewedness of Tikhon's face, for instance, is modulated by pockmarks and by raindrops that look like "silvery glass-beads" (40). The hollows of Tikhon's neck accentuate that his head is "like a horse's head" (64) and advance him further to rebirth.

Also, Tikhon foreshadows impending demise by wrapping his remains in a *poddevka:* a light, tight-fitting coat that, with its upturned collar, resembles a burial shroud. The narrator, too, intimates interment, since he mentions that Tikhon's face and boots are splashed with mud and that he sinks his feet deep into muck.

The final profile of Tikhon at the end of part 1 of *The Village* paves the way for his imminent demise. Passive and still, he gazes mutely and glumly upon the world. Nevertheless, Tikhon is afforded one final opportunity for escape, for enlightenment. He stands on the threshold of his hut—that is, on the border between his inner and outer worlds physically, and between dead ends and new beginnings metaphysically. To the self-obsessed Tikhon, however, such a demarcation only worsens his dilemma. Behind him, he sees the grease and grime of his home, his dreams of power and glory reduced to soot. In front, he is assaulted by a Buddhist folk image of evil and destruction: a train, a "chain of electrically lit windows," which spouts smoke like "a flying witch's loose gray hair, redly illumined from below" (64). In younger days, secure in his business prowess, Tikhon could have matched ego against his milieu. Now, though, standing on the threshold of his home, he sees only the filth that he has created on one side, and the chaos he can no longer control on the other. All that seems left to Tikhon, a failure in both worlds, is a perverted image of his flawed procreative acts: he urinates on the threshold and clamps his jaws to repress the anguish that wells up from within.

KUZ'MA KRASOV

Tikhon's story told, his alienation complete, he turns to his brother, Kuz'ma, for solace and support; but to Tikhon's dismay, Kuz'ma has continued the Krasov tale of woe. As rendered by Bunin's narrator, Kuz'ma's story is rougher and more truncated than Tikhon's, even though it also repeats earlier themes and details. Physically, for instance, Kuz'ma is already an "aggregate" pencil sketch of lines, angles, and dots. Ailing and fragmented, he, even more than his brother, thinks frequently and morbidly of death. Paralleling Tikhon's *poddevka,* Kuz'ma wears a *chuika,* a wraparound overcoat that conceals his torso but that could double as a shroud. Kuz'ma's face is pelted by rain, snow, and hail that obscure the lines with dots and create the mud that splatters his body.

Kuz'ma shares Tikhon's disintegration. His hands shake, his teeth are clenched, and his mouth "spits out" words (33). Kuz'ma is also wracked with sickness and pain. Feverish moments alternate rapidly with frozen ones; he suffers several heart attacks, and by the end of his story he, too, stands exhausted and drawn. Kuz'ma's inner turmoil exceeds Tikhon's. His thoughts include nightmares from the past, fears for the future, diatribes against Russia, superstitions about the Deity, and regrets about chances taken and opportunities missed. When Kuz'ma feels compelled to write his life story, he realizes, as Tikhon had, that his life has been "so plain, so ordinary and squandered on trifles with such inexplicable speed . . ." (70) that there is nothing of value to say. In short, Kuz'ma, too, is mercilessly disenchanted with life. Like his brother, he is a loner, an outcast who stumbles through lodgings that are congested and noisy and who wanders amidst settings that are dark and dotted with tombstones and iron slabs. It is not surprising that, when the brothers reconcile, Kuz'ma craves the same things that Tikhon does: rest, a good woman, and a cozy home.

The False Pilgrim

Despite the parallels between them, Tikhon had stayed most of his life to pursue capital and career, but Kuz'ma has wandered throughout Russia to break life's bonds. Kuz'ma might seem better suited for liberation than Tikhon because he has spent some time on the Path of Return. He has abandoned "home," scorned security, and welcomed change. Unencumbered by material things, he has been well poised to savor the past, embrace Russia, and serve as a prophet in the wilderness of his native land.

At times, Kuz'ma's insights into life are so valid that he seems well on his way to enlightenment. For instance, Kuz'ma sees that his brother's yearnings for power and wealth have caused Tikhon pain, not joy. Kuz'ma also claims to elevate morality over politics and declares that individuals should live "like human beings" (34), with the right to think and to receive a decent wage. Kuz'ma is even honest about his own failings. Years before Tikhon, he condemns his own peddler's career as a "waste" (68).

Kuz'ma is a true Krasov, however, so individual good actions or attitudes do not bring him authentic peace. Kuz'ma has used his opportunities as a traveler with no more honesty than Tikhon had used his chances in his pose as an entrepreneur. Accordingly, Kuz'ma is as unfulfilled as Tikhon and has been at least as unwilling to renounce his illusions and desires.

Kuz'ma has good reason for loathing his life of wanderlust. In his youthful sojourns through Russia, Kuz'ma sought only the external freedom that travel seemed to afford: the self-seducing escape from the "yoke" (69) of daily obligations. When traveling, Kuz'ma would choose either good or bad with abandon. He was as charmed "by the steppe's expanse . . . by the exciting smell of the road," as he was by the smell of dust, tar, and the "asphyxiating stench of catskins" (68). His wandering did not bring him to memory, or to ancestry, culture, and primordial existence; it did not attach him to soul and soil. Wandering only made his rootlessness total and isolated his being from the things that might have given him peace. Kuz'ma's youthful physical jaunts are thus represented by the narrator as pointless and pathetic. Kuz'ma's life was a frenzied one, without purpose or goals. Indeed, the neophyte Kuz'ma was always in motion. If he was not in a cart, then he was at a train station, going from city to city or job to job; he was invariably drunk, idle, or promiscuous in between. Since Kuz'ma used travels to gratify self, not to renounce it, it is ironic but not surprising that his wanderings through Russia caused him "to touch bottom" (73) and to confront everywhere the very cold and dirt, poverty and loneliness that he had sought escape.

Bunin's narrator shows that Kuz'ma's superficial dips into intellectual realms have failed to mature him. A *samouchka*, or "self-taught person," Kuz'ma began his quest with high-minded goals, like his belief in Tolstoyism and in Russia as a national ideal. Pronouncing his countrymen a "great people" (67) and paying conventional tribute to the past, Kuz'ma also celebrated national culture in the lore of Kievan Rus', Platon Karataev as a national type, and church bells and religious processions.

Like his fruitless physical wanderings, though, Kuz'ma's intellectual pursuits were ephemeral because ego, not memory, has served as mentor. For instance, Kuz'ma remains ignorant of beauty or culture because he has sought out teachers who dwell on ugliness and evil. Among these, Balashkin is the best example. Balashkin propounds a victim's view of the world: existence is bad, never good; the individual must constantly watch for threats to survival. Balashkin himself clearly bears the imprint of chain and circular return. In addition to his teachings, "silvery bristles" speckle his "gray cheeks" (67), and a dot hernia ends his days.

Furthermore, Balashkin seeks only to fetter his student alongside himself. For instance, he quickly disabuses his pupil of the value of the past, by simplistically summarizing world history in terms of religious tragedy: coliseums, crusades, religious wars, and splinter sects. He dismisses Russia as a nation that is cursed and regressing to Scythianism. "It's really all over with us now," Balashkin tells Kuz'ma, "We're tearing back to Asia, as fast as we can go!" (68).

Balashkin also attacks Russian culture and undermines Kuz'ma's sham appeal to national ideals. As the national type, he champions not Karataev but the scoundrel villains of Russian literature. "Why Karataev . . . and not Karamazov and Oblomov, not Khlestakov and Nozdrev? The lice have eaten your Karataev! I see no ideal here" (68). Balashkin claims that Russia does not revere its writers; in fact, he swears that it has brought them to execution. "Good heavens above!" he continues, "Pushkin was killed, Lermontov was killed, Pisarev was drowned, Ryleev was hanged . . . Dostoevskii was taken to the scaffold, Gogol' was driven insane. . . . Oh, if there is another such country in the world, be it thrice accursed!" (67).

Kuz'ma emerges from such tutelage a cultural barbarian. In truth, though, Kuz'ma shares the blame for his own ignorance, since he has not been a serious student. For instance, Kuz'ma discusses Schiller with Balashkin not to study idealism but only as a ploy for asking to borrow his adviser's accordion. Kuz'ma does not read the poet Kol'tsov but only copies illiterate inscriptions from the writer's tombstone. Also, Kuz'ma appeals to Russia's medieval heritage only to titillate his being. His "pilgrimage" to the Cathedral of Saint Sophia in Kiev is a good example. Kuz'ma does not respond to the church's bells as a testament to lives past or as invitation to enlightenment. Instead, he is so perverted that their pealing brings him to self-induced orgasm: clenched teeth, eyes closed in "sweet agony," and beard falling limply on his chest (72).

The Failed Author

Kuz'ma's refusal to learn about his ego or the culture of the world equips him poorly for a career as a writer, but it is Kuz'ma's stance toward his craft that ensures his failure. Unlike Bunin's narrator, Kuz'ma would not see himself as a teacher of humankind. He would write instead from "festering ambition" (69), to forestall dissolution and decay, to keep from "withering like a burdock in the field" (69).

Kuz'ma's writing mixes pulp and plagiarism: complaints about cruel fate, tales of robber bands, and (jabs at Tikhon) stories of murdered merchants. In desperate moments, Kuz'ma regards his fiction as the achievement of his life, but in more honest ones, he admits that his work is crass and crude: a "rotten little book" (34). Even in such a moment of candor, ego severely limits Kuz'ma's vision.

Bitterness and Decay

Having returned to Durnovka, and looking back on his life, Kuz'ma sees himself as an "anarchist" (33) and a "strange type of Russian" (34). His sense of regret over his wasted life complements and rivals Tikhon's. Too late Kuz'ma realizes that, in his craving for the wrong things in life, he has missed chances for growth and peace. Worse, the banal lessons that Kuz'ma has internalized will now influence his present.

For instance, Kuz'ma adopts not only Balashkin's ridicule of Russia but also his ploy of lecturing gullible people—for example, his brother, Tikhon. As rendered by the narrator, Kuz'ma becomes a modern-day *raisonneur:* "an ass-head" (67, 69), who, en route to rebirth as a dumb animal, pontificates on life with hatred and spite. Kuz'ma comes to see Russian history as "all treachery and murder" (39), but to prove this, he offers only empty generalizations about Mongols and time-worn comparisons of Russia to Europe. Kuz'ma also censures national culture. Folk art he relegates to the Stone Age; proverbs and tales he condemns for their praise of cruelty and strife.

Kuz'ma's forays into the speculative realm are even more pathetic than his ridiculous cultural ones. He lacks the grandeur of an ideé fixe. Rather, it is a measure of how far Kuz'ma has wandered from his roots that he questions the villagers so relentlessly about their lives and that he arouses the same suspicion and resentment in them that his brother does. Kuz'ma judges his fellow countrymen as severely as Tikhon does. Russians are dull, lazy, stingy, godless, fierce, resigned, hypocritical, superstitious, and mean-spirited. Citizens teach one another to masturbate, and they mock prostitutes who gobble bread while plying their trade (39–40). Kuz'ma's hatred of Russia and life so emaciate his body and soul that he becomes even more linear, circular, and predatory than Tikhon. Kuz'ma is shorter, bonier, leaner; he has prominent cheekbones, knitted eyebrows, and small eyes. If Tikhon is daubed with red and black, Kuz'ma is gray and "iron-colored" (125). Also, while the samsaric dots that curved Tikhon's face and torso were mostly external and were caused by rain, hail, and snow, Kuz'ma's dots well up from within, from tears he sheds in drunken stupor or despair.

Returning Home

Kuz'ma's most bitter disappointment in life is his return to his family and his roots. Kuz'ma finds that Durnovka has changed but little; and, like Tikhon, he spurns nature's embrace and spends his waking hours in a world of peasants and dogs, rain and weeds. Kuz'ma's stay at Durnovka brings on additional miseries. For instance, he shares his quarters alternately with Youngbride, who, except for an occasional tryst, stands aloof, and also with a woman known only as the "Widow," a regressed spirit who rises up as "something huge and dark . . . flooding the fields, screaming in horror, and swelling monstrously against the faintly smoldering streak of sunset" (97).

To dull his pain and its latent enlightenment, Kuz'ma, like Tikhon, numbs his senses with drinking, sleeping, and smoking. He continues to presume to "self-development" (34), but, with his ego losing ground, he becomes more samsaric with each passing day. His eyes are sunken; his skin develops pink, mauve, and black dots. Kuz'ma is almost always sick, often delirious, and by the novel's end, he seems to lie in state. As was the case with his father, Kuz'ma is unattended in a tomblike room; Youngbride, the Widow, and his daughter, Klasha, ignore him, as if he is already dead. As the narrator had remarked about Tikhon, Kuz'ma also gazes upon a dead bird in its cage: "its inflated red crop" (115) suggestive of a puffed-up self trapped in a prisonlike existence. Indeed, it is the tension between Kuz'ma's fear of death on one hand and his desire to escape his life at Durnovka on the other that keeps him living at all. Like Tikhon, he remains deaf to the past and blind to the future. He experiences only the present, and that is finite and empty.

THE CITIZENS OF DURNOVKA:
ATAVISM AND HUMAN BEASTS

Bunin's narrator intersperses the tragic tales of Tikhon and Kuz'ma with unpleasant vignettes of the villagers. Initially the inhabitants of Durnovka

Self as Peasant

resemble the brothers Krasov in their wanderer-outcast qualities. They carry chainlike "gray suitcases, lavishly speckled with tin studs" (53); they suffer exhaustion, from malnutrition and sexual excess. Early on, their bodies are lines and curves. Their clothes—spotted, striped, shroudlike, and trimmed with braids and lace—conceal their faces and bodies. Their attire also features gray capes and wide-brimmed hats; it even shows a Belyi-like, Scythian flourish: Manchurian hats (46, 76).

Together with Tikhon and Kuz'ma, the villagers are trapped in the present. Their access to the past has been cut off by upheaval and change; their hope for the future diminished by children who are deformed or stillborn. The folk of *The Village* stand on the brink of madness and, in the view of one critic, with "one foot already across the threshold."[10] In the context Bunin is providing, however, the inhabitants of Durnovka are crucial to the Buddhist mythos of *The Village*, since they have actually entered rebirth and now reappear as primitive life-forms: cavemen, humanoids, ghosts, and animals.

The inhabitants of Durnovka are little better than skeletons and scarecrows. They also appear as giants with small heads, midgets with legs shorter than the trunk, or phantoms, dressed in white and processing in ghostlike "blurs" (93). Any given torso can be cruelly swollen or truncated, grotesquely arched or bent, or severely angled like an "Egyptian" (37). A peasant body can also devolve into a tangle of "lines," "circles," and "dots." Villagers tend to have chapped hands and feet and backs cut to ribbons by whips. Some of the folk of *The Village* are stooped and round-shouldered; they may have protruding stomachs, gnarled fingers, and legs "as crooked as a dachshund's" (130), or they can be speckled with rain, sweat, and warts. They have been ravaged by smallpox, frostbite, calluses, even hemorrhoids, or still suffer from these, as the case may be.[11]

Bunin's narrator is particularly cruel with faces. To capture the regressed disintegration of the folk, he uses a meld of folk, iconographic, and modernist modes. Sometimes Durnovka visages are like those of a witch or "an old woman from a fairy tale" (21, 110). At other times, folk countenances are "Old Russian and Suzdalian" (85, 89): narrow, gaunt, and shrouded in wooden folds. At still other times, faces are stretched like pieces of canvas on wooden frames and delineated in an avant-garde riot of colors, lines, and dots. Faces can be blue from cold, purple from anger, and red from sun. Harelips, buckteeth, and puffy cheeks are relatively normal.[12]

It is, however, the rebirth of many of the peasants in *The Village* as barnyard animals that best illustrates the karmic regression. Bunin's narrator initials signals of the reversion of the peasant self from human to beast with the brothers' comments that the folk are like dumb animals, or with the nicknames that the folk have for members of their caste-herd, such as "Donka the Nanny Goat" (95), "Motka the Goosehead" (38), and "Polukarpia," or "Half-Carp" (64). Bunin's villagers sometimes have bodies covered with "golden fur" (72) and are compared to apes, bears, even camels. Most often, though, they resemble the livestock in their care. They walk like ducks, grunt like pigs, and bray like donkeys; they growl like borzois and flutter like hens. They huddle in huts or inns, hobble along in dreary processions, and moan from hunger. With the agitation of flocks, they are seized violently by change and by rumors of revolution and war.

Music and Theater: Carnival and Liturgy

To give a wild, elegiac expression to their lot in life, the regressed peasants and animals in *The Village* employ devices of "modern" music and theater. Man and beast orchestrate an atonal symphony or resort to gesture and kinesics to show signs of distress or explosion. In transit to new "rounds" of life, bodies convulse in shivers and hiccoughing; faces glare and sneer; and voices let loose in bellowings, gasps, and chatter.

Furthermore, Bunin's narrator in *The Village* often lets the modern spirit of his tale use music and theater to construct mass carnivals and liturgies. At a fair, for instance, Tikhon confronts a "discordant hubbub" (18): shouting voices, neighing animals, and the blaring music of marches, polkas, and merry-go-rounds. This cacophony deepens his anxiety and restlessness. Ironically, the dissonance makes him crave home and the very environs from which he had sought to escape.

The citizens of Durnovka also use modern liturgies to vent frustration and pain or to seek protection from menacing powers in a hostile world. Such proceedings are, of course, empty shells, the "performance of a ritual and not an expression of feelings" (41). For instance, pilgrims sing "something that is immoderately loud, crudely harmonious, ancient-religious, imperious, and menacing" (51). Half-demented women rend the air with screaming, savage chants, and the beating of pots and pans.

Apocalypse

Peasant life in Durnovka witnesses to a universe in the throes of regression, atavism, and apocalypse. Alternately, the Russia of *The Village* burns with lightning and fire, dissolves in "watery mist" (46), or congeals in the ice and snow. The sky presses heavily upon the earth, causing planes and squares to become circles, spirals, and arcs. Land and roads buckle in wavy lines, rush upward in slopes, or plunge downward in ravines. Dust and rain dot the terrain. Spiraling smoke makes dwellings seem to whirl samsarically in the distance. Markings of death and bondage are everywhere. The soil exudes "sepulchral blackness" and supports tiny crosses in the snow (88, 116). Wet roads feature "leaden puddles" (44). The firmament radiates "deathly blue light" that turns foliage "metallic green" (90), and "leaden" rainclouds threaten a second Great Flood and a Devil's Island ruled by shaggy demons with spindly legs (85, 90, and 106).

THE WEDDING

Bunin brings the portraits of Tikhon, Kuz'ma, and the villagers together in the final scene: the marriage between Youngbride and Deniska. Like a coda, the wedding of the two peasants echoes and underscores many of the motifs in *The Village*. It suggests that the narrative itself is entering circular rebirth.

For instance, the characters of the novel follow established patterns. The Krasov brothers are at the nadir of degradation and despair. Tikhon is implicated in, if not directly responsible for, the murder of Youngbride's first husband, Rod'ka. He is a shattered, broken being. Compulsively, he succumbs to tears and trembling because he is progressively aware of his wrongdoing. He confesses to Kuz'ma that he has lived "like a chained dog," and that he now sees that "all things are vanity . . . a shadow, a dream" (124, 125).

This self-knowledge brings to Tikhon new terror of death and oblivion. Earlier, Tikhon had wanted to sell all and to become a pilgrim, wandering through Russia. Now he wishes to move to town and to resume making money. The dotlike "fisted hands" that Tikhon displays throughout *The Village* are thus to be understood physically and philosophically. Physically, they represent the vicelike grasp of an ego clutching to save its own fearsome existence. Philosophically, they show Tikhon's clinging to the very desires that have brought him ruin. "I haven't lost my grasp, mind you," Tikhon boasts to Kuz'ma. "It's too early for me to retire. . . . I'll break the devil's own horns yet" (121).

Kuz'ma similarly moves toward his end. More than anyone else in *The Village*, Kuz'ma has caught a glimpse of the depths of depravity of modern life, but he, too, has refused to admit that his craving is the locus of personal evil. With his brother mad and the people in revolt, Kuz'ma can, at least, examine the collapse of his worldview and the emptiness of his life. He realizes that for all his "thinking," he knows little about God or life. "I don't know right from wrong anymore!" he tells Tikhon. "I don't understand anything anymore!" (122). By the novel's end, Kuz'ma is "completely indifferent" (116) to everything. Such lack of interest, though, is not a form of Buddhist-style liberation as much as it is a modern man's numbed response to his world.

More than either brother, however, it is the villagers themselves who dominate the wedding scene and who bring the tragedy of *The Village* into full, uninterrupted light. In the marriage between Youngbride and Deniska, the inhabitants of Durnovka reaffirm the composite folk self and its relish for rituals that celebrate ends, not beginnings. The choir is situated like the massed groups of figures in icons: "chains" of illumined but bodiless faces frozen in meekness and fear. Folk songs of betrothal and lament are paired with Orthodox chants in a "strident chorus" (129).

The citizens of Durnovka have not assembled for this liturgy to wish Youngbride and Deniska well. They do not invoke memory or uphold the ideals of love and family that such Christian folk assemblies would typically affirm. Instead, they come together to sacrifice two of their race to rebirth. Indeed, it is the villagers' obsession with self-preservation that leads them to conduct this particular marital service with frenetic energy.

For instance, if on other occasions the folk slept or skulked about, at this one they sing and dance with such abandon that they might be modern cavemen, hoping to stave off night spirits until the dawn. A peasant woman dances like a "shaman" and shrieks "in a wolf-like howl" (132). Deniska's father, Seryi or "The Gray One," is like a high priest, skirted in a cassocklike *chekmen* and brightly illumined by fire. Bride and groom, undaunted, are ready participants in the frenzy. When Youngbride is led away to be dressed, she moans and trembles, like an animal being prepared for slaughter; she then falls forward, dropping her face on her knees, grotesquely reminding one of a fetus facing rebirth. Because she arrives at the church in a blizzard, Youngbride is shrouded like a corpse. Her dress and her overcoat are pulled over her head which is bound up in kerchiefs and shawls. A lace curtain serves as a veil (recall the "silken nets" of Gautama's world). During the ceremony, the couple receive copper crowns. Deniska's is like a huge shackle, crammed down low over his ears and making him "both uncomfortable and scared" (132).

Clearly, the marriage is a ceremonial sacrifice in which signs of regression and return abound. Seryi's shadow is that of an "idol-worshipper" (128). Women appear as birds: "crudely powdered and rouged with curly rainbow-colored feathers" in their hair (128). The universe itself moves in circles, spirals, and arcs, as whirling snow accompanies the dervishes of the peasants and enshrouds humans and beasts as ghosts. The land is frozen in a series of wavy humps, and the sun is chained behind rings of frost. Droning trees and creaking iron rudders contribute to the ritual disharmony to the world (114).

Suddenly, with the shriek of the shaman woman's imploring the Holy Spirit as a "gray dove, with a golden head" (132), the narrator abruptly ends *The Village*. The performance of the folk self comes to nothingness, to oblivion. Earlier, Kuz'ma had insisted to Tikhon that their life on this earth was finished and that "no candles in the world can save us" (23). Bunin's narrator agrees, snuffing out the narrative as he would the candle that any of his villagers might light against one more dark night.

CONCLUSION

In *The Village,* Bunin portrayed Russian peasants as avid hosts to ego, as victims of regression. As he saw it, Russia could not look to entrepreneurs, dreamers, or simple villagers to save it from enchainment. Indeed, they move the land and the inherited culture one step closer to the abyss. Bunin did not confine his pessimism to the folk alone, though. He believed that the Russian gentry suffered a similar, self-bound fate. In his next major work, *Dry Valley,* Bunin turned his attention to the yearnings and desires that plagued the other half of gentry life. In this way, "master" and "man" are seen in parallel, and the damnation of the land literally runs full circle, or chain.

Chapter Three

Self as Lord: *Dry Valley*

INTRODUCTION

"Who are we?" a critic asked in a review on Bunin's *Dry Valley* in 1912.¹ In truth, few Russians knew, for they saw their land as a fatally infected organism. "What kind of life can Russia have," another critic had noted a year earlier, "when it is infected by typhus, oozing with pus, and raging with fever . . . ?"²

In an effort to diagnose their country's ills, many Russians overlooked the peasant and isolated the gentry as the source of national infection. However correct the diagnosis may have seemed, it was at best partial. The gentry were victimized as much as any class in Russia at this time. After the Emancipation, the noblemen who had not left their estates for the cities suffered severe social and economic change. Some clung to lineages and codes of conduct for a time; others sank directly into poverty and despair. Urban Russians scapegoated the gentry for the disarray in the provinces. "The gentry is the most rotten sector of society," one reviewer raged. "It is incapable of creative work . . . and with its purely animal egoism, it preserves the status quo. Our nobility inhabit a genuine kingdom of stagnation, a swamp where miasmas of rot and corruption find a most favorable soil."³

Given the antipathy of urbanites to the gentry, it is not surprising that many Russians grew nostalgic for the "masters" of the pre-Emancipation. In fiction, they disavowed the sordid gentry chronicles of Aleksei Tolstoi and longed for Rostovs and Levins, for loving families and wise serfs. As one critic wrote, "There is no value which our revolutionary literature will not reappraise, no idol which it will not profane. . . . Only one relic seems unshakable . . . the beauty and poetry of the old gentry."⁴

BUNIN AND THE GENTRY

Bunin, too, pined for "gentry" Russia. He believed that the estate was a seedbed of memory, that it was a museum and a haven, scarcely touched by time. Bunin, though, was no stranger to gentry decline, for he knew that the noblemen of his day were diseased and destructing. He could see that his own family estates were totally unlike the romanticized manors of Turgenev and Tolstoi; and he could recognize that his immediate ancestors were living prototypes for the depraved gentry heroes and heroines in *Dry Valley*. For instance, Bunin's grandfather, Nikolai Dmitrievich (Grandfather Petr in *Dry Valley*), was a simple soul in the era of the post-Reform. Ol'ga Dmitrievna, Nikolai's sister (a partial model for Aunt Tonia), was a religious fanatic who, after having taken a vow of virginity, would run about at night and scream that "the snake of Adam" had entered her—attitudes and events that Bunin would include in the work.

Nikolai's two sons were also unlike "classical" literary types. One, Nikolai Nikolaevich, Bunin's uncle (Uncle Petr in *Dry Valley*), was fired by desires for power and fame. Having failed at a military career, though, he returned home to an undistinguished life and an early death. Nikolai's other son, Aleksei Nikolaevich, Bunin's father (Arkadii in the novel), was no less tragic. A hot-tempered but kindhearted man, he helped defend Sevastopol' in the Crimean War, but he also ended his days at the estate, squandering both his and his wife's inheritances on wine and cards.

To complete the model for Aunt Tonia, Bunin used Nikolai and Aleksei's sister, Varvara Nikolaevna, who needs special comment. As a young girl, she fell madly in love with, but rejected, a visiting officer. Varvara bitterly regretted this decision for the rest of her life, afterwards living alone and wearing nothing except an overcoat and cap. In literal truth, she seemed to be a victim of regression. Bunin's wife, Vera Muromtseva-Bunina, recalled that Varvara was "hunchbacked, with a waxen oval face, a hooked nose, and a sharp chin . . . like the bill of a bird . . . and that when she played the piano and tried to sing with her toothless mouth, she was somehow not normal."[5]

BUNIN AND "ESTATE" FICTION

On the basis of conditions he knew as facts, therefore, Bunin dismissed classical gentry literature as resolutely as he had disavowed idealized peasant fiction. He told an interviewer in 1911: "We know the gentry of Turgenev and Tolstoi; but . . . the life of the gentry in Russia was much more rudimentary, and their soul was much more Russian than either Turgenev or Tolstoi depicted. This life has not yet been captured in fiction about noblemen" (9:536–37).

Just as Bunin had brought the peasant squalor and brutishness of his earlier stories together in *The Village*, so in *Dry Valley* he synthesized all that he had written previously on gentry decline. In fact, he saw the novels as companion pieces (9:536). Specifically, in *Dry Valley* Bunin portrayed "master" and "man" as brothers related by blood and soil. "The nobleman and the peasant have the same life and soul," he told the same interviewer. "In *Dry Valley*, I attempt to portray this similarity . . . to study the Slavic psyche" (9:536, 537).

DRY VALLEY: PREFATORY REMARKS

Bunin's disaffection with estate fiction, his merging of master and man, and his affirmation of the memory of gentry Russia serve as starting points not only for an in-depth analysis of *Dry Valley* but also for aligning this work with the Buddhist underpinnings in his writing. Indeed, it is possible to see *Dry Valley* as a new stage in Bunin's teaching his readers about craving, self, and rebirth.

Dry Valley echoes many of the themes and images of *The Village*, but it also departs radically from its predecessor. For one thing, Bunin's inclusion of master *and* man invests *Dry Valley* with a symmetry that was absent in *The Village*. In *Dry Valley*, Bunin also replaces the omniscient homilist narrator of *The Village* with an intimate *Ich-Erzählung*. By means of this device, three members of an "estate" clan—the anonymous duo, "my sister and I," who are the last surviving members of the Khrushchev clan, and the house serf, Natal'ia—structure their tale as a poetic sermon reflection on the passing of their family and of gentry Russia. Together, lords and peasant grieve, reminisce, and try to make sense of their lives and of their nation's character and past. In *Dry Valley*, Bunin again portrays the fall of a Russian estate, but he avoids a cold, brittle chronicle like the Krasovs' by appealing to memory—the warm and supple recollections both of Natal'ia and of the noble family with whom she has spent her life.

"MY SISTER AND I"

The Khrushchev siblings, known in the work only as "my sister and I," enter *Dry Valley* as individuals who are aware of the illusion of self, as well as of the Paths of Egression and Return. They have ego in check. They reveal only that they are urbanites and members of the clan, feeling no compulsion to suggest importance by disclosing their names, ages, or accomplishments, or telling what they look like or where they live, or even mentioning their economic or marital status.

Moreover, and in stark contrast to many first-person Russian narrators, the Khrushchev siblings do not belabor their own dilemmas or designs. They do not hate the present, fear the future, or dread death. "My sister and I" are also detached from the sociopolitical concerns of their day. They do not talk politics, confront peasants, or pit themselves against the world. Instead, they wish only to rest from "modern" life and to seek enlightenment both for themselves and for Bunin's readers. Specifically, the Khrushchev siblings in *Dry Valley* wish to travel back to their childhood and adolescence; to live surrounded by the ancestors, culture, and nature of other times; and to use insights drawn from the past to illumine their life in the present.

Self as Lord

Starting Difficulties

By virtue of their desire for enlightenment, "my sister and I" adopt a more tentative and probing approach in *Dry Valley* than the narrator did in *The Village*. Indeed, they claim only one certainty: their nobility. The Krasov brothers in *The Village* could barely remember their parents, but the Khrushchev siblings take great pride in their lineage and proclaim it as the starting point for their search. Their family name is inscribed in the Sixth Book of Noblemen, and their ancestors hailed from both the Scythian East and the civilized West and include Tatar princes and Lithuanian noblemen. The Khrushchev narrators also reiterate that they are the children of Arkadii Petrovich Khrushchev, one of the most recent masters of the estate, and that they were the charges of Natal'ia, a house serf with the clan for its final two generations.

"My sister and I" are aware that they do not know the past of Dry Valley well and that their ties to the estate are tenuous. They have come into contact with Dry Valley only twice. As children, they passed it on a journey, and, as young adults, they actually visited the place—a high point in their lives. These two contacts, together with family legends, the sporadic visits from Dry Valley peasants, and the accounts of the serf Natal'ia, are all that this sibling duo actually knows about the estate. Nonetheless, they conduct an energetic investigation into Dry Valley. Almost compulsively, they gather facts, seeking to puzzle out the waning fortunes of the clan. Sometimes, the siblings question Natal'ia about the family and her attraction to the estate; at other times, they rummage through their own recollections of childhood and youth to reconstruct the past of the clan.

"I Remember"

Because of their openness to other times, when the sibling narrators of *Dry Valley* use the phrase "I remember," they accomplish several ends. For one thing, they can spontaneously leave the present and enter upon many "pasts." Indeed, for them, the phrase "I remember" is a type of incantation by which they can discard bleak, everyday reality for worlds of primordial mystery and delight. The brother and sister care little whether the images evoked by "I remember" are real, unreal, ethereal, or symbolic. The important thing is that "I remember" allows them to drift into the past and to warm the present with memory, with excitement, creativity, and love.

For another thing, the phrase allows the duo to take liberties with the content and form of Russian "family chronicles." When they recollect the estate, they do not try to recreate the chainlike progression of precise chronology, linear movement, and cause and effect that Tolstoi, Aksakov, and other family writers observed. Instead, they generate a personal ambience by moving at will among their childhood, adolescent, and adult years.

If You See the Buddha

For instance, as they begin their tale, "my sister and I" disclose the fate of each protagonist before they actually introduce the character into the narrative. As they move along, they scatter fragments of family history throughout the tale. This approach enables them to observe such individuals as Natal'ia and Aunt Tonia from different angles of vision and at various points in time. The result is a diffuse and lyrical narrative in which memory enfleshes and animates the bare bones of people and events.

Above all, the phrase "I remember" invests their story with equanimity and balance. If at times the siblings romanticize the past, they also show the sickness and suffering that they find there. The poisons that destroyed *The Village*, though, are not fated in *Dry Valley*. Rather, when "my sister and I" tell their story, they let memory expose and heal the diseased and wounded of life. The teller of the tale of Durnovka blasphemed estate Russia; by contrast, the nobly born siblings in *Dry Valley* narrate the clan's tragic struggle with self and chain, partially to disclose their triumph, as the last two survivors, in escaping both.

Child, Adolescent, Adult

Throughout their tale, "my sister and I" make it clear that the Path of Return to enlightenment is often a "dry valley" and that progress demands stamina and growth. Their own life story is a case in point, and they use the first three chapters of *Dry Valley* to tell of their own passage to awareness. In so doing, they seek to legitimize their authorial "voice" and to make it the standard by which all other voices in the work can be measured.

In an approach akin to Buddhistic thought, brother and sister Khrushchev view awareness as a series of "flashes" or "moments" by which they gain insight into their world. To this end, they often let memory refract light through the prism of their childhood and adolescent years.

Key themes emerge in the discourse of the siblings. Whatever their age or awareness, "my sister and I" seek to shed light on the estate and the clan. To do this, they appeal to Natal'ia as guide, and, together with her, they explore seminal events, such as the murder of Grandfather Petr Kirillovich by the peasant Gervas'ka, Natal'ia's love for Uncle Petr Petrovich, and Aunt Tonia's liaison with the officer, Voitkevich. The reconstructed tales disclose the rudimentary life of the gentry as well as the Slavic psyche, linking master and man.

The Child Voice

As would be expected, the Khrushchevs' view of Dry Valley changes as they move from childhood to adolescence to adulthood. Indeed, their enlightenment as adults is all the more noteworthy, since in their early years they did

Self as Lord

not ponder the regressive tragedy of the estate but presupposed a Dry Valley of their own imagining. Like the young Kuz'ma Krasov in *The Village*, they lacked discrimination. They embraced the good and the bad, the romantic and they real; they were simply heedless of values or truth.

In all fairness, the Khrushchev youngsters cannot be judged by what they communicate in their child voice. They are, after all, only children, and they know Dry Valley only from fleeting impressions of the family abode: a passing glance at the estate, occasional visits from its peasants, and the snatches of conversation they hear from Natal'ia and others. The child voice in the siblings' account is important, though, because it underscores the dilemma that all the characters in *Dry Valley* confront—the tug-of-war between fantasy and truth and the highly divergent outcomes when one of these triumphs over the other.

As children, the brother and sister are model storytellers. They boldly introduce Natal'ia into the narrative and confirm her as the heroine of the work. From the repository of their own early reminiscences, they grace *Dry Valley* with the first softening touches of memory: excerpts from family songs and legends and the recollected smells of honey and hemp. Such recollections are short-lived, though, since the young siblings are also hosts to burgeoning egos that resist moderation or even reality.

For example, as children, the Khrushchevs are highly self-protective about their position in life. Without reflection, they stand firm on their gentry status. The cruelty and contradictions of the estate simply excite them; they neither understand Natal'ia's attachment to Dry Valley nor censure the suffering that the family has inflicted upon her. At this early age, "my sister and I" are not yet aware of chain and rebirth. They are oblivious to Natal'ia's brownish-black hands, thin smiles, and pursed lips; they are unmoved by the undulating fields and stone-filled gullies that mark their first glimpses of the estate.

Worse, the Khrushchev children do not regard the evil threatening the estate as a stimulus to "endless fantasies"[6] about their roots. They cannot anticipate when Dry Valley will become, for them, a refuge for ancestors, culture, and primordial existence. To their childish minds, Dry Valley is only their particular place of gothic horror, the abode of mythopoetic heroes stained with blood and gore. The siblings "all but swoon" (135) when they fancy the estate as the site of murders, insanity, and intrigue. They "exchange ecstatic looks" (135) when Natal'ia tells them that their ancestors were "hot-tempered like gunpowder" (135), or that they threw bones to glowering borzois, or that, faithful to their Scythian origins, they sat down to meals at the manor with Tatar whips on their laps. As children, the siblings never question the depravity of what they see or hear. They not only enjoy their myth making, but they also assume that someday they will follow their ancestors'

If You See the Buddha

example. Potentially, the youthful Khrushchevs are already unconscious victims of karma.

The Adolescent Voice

The children of *Dry Valley* mature into more sensitive adolescents, however, and begin to develop a radically different view of the world. They look upon the estate soberly and somberly, attentive to discrepancies that had eluded them before. They notice—but do not resist—their changing awareness. "As we grew older," they confess, "we listened more attentively to everything . . . about Dry Valley; and what we had failed to understand before grew clearer now, so that the peculiarities of life there stood out more sharply" (134).

The most notable shift in the account of the adolescent siblings is their emerging sense of realism and balance. The two have abandoned the romanticism of their childhood. They neither see themselves as the center of the universe nor view the family estate as a gothic memorial over which they will rule. Furthermore, the compatible pair grasp that, though suffering is part of life, the pain of the present can be greatly assuaged by their recollections of the past.

To the Khrushchev adolescents, Dry Valley is a homestead in ruins. It is the final resting place of people long since gone and the haven of some who are breathing their last. They readily relinquish their earlier fantasies about the clan's whips at dinner and accept the regressed reality that the dining hall is only half its original size. The youths even intuit that a source of disorder is present and that the "gentry" are dissolving into geometric and gray tinged shards: "aggregates." When they arrive at Dry Valley, a fierce thunderstorm suggests both the treachery of Mara and the myths of Fall and Flood. Like an evil spirit, a dark mauve thundercloud slumps heavily upon the earth, and lightning flashes "in swift fiery snakes" (138) across the sky. The constellation of Scorpio "shines in a triangle of silver, like a gravestone with a little roof over the cross" (143).

As they investigate more deliberately, the siblings are particularly struck by what will be a key image in the work: the icon of Mercurius of Smolensk. Somberly, they recall the ancient legend. With the help of the Virgin, Mercurius had defeated the Tatars. Later, his enemies beheaded him as he slept, but he returned home with his head in his hands, himself a victim of regression. The icon is also shrunk, splintered, and framed in heavy silver; on the reverse side, one can read the family lineage inscribed there. Mercurius has a bluish-gray head and an iron helmet and sandals. Natal'ia and the senior Khrushchevs cherish this sacramental, but the adolescents see it as auguring the clan's fragmentation, shrinkage, and "manacled" existence.

The adolescent Khrushchev duo also takes in-depth note of the regression afflicting the humans and animals of the estate. As the narrator in *The*

Village used composites and types in his pictures of the peasants, the adolescents combine folk, iconographic, and modernist modes to portray the family's decline. The protagonists of *Dry Valley* are "prisoners who love their shackles," victims of "hostile forces" in a "world of goblins and ghosts."[7] Indistinctly sexed torsoes, lines and circles, and daubs of reds and blacks are typical features. Natal'ia has a dark wrinkled neck, jutting collarbones, and tired, sad eyes. Aunt Tonia is seen, alternately, as Baba-Yaga, the witch of Slavic folklore, and also a pathetic grande dame whose shawl of gold lace (recall Youngbride's lace-curtain veil in *Dry Valley*) hangs like a chain of mail about her shoulders.[8] Further, Tonia has entered samsara. She screeches likes a parrot, her shriveled body is shrouded in a dressing gown and hood, her face is "dotted" with flies, and her sex is often indeterminant.

The adolescents see that the animals of Dry Valley are also in rebirth. Horses are shockingly lean in the summer lightning; rabbits have split lips and squinting or goggling eyes. It is, however, a barn owl that shows the loss of its persona most poignantly. The bird has triangular ears and, like Aunt Tonia, looks "wild and fiendish" (142). A soul "reborn" as an animal, the anguished owl serves as a warning that the clan will suffer a similar fate. The creature "struggles to remember something" and lets loose "a wail of amazement" (143) when it grasps the wisdom that has eluded it for so long. Such "enlightenment" does not console the bird, though, since it is past the time for insights into life. The owl's moans "presage disaster" (142) to all; its "hysterical screeching and laughter" (143) mock the vainglory of ego and herald the rebirth awaiting humankind.

"My sister and I" respond to the plight of Dry Valley neither with the fantasies of their childhood nor with the distemper of the people and animals they find at the estate. Rather, their recollections function as a catalyst to self-knowledge and to a better understanding of the world. Like travelers in ancient myths, they win out against obstacles that could impede their search. Tonia, Mercurius, and the owl capture their attention but not their minds and hearts. As disciples to truth, they press on bravely, moving down the dark corridors and rooms of the home until they find openings onto a fresh and pristine world.

The adolescents are thus able to succeed in their quest only because they are innately open to their milieu. For example, if the peasants in *The Village* saw the lightning that flashes about Durnovka as portending apocalypse, "my sister and I" see the lightning that illumines the Khrushchev estate as revealing "mountains of roseate gold" (140). Such an image is welcome in the "dry valley" of life and can be interpreted as encouraging their ascent to enlightenment. Nature also supports the siblings. Warm, moist breezes and the aromatic smells of trees and the earth enter the siblings' memory. The young people sense the very "depths of Russia" (140). They "think and think" (141), countering samsaric images of regression and death with Nirvana-like impressions of beauty and light: the streaming sun, the spreading trees, and the joyous sounds of animals and birds.

It is also during their encounters with nature that "my sister and I" discern the ego-laden pitfalls in romantic love. Earlier as children, they had listened spellbound when told how Aunt Tonia had gone insane from love. They can now reconstruct her affair with Voitkevich as entry to rebirth. Voitkevich, they note, is Kalmyck—that is, he was born a Buddhist Tatar—but as an officer, he has rejected his heritage for Scythianism and self. Tonia's lover is thus recalled by the siblings as a regressed, formless "*he*" (141, their italics), who is marked only by clamped jaws and a lined brow. Voitkevich has a penchant for the kind of violence that sends his victims to new "rounds" of life. In a fit of anger, for example, he crushes a butterfly into "silvery powder" (141): an act which augurs the devastation that will come to Tonia, the crushing of her existence.

The Adult Voice

As adults, "my sister and I" advance story lines that they had only dimly surmised as children and adolescents, making clear who loved, ruined, or murdered whom. More important, they seek to make amends for wrongs, their own included. They redress their previous arrogance toward Natal'ia by according her full status as a member of the clan. By proclaiming that she is "really one of us, gentlefolk of ancient lineage" (134), they point to other bonds of unity between master and man—for example, Natal'ia and Arkadii had been suckled at the same breast, and Arkadii and Gervas'ka had exchanged baptismal crosses.

The adult siblings concede also that the family's ties to the peasants have triggered social regression in the Khrushchev clan. Patrician "fathers" have sired plebeian "sons." "From time immemorial," the siblings state realistically, "the blood of the Khrushchevs mingled with that of the servants and villagers" (136). They also make public the questions of paternity that surround Grandfather Petr Kirillich, his legitimate sons, and the bastard son and peasant, Gervas'ka.

When the adult Khrushchev siblings talk about master and man at the estate, they do so not as "repentant noblemen," internalizing guilt over the lot of the folk. They see the people as "desperate idlers and dreamers" in need of "spiritual satisfaction" (136). They bring the peasants of the estate into the clan because their enlightened state urges them to assuage earlier wrong and pain. To act otherwise, the siblings believe, would imperil their own hard-won spiritual independence and undermine the truth they wish to proclaim to the world.

When they recollect the estate as adults, therefore, "my sister and I" do not focus on the misery and regression that had intrigued them as children and adolescents. They recognize that the history of a family is often a gruesome affair and that legends are often "poison to the Slav," since they can give rise to "dreams stronger than reality" (136), but the siblings are now able to use what they have learned from their own visits to the estate. They know that the clan's love for the past and its reverence for the language, legends, and songs of the estate are the embryo of consciousness and phenomena that resist rebirth and the ravages of time and space. In their enlightenment, they grasp that "what is bred in the bone, is in the flesh" (133) and that Dry Valley—despite its many inadequacies—is their wellspring of memory and of their definition in life. They let "recollections" (136) reveal the rhythmic unity of existence: "the sway of the steppe, the ancient clannishness that united the village and the manor-house into one" (136). With these "truths" in mind, they proceed with courage, faith, and love.

THE VOICE OF NATAL'IA

After the Khrushchevs have disclosed their own passage to awareness, they allow Natal'ia's story to be heard in her own voice. Their purpose here is twofold. Through the testimony of another member of the clan, the siblings validate their own experiences with self. Also, by allowing Natal'ia to discourse upon her life, they provide a balance of voices between master and man and affirm that the path to awareness is open to all.

"My sister and I" prepare for Natal'ia as a spokesperson into *Dry Valley* by conversing with her during their accounts as children and adolescents. To the very young Khrushchevs, Natal'ia is a startling witness to the cruelty of the clan. She is the first to tell the children of the trials of Grandfather Petr, Aunt Tonia, and Gervas'ka, and to give hints of how she herself nearly went insane from her unrequited love for Uncle Petr and remains unmarried by order of Aunt Tonia.

The Natal'ia recalled by the very young Khrushchevs has markings of physical regression—her dark hands and her thin lips and smile. Natal'ia tells the children only the evil of Dry Valley, never the good. They can see that her stories come from a source of "great bitterness" (135) and thus serve as an admonition against their own specious fantasies. Natal'ia is thus not the totally otherworldly and selfless servant that some critics of *Dry Valley* have claimed her to be.[9] She, too, capitulates to ego when she firmly insists to her charges that she is not a lowly peasant but is on equal footing with her masters: a "real and proper miss," and "a second aunt" to them (134).

Several times in the children's account, though, Natal'ia seems well poised for enlightenment. She is without a "corner and ties of her own" (135). She is sufficiently self-sacrificing to care for the children, a fact that wins her their acceptance in later years. Equally important, Natal'ia passes on to the Khrushchev children the memory of Dry Valley. Finally, Natal'ia does not

If You See the Buddha

seek revenge for all that she has endured. Rather, she sees her misfortune as "God's will" (133) and accepts the many injustices of her life.

The contradictions in the children's portrait of Natal'ia—her bondage to the chain and her attempts to escape it—continue in their account as adolescents. On the one hand, Natal'ia shows new signs of decay. In fact, she often seems to have left this world and to have entered the next. Her eyes, neck, and torso are iconlike; hands and arms are bent, folded, or crossed; and her voice alone often tells of her presence. Furthermore, Natal'ia is still tainted by ego and the evil of the estate. She still considers herself to be above the other servants; she is unnerved by the regressed owl's screams; she worships the ironclad Mercurius, bowing low to "the invisible saint in the darkness" (143).

Natal'ia's recollections grow darker with age, since she furnishes new details on the gloomy house, the deranged clan, and her banishment to Soshki. In the adolescents' account, Natal'ia does not direct her charges to enlightenment. She does not shelter the youngsters from harm, nor does she urge them to look beyond the storms, Tonia, and the ominous owl. She does not escort the adolescents through the dark house or open windows and doors onto the garden. Indeed, Natal'ia is simply not part of the siblings' search.

On the other hand, as described by the Khrushchev adolescents, Natal'ia does make some progress toward self-knowledge. She offsets much of her apparent regression with her soft smile and kind face. Natal'ia also seeks to hold her ego in check. "My sister and I" see her as a "kind and gracious soul" (143), who, as the "bard" (140) of Dry Valley, sings lovingly of her roots and brings a "feminine" touch to life.

After their long separation from the estate, Natal'ia is, in fact, memory incarnate. She is a spirit-anima who speaks and moves softly, sits near open windows, utters a discourse rich in sayings and songs, and suggests a life view of forgiveness, hope, and love. It is also Natal'ia who introduces them to the healing power of the past. When she recalls her youth, she draws solace from the very people who later caused her ruin. For all her pain and suffering, she can admit that life at Dry Valley was often "good in the old days" (144), or that she was enthralled by her first love. Drawing on the softening power of memory, Natal'ia can reinterpret her exile at Soshki in terms of adventure and as a light punishment for her "sins." She can still love and pray for the deceased Uncle Petr, and she can even forgive Tonia. Simply put, Natal'ia evinces the triumph of her past over her present.

The siblings devote chapters 4 to 9, roughly half of *Dry Valley*, to Natal'ia's memories of the estate. At first, the second part of *Dry Valley* seems like the first. "My sister and I" continue to control the narrative, using Natal'ia's voice as a type of reported speech to clarify and embellish their own emerging ideas about the Khrushchev clan and the bonds between master and man. In this second part the young Khrushchevs also repeat earlier images and events. Demented masters, Tatar whips, ironclad icons, and glowering borzois are the thematic refrains in their narrative symphony.

The second part of *Dry Valley* differs from the first part, however, in that "my sister and I" speak only in their adult voice. Both their actions and their reactions identify them as wayfarers who turn back the clock some fifty years, and, with Natal'ia as guide, "return" to Dry Valley to view, firsthand, the tragedy of their ancestors.

THE MEN OF DRY VALLEY

The Lord Fathers

Another difference in the second part of the narrative is that "my sister and I" take up a topic that had not come up earlier, the men of Dry Valley. These include Grandfather Petr, his two sons, Gervas'ka, and the unrelated procession of wizards and holy men who pass through the estate.

The last of the Khrushchev men of Dry Valley are consummate egos. They live for the present and function well only in self-secured systems of manorial power and order. "Masters" can be content and carefree; "men" are expected to be humble and true. Indeed, so long as both groups subscribe to estate "etiquette," they can both live with the changes eroding sociopolitical distinctions.

As Natal'ia and the siblings show, however, the men of Dry Valley cannot accept sudden or overt threats to the established routine. Their reaction is always the same: fear, disorientation, force, appeal to "roles," and, ultimately, a struggle to the death by which they seek to fend off perceived loss. In each succeeding crisis, the men of Dry Valley find that their efforts to reimpose themselves on their milieu are less effective. The more they struggle to reassert themselves, the more ground they lose, and the more threateningly the specter of rebirth looms over their horizon. Invariably, the men of Dry Valley self-destruct, since they cannot live by any rules other than their own.

The masters of the estate—Grandfather Petr Kirillich and his two sons, Arkadii and Uncle Petr—are cases in point. As recalled by Natal'ia in her account to the siblings, the masters of the Khrushchev clan hail from longstanding positions of power and prestige. Great-grandfather Khrushchev, Petr Kirillich's father, cut a wide swath through life. Even as an old man, Great-grandfather not only asserted himself against nature, destroying the primeval forests that stood in the path of his future home, but also enforced a code of self-governance, regulating titles and conduct, time and space: "masters and owners, rule and obedience, holidays and weekdays" (149).

Proving the transience of ego, though, Great-grandfather's self-inscribed code does not survive one generation. When Grandfather Petr Kirillich comes to prominence, all that he is master of is only Dry Valley, the smaller and poorer part of the original patrimony. Furthermore, apparently giving sustenance to rumors that he was, in fact, fathered by a peasant, Grandfather Petr does not protest his diminished lot. Whereas a full-blooded offspring would surely have revitalized the code, reunited the estate, or, at the very least, reclaimed his wife from the arms of a "serf-scoundrel and thief" (181), Petr does nothing. Like the icon of Mercurius, he accepts himself and his world as truncated. When he is confronted by the abrupt and permanent change caused by the death of his wife, though, Petr himself changes immediately from hapless patriarch to despotic tyrant. Earlier, he had been generous, flexible, and carefree; now he is compulsive and consumed by conflicting needs for self-preservation, on one hand, and for renewed law and order, on the other.

For example, Grandfather Petr plans for visitors, who, he hopes, will honor him as the paterfamilias of the estate, but such measures are futile. Petr regularly sits down to dinners that lack taste and nutrition but that are rife with chain and rebirth: bubbling (dotted) *surovets* and great quantities of coarse, gray salt. Grandfather Petr also cannot fulfill his cravings for deference and attention. Visitors rarely come; his family chases him from their rooms; even the servants abuse him. Also, like Tikhon in *The Village,* Petr makes himself dreadfully ill. His face becomes clouded, his shoulders rounded. His housecoat and high boots barely conceal his emaciated body.

Petr's mind is similarly disordered. For instance, when he roams the estate, Petr does not enter the garden but is moved only to imagine jangling stagecoach bells and (dot-inducing) hail clouds in the sky. In fact, his premonitions of chaos become self-fulfilling prophecies. Like menacing phantoms, storms "creep up from behind the garden" (148) and mercilessly pound the estate.

It soon becomes apparent to the clan that since Grandfather Petr is no longer in control, the system of governance that had prevailed at Dry Valley is defunct, and that the issue of "who rules whom" (148) is an open one. The clan, though, fails to call a conclave, choose a new leader, devise a new code of conduct, or revitalize the old one. Rather, they opt, however unconsciously, for disintegration and decline. They value the old ways only as screens for acts of power and greed.

The so-called French people of Dry Valley are the first samsaric victims of the estate. As tutors to Tonia and her brothers, they have helped preserve a modicum of decorum at the estate, but, they are readily affected by the chaos invading the home. Indeed, they regress even more rapidly than Grandfather Petr. Mademoiselle Suzie always shivers. Monsieur Louis Ivanovich is sketched with sweeping curves—for example, "long moustaches," "exceedingly wide trousers narrowed at the bottom," and "hair plastered across his bald pate from ear to ear" (148). Also, the phrase that the French

Self as Lord

people make the children practice—*Maitre corbeau sur un arbre perché*—suggests that the tutors are in transit to a lower, animal state.

The tutors depart, but they leave behind a void that is filled by an almost palpable spirit of evil. Icons disappear in the unlit darkness; borzois are allowed to be present at dinner. The house loses living color and is depicted in stark contrasts: whites from lightning outside, blacks from the shadows within. The growing chaos at Dry Valley brings Grandfather Petr to a breaking point, to a life-and-death confrontation with his environs.

Like Tikhon, Grandfather Petr attempts to regain control by means of superstition and ritual. He hangs towels and lights candles to placate evil spirits and to win the Almighty to his side. More revealing, though, are Petr's futile attempts to restore himself and the code of family conduct. Gervas'ka is the focus of his efforts. In truth, Grandfather Petr fears Gervas'ka greatly. As Natal'ia tells the siblings, Grandfather avoids the servants' hall and regularly takes abuse from his bastard son and adversary. Almost out of necessity, Grandfather believes that Gervas'ka is the source of his ills. He thinks that if he takes this insidiously powerful serf in hand, he can regain full authority on the estate. A party at Dry Valley gives Grandfather the opportunity to try.

To regain his role as lord of the estate, Grandfather Petr seizes the spotlight. He acts the proper host, expands a party into a three-day holiday, and then takes the opportunity to lodge a formal, public complaint against Gervas'ka. Although Grandfather is "blissfully happy" (158) with his efforts, the clan sees him both as a buffoon who reduces estate rituals to "farce" (162) and as a person regressed to childishness. They have ample reason for such views. Petr bursts out crying when he denounces Gervas'ka, and then he blurts out that Tonia is with her aunt, thereby abetting rumors that his daughter is pregnant.

Grandfather Petr acts not as a patriarch but as a man facing execution. During the party, he tugs nervously at his collar, speaks in a thin voice, and becomes agitated for no apparent reason. He also feels menaced. Petr does, however, accomplish one thing: He turns the gala event at Dry Valley into his own metaphorical wake. The guests celebrate a ritual that lays to rest both Petr as the leader of the clan and the code of conduct that he has endeavored to restore. Hours of muffled conversation take place in darkened rooms amidst "great clusters of lighted spermaceti candles" (162). The last image is rich in implication. On one hand, the candles recall the plight of the Krasov brothers in *The Village:* their aroused-but-failed manhood, their golden cagelike existence, and their impending end. On the other hand, the candles invest *Dry Valley* with a liturgical aura, since they evoke the "glitter of a church" (162), and consume gentry life in "expensive, aromatic smoke" (162): incense.

As recollected by Natal'ia and the siblings, Grandfather Petr's death surprises no one. His self has not only refused to live in a world that it can no longer control, but it has also blinded its host to enlightenment. Although Petr does several potentially salvific things before his end—for example, at the party, he moves back the heavy furniture, undoes the iron bolts of doors, and stands on the threshold of his home to welcome guests—he does so not to attain movement or freedom but only to "conform to ancient custom" (159) and to nurture his image as patriarch of the estate. Even worse, Petr does not heed nature, which calls to him only moments before his death. He looks at the dawning universe only from behind glass portals or as it is reflected in the mirrors of his home. He thus misses not only the joyous beauty of the creation but also symbols and warnings of the chain—for example, the "silver and saltlike frost" that "dot" and congeal the land (163).

Natal'ia and the siblings regard Grandfather's end as "ridiculous" (158). After a short, pathetic encounter with Gervas'ka—two bastard selves united in blood—Petr slips and strikes his temple. He does not die so much as he shatters, a vessel gone brittle from ego and age. The lines and circles that mark Petr's face and body indicate his fate. Circular adornments, a golden amulet and a wedding ring, may have given Petr security in life, but now, when joined to "senselessly slanting eyes" (Tatar/Scythian) and a "gaping mouth" (164), they suggest a fixity from which he will never escape.

The Lord Sons

The sins of Grandfather Petr are visited on his sons: Arkadii (the siblings' father) and Petr (the siblings' uncle). Rumors about the sons' own illicit paternity seem legitimate because they take possession of their surroundings not as "master" but as "man." Arkadii and Uncle Petr have never known a restraining hand. Neglected once the French people leave the estate, they are ignorant of memory and of the codes that keep self in bounds. They thus follow in their father's footsteps, unconscious victims of karma.

Arkadii and Uncle Petr are unseasoned and roughly hewn. Unlike the sibling narrators, they have failed to move from childhood to adulthood. They take refuge in roles and make no attempt to restore the estate. They are too preoccupied with prolonging pleasure and avoiding pain to heed the dangers about them. Indeed, they actually nurture the very people who can do them harm.

Initially, Arkadii, the father of the siblings, seems free of inner shackles. Tramping about in woods, playing the balalaika, and seeking equality with Gervas'ka suggest that he has stilled the cravings of self, and that he has even had a glimpse into Nirvana. Close analysis, though, reveals that Arkadii is a mere child, a "sheep among wolves" (149). He is restless and shallow. He seeks out nature, music, and the common man, yes, but only to escape life's real challenges and to fill in the empty hours of his existence. Furthermore, Arkadii handles sudden threats to his routine with the same defensive strategies his father, Grandfather Petr, used to use. He claims to love Gervas'ka like a brother, but he slaps Gervas'ka in the face when the serf steps out of bounds.

Uncle Petr has a more tortuous experience with self. To the surprise of the clan, Petr suddenly retires from the army and reappears at the estate. In so doing, though, he has sown the seeds of his own demise. Petr has given up his military career not because he curses ambition or glory or because he wishes to find his roots. He returns home to Dry Valley believing that he is a savior of "the family honor and the estate" (158). In short, Petr has merely exchanged codes of conduct and has adopted the more subjective and pleasing one. Ambition to do anything brave or noble sinks, gradually, into the quicksand of unearned and arbitrary power at Dry Valley.

Like Kuz'ma in *The Village*, Petr has learned little from his time away from home, for when he returns to Dry Valley, he is even more childish and contradictory than Arkadii. Though at times, Petr is "awkward and boyish" (151), an individual who blushes easily, frets about appearances, and becomes confused to the point of tears, at other times, he is vengeful, harsh, and cruel. Petr welcomes the chance to rule the estate, but the results are tragicomic. He is a model "autocrat" (158) given to "gentry" notions of titles and conduct. He dresses in regal clothes, proclaims his sacrifice to all, and nurtures a "holiday atmosphere" (152) to offset his earlier brooding and discontent.

Petr's efforts to exalt himself, though, only betray his impotence and naïveté. Despite an ample body build, Petr has small hands and feet. Tatar slippers, turquoise rings, and a face "as delicate as a young lady's" (152) identify him as effeminate, ill-formed, and Scythian. Very clearly Petr is in regression.

Like his father also, Uncle Petr does not restore law and order to the estate. Although he seeks to steer Dry Valley on a "new course of glitter and leisure" (151), he cannot placate Grandfather, soothe Tonia, or stabilize Arkadii. In the Khrushchev manner, he overreacts to sudden threats but lets genuine evils go unheeded. For instance, Petr sends Natal'ia into exile merely for stealing a mirror, but he tolerates the tryst between Voitkevich and Tonia, and he seeks to curry favor with Gervas'ka. Also, Petr spends his days both fearing and yearning for death. By analogy to Mercurius, he regularly clutches his head; like Tikhon, he arms himself, takes to drink, and charges off into the wintry night. In the end, Petr is killed either by a serf or by a spirited young mare: the truth will never be known. Revealingly, Petr's progeny is simultaneously in rebirth. His infant son is seen as inscribed circles: the babe has milky eyes and blows bubbles from his mouth; in a new variation on Mercurius, he topples over because of his heavy head.

The Peasants

Physically, the serfs of *Dry Valley* resemble the peasants in *The Village*, but they differ from their brothers at Durnovka in that, like their "masters," they also appeal to the etiquette of the estate, and for similar reasons. The folk of *Dry Valley* see the line between "master" and "man" as an anchor in their lives. Inertia, yearnings for security, and fears of alternatives motivate them to uphold flagging codes of conduct and to function as associates of the clan.

Two peasants of *Dry Valley*, however, exempt themselves from this protocol. Gervas'ka and the monk Iushka both compete with the other males for control of the estate. Gervas'ka exploits estate etiquette to assert his insolence; Iushka, one of the most depraved souls of *Dry Valley*, dispenses with rules altogether.

To Natal'ia and the siblings, Gervas'ka is a special type of serf: a frightful hybrid of "master" and "man." Gervas'ka does what Grandfather Petr and his sons cannot. He commands fear and respect from everyone at the estate. He is addressed by his formal name and patronymic; and he becomes such a devotee of manorial etiquette that he translates the clan's yearnings for order into action. "A genius!" Uncle Petr Petrovich proclaims, "with hands of gold!" (161). As described by Natal'ia, though, Gervas'ka's atavism cannot be disguised: he falls between an "ancient Aryan or Persian and a borzoi" (160). He has an oversized body, an undersized head, and "disproportionately long legs" (160). His face has deep eye sockets, a razor-sharp mouth, and strands of curly hair.

Gervas'ka is regarded by the clan not as an open threat but as a hulking presence that sets all on edge. He engages everyone in battles of will, assured that he will be the winner. For instance, Gervas'ka scolds Grandfather and almost kills Arkadii in play, but he goes unscathed even when he demands punishment for his sins. Regressive, bared teeth and his doglike grin are the only weapons that Gervas'ka needs to drive Dry Valley into submission.

At a farther reach of samsara, the monk Iushka is the devil himself. Iushka openly disparages the codes and roles of the estate. He poses as a village Rasputin, a herald of divine might, on one hand, but a vaunter of his lechery on the other, with "more rut in him than a goat" (179). Iushka succeeds in his effrontery for several reasons. For one thing, he chooses his time well. When he arrives at Dry Valley, the clan's men are dead or absent from the estate. For another thing, Iushka's instincts tell him that he can command a warm welcome from Dry Valley and from "Rus" (179), his regressed medieval homeland.

Iushka quickly gains the confidence of the clan, although its members soon realize that he will drag them to ruin. Their impotent response is to give him greater license to wreak havoc on their lives. Iushka is ego unbounded in sexual appetite. He beds Tonia and regularly rapes Natal'ia, impregnating her before he departs from the estate. The monk of Dry Valley disappears as quickly as he has arrived, leaving shattered lives and chaos in his wake.

Self as Lord

THE WOMEN OF DRY VALLEY

Aunt Tonia

Upon first glance, the women of Dry Valley are like the men of the estate, but the two key women, Aunt Tonia and Natal'ia, vaunt ego more subtly than their male colleagues. Their driving force is a Buddhist taboo, romantic love.

Initially, Tonia and Natal'ia observe the restraining rules of sex and caste. Tonia reads poetry and plays the piano; Natal'ia feeds the chickens and shines the boots. Both women see their lives as "dull and shut in" (151), until the arrival of Uncle Petr and his fellow officer, Voitkevich, at Dry Valley. This event ignites fantasies for power and prestige. Uncle Petr and Voitkevich make life at Dry Valley exciting, but the situation degenerates quickly, since the two women become so taken by a self in love that they lose all sense of reality. Each sees herself not as a member of the clan but as a solitary princess yearning to live happily ever after with her prince. Both Tonia and Natal'ia pay a high price for these projections of love. Sweetness and dreams yield to violation, madness, and despair. Worse, the two do not learn from their mistakes but repeat them on a cosmic scale.

In truth, Tonia has always lived in the shadow of the chain. Like her brothers, she has been left to her own devices, since the French people have left the estate, and she is particularly unschooled in the ways of ego. When Tonia meets Voitkevich, therefore, her aroused feelings fire her being and cause it to break from estate etiquette and restraint.

The scene of Tonia and Voitkevich at the piano dramatizes their tragic relationship. As Natal'ia tells her charges, Voitkevich approaches Tonia with "honorable intentions" (159). He brings her flowers, plays duets with her, and reads her poetry, all of which, incidentally, he does amidst open doors and the cool fragrances of the garden. Tonia, though, quickly moves from infatuation to eros; but her first tryst with Voitkevich leaves her both angry and confused. Tonia has learned too late that her lover is not a prince. He is, however, a catalyst for emotions that, once aroused, she cannot restrain. In fact, Voitkevich's crime against Tonia is not that he has destroyed her sexual innocence but that he has awakened her latent self to realize her reduced lot in life.

Tonia changes immediately after the tryst. She becomes more like her father and brothers. Her confusion—the result of guilt mixed with passion—is symbolized by her hands. Tonia alternates from constantly pulling down the sleeves of her dress to executing anguished polonaises on the piano. Also, Tonia flares wildly whenever Voitkevich tries to be civil, and she sits alone and with her back to the sun, preferring the darkening shadows of the house.

When Voitkevich leaves the estate, Tonia experiences still greater regression and pain. As she is now completely deprived of the object of its yearning, life is even emptier than before. Very much like Grandfather Petr had done in his crisis, Tonia becomes paranoid, restless, and cruel. Silence and bitter sobs betray the presence of a distraught ego. Indeed, in her anxious state, Tonia responds as if "someone else were doing the talking for her" (166).

Tonia finds little respite from her pain. Relics, wizards, and visits to holy places only underscore her captivity in rebirth. For instance, when Tonia seeks help from the sorcerer Klim, she is frightened by his chain-gray beard, curly gray hair, and steel-gray coat. His incantations, a grim parody of Jesus' raising the daughter of Jairus, make her eyes bulge and her body shake. Tonia, of course, cannot learn from this frightening experience, so she repeats her underlying mistake by seeking out other, more unnatural princes for her fantasy world. Selecting the Prince of Darkness in Iushka, she abandons poetry and piano for nights of "voluptuous and wild moaning" (180); she casts herself as a modern-day Eve "being strangled by the snake of Eden" (180).

After Iushka, Tonia goes to the opposite extreme and declares herself a "bride of Christ" (180)—that is, she wishes to possess the Prince of Light and to be a princess of the world. Natal'ia and the siblings are silent about whether Tonia delivers a child or whether, in fact, she was actually ever pregnant. The issue, though, is moot. The self in Tonia, like a ravaging disease, cannot support new life or a rival ego within the confines of the estate.

Natal'ia

Natal'ia is also a woman in "love"; but her story is more important than Tonia's for several reasons. For instance, when Natal'ia tells her tale, she resolves many of the riddles and half-answered questions that have troubled the sibling narrators from the beginning: for example, why she was exiled from Dry Valley, why she prays daily for the soul of Uncle Petr, and, why, for all her kindness and simplicity, she shows increasing decay.

Also, Natal'ia's "love" differs from Tonia's in quality and degree. Although Natal'ia is never intimate with Petr, she is deeply, often erotically stirred by her fantasies of him. As noted earlier, Natal'ia is drawn to Petr because he enlivens the stultifying life of the estate. Natal'ia's fantasized love for Petr allows her, in her mind at least, to establish a place for herself in the world. She aspires to escape her peasant status and to be equal with the clan.

Natal'ia begins to revere and to covet everything of Petr's, including a small mirror of his that she steals. Although her act is of little consequence initially, it causes a chain of events that Natal'ia cannot halt. Possessing the mirror, she no longer relates to Petr as servant to lord but as "princess" to "prince" (155). Like Tonia, Natal'ia fosters ego in private; indeed, her emotional outpourings are often so intense that they move her to erotic ecstasy. Peering into the looking glass, Natal'ia "creates an imaginary intimacy between herself and Petr" (153). She becomes so aroused by such thoughts that her head "reels" (152) from the "encounter."[10]

Self as Lord

In such a state, Natal'ia loses her grip on reality and misreads cues of her wrongdoing. For example, she is blind to the threat that Petr's mirror represents. It may bring a heady lightness to Natal'ia's cold, dark life, but it also provides a one-dimensional, sterile reflection of existence. Also, since Petr's mirror folds and is framed in "heavy silver" (153), it augurs the collapse of Natal'ia's dream and her bondage in the chain.

Natal'ia's fantasy ends in disgrace. Petr, unnerved by yet one more challenge to his "rule," banishes the serf from the estate. In so doing, he unwittingly subjects Natal'ia to further decline. The hair of the would-be princess is shorn; she is dressed in ticking and perched on top of a manure cart for public view. Like a prisoner, she is banished from her Edenic world to a life of labor and exile in the hot steppe.

In Exile

Traveling into exile, Natal'ia is confronted by an expanse of blinding whiteness, smelling of iron and rot and streaked with silvers and golds. A cathedral in the distance has "white metal domes" that shine like "silver stars" against a "bleak and bluish-white sky" (156).

At first, Natal'ia staves off the assaults of the dismal scene with the help of the past. Recollections of Dry Valley's cool garden scents and warm kitchen fragrances distract her from the dust and heat of the road. The exiled serf does not understand, though, what mechanisms are at work in her. She does not suspect the viciousness and tenacity of self, or the ways in which ego blocks enlightenment. Misapprehending her situation, Natal'ia also misuses her memories. She uses these to reconstruct her fairy-tale life with Petr in the garden.

Natal'ia's actions are catastrophic. Fantasy transmutes to nightmare. Just as rural disharmony had unnerved Tikhon in *The Village*, jangling bells, swishing wheels, and thudding horses and troikas bring Natal'ia nearly to delirium. She conjures up Petr not as a tender lover but as an apocalyptic horseman who charges toward her from the steppe. The image cuts two ways. On one hand, Natal'ia's fantasy of Petr brings her to new suffering. Terror and feelings of separation and loss "pierce her nervous heart" (157). On the other hand, Natalia's hallucination about Petr's coming is salvific because it shatters the serf's love for her master. When Natal'ia realizes that what she sees is not Petr, she first loses consciousness and then is overcome by nausea. Symbolically, she has escaped the grip of self and has even disgorged it from her body. At this critical juncture, Natal'ia also glimpses Nirvana. Her torso becomes cool and limp, and she feels as though "she has no body at all, but only a soul that is as happy as though it were in heaven" (157).

Holding Firm

Natal'ia does not manage to keep free; rather, she resumes yearning for Petr and the garden. Masochistically, she seeks to "master the torments of her love for Petr" and to "bury it deep in the depths of her soul" (157). Thus, as was the case with Uncle Petr during his years in the army, Natal'ia gains little from her time away from home. In her case, such an outcome is very sad, for it can be argued that Natal'ia, more than anyone else in *Dry Valley*, consciously assents to her ruin.

For instance, in exile at Soshki, Natal'ia craves Petr and her fairy-tale world so much at times that she regards images of "shackled" life with "awe-struck fascination" (169). For instance, she is attracted by people in rebirth. Her new master, the peasant Sharyi, or "Sphere-like," is nicknamed "Badger." He has a wedge-shaped head, silver hair, a Tatar moustache, and a face that is wrinkled and burnt black by the sun. Sharyi's wife, Marina, has skin like "polished wood" (169) and clothes marked with spirals and circles (e.g., a turbanlike kerchief with red dots).

Keeping Petr uppermost in her mind, however, Natal'ia reinforces herself with its emotions, passion, and woe. She feels anew the "agony of jealousy and shame"; she drinks "to the dregs the bittersweet poison of unrequited love" (169). In fact, Natal'ia is so obsessed by her love for Petr that she psychically hastens her lover's entry into rebirth. Like Tonia's lover, Voitkevich, Petr gradually becomes only a *"he"* (170; Natal'ia's italics), a regressed figment of Natal'ia's imagination.

Natal'ia pays dearly for her unrestrained desire. News that Petr has gotten married and that he is fighting in the Crimea sharpens her feelings of longing and loss, advancing her in rebirth. In her time away from the estate, Natal'ia's appearance assumes "modern" lines: black and brown transmute to red; lines and angles multiply along with circles and dots. During the day, Natal'ia is sunburnt, freckled, and dressed in checkered clothing. At night, she suffers immeasurably. She is repeatedly tormented by dreams of a dwarf and a goat who, "obscenely excited" (171), proclaim themselves her mates.

Like her Khrushchev "masters," Natal'ia responds to the growing chaos in her life by taking cover in a "role" (171). Following in Tonia's footsteps, she also becomes a bride of Christ—a nun. The ruse fails for several reasons. For one thing, Natal'ia continues to love Petr, not God. For another thing, Natal'ia uses her religious stance to hide from life and to prevent other men from usurping Petr's place as her prince. Thereby, she sustains her hope. Natal'ia "glories in the part" (165) of Christ's bride only because she wishes to "convince herself of something that she herself has invented" (171).

Return to Dry Valley: Natal'ia and Iushka

Natal'ia fools no one with religious imposture. When she is finally allowed to return to Dry Valley, the peasants see her as "ugly" (165), and the family regards her only as one more self to fight and feed.

Natal'ia's actual return to Dry Valley, however, affords her a new chance at liberation. Seeing the fields, flowers, and the people of her youth, Natal'ia delights in memory. She happily recalls her life as a young girl and even supposes that the estate has grown younger with age. Most important, Natal'ia finally grasps the nature of her wrongdoing. She sees that "everything at Dry Valley is peaceful, simple and ordinary" and that all that is "alarming and extraordinary is in her mind" (173). Unfortunately, Natal'ia does not pursue her insight. She again capitulates to an ego that, fearing vanquishment, rises up to blind her to the truth. Natal'ia thus becomes "utterly dazed" (173) by what she sees and recalls. Her youthful feelings vanish "without a trace" (174), and she refocuses images of death and rebirth: empty birdcages, rotting tombstones, and the "fatal silver-framed mirror" (173).

Natal'ia becomes, in fact, the latest scourge at the estate; her return even seems to trigger new evils there. Comets, storms, fires, and an "endless stream of vagabonds, half-wits, and monks" (176) nearly overwhelm her and the family. Natal'ia is now more susceptible to supernatural menace than the other members of the family. For instance, when the wizard Ierokhin attempts to exorcise demons from Aunt Tonia, he inadvertently whisks Natal'ia "off to some wild, fabulous and primordially coarse world" (175–76): a travesty of her fairy-tale life.

It is, however, Natal'ia's assault by the monk Iushka that seals her fate. Natal'ia's ravishment by Iushka in *Dry Valley* differs markedly from Youngbride's rape by Tikhon in *The Village*. Whereas Tikhon sought to perpetuate himself in posterity, Iushka is moved by lust alone. Also, whereas Youngbride was akin to a regressed animal in heat, Natal'ia seeks to consummate a fantasy with a prince. Finally, the rape in *The Village* occurs only once and bears little reference to the pervading milieu; by contrast, the rape in *Dry Valley* passes through several stages, occurs many times, engenders nightmares, embraces Satanism, and trips off cataclysms in the universe.

Natal'ia recognizes that Iushka is the dwarf-goat of her dreams. She sees that "it was *inevitable* [her italics] that she should perish along with Tonia" (180). She finds that the very thought of a liaison with Iushka can bring her to sexual climax. With the monk close by, Natal'ia feels "the first attacks of a grave illness which was to possess her for a long time to come" (180). Hers is an especially brutal type of regression. Natal'ia's feet itch; cramps twist her toes inward; spasms contort her nerves "cruelly and sweetly" (180); and she shrieks "more madly and with more ecstasy than Miss Tonia ever shrieked" (180). Additionally, Natal'ia bears the responsibility for the tryst. Aroused by a universe that, like her, quakes in orgasm—for example, lightning "swells and trembles" (180)—Natal'ia actually recites incantations to summon forth her dwarf-goat mate.

Natal'ia's repeated ravishment by Iushka exacerbates her dilemma. The serf-princess is so charged sexually that she yearns, with new energy and vigor, for what she cannot have. This is an old pattern that leads to even more tragic consequences. For instance, the night that lightning sets the house afire, Natal'ia runs into the garden not to seek safety or peace of mind but to conjure up Petr as a Cossack wearing a gold-braided (read: chain) hat. This time, though, the erotic yearning hurts a being other than herself. When Natal'ia "sees" Petr, she miscarries the child conceived by Iushka. Natal'ia experiences no remorse for her wrongdoing. She feels pity only for her own situation in life—that she is "fading" (182)—entering rebirth.

Natal'ia's response to her dilemma is increasingly neurotic, for she juxtaposes God and Petr as her lovers. After taking Eucharist, she kisses the dark, ringed (read: samsaric) hand of Uncle Petr, who excites her "youthfully, tenderly, and thrillingly" (182). Given this renewed surrender by Natal'ia to desire, it is not surprising that when Petr dies, Natal'ia experiences sexual climax, not grief. Holding the regressed body of her lover—Petr's face is icy and "crushed in" (184), she engages in necrophilia. She "showers Petr with kisses, screams . . . a wildly joyous scream, and chokes with sobs and laughter" (184). Natal'ia finally attains what she has desired for so long. She does not notice that the object of her fancy is chain-bound. Given the perversity of her self, it can be assumed that Natal'ia genuinely does not care.

DRY VALLEY: CODA

Having enticed Natal'ia to tell her story, "my sister and I" bring the chronicle of *Dry Valley* to closure with a coda that repeats the key refrains of the work: whereas ego engenders suffering, memory can have a salvific role in life. In their coda, the siblings review the last years of the clan. Initially, "my sister and I" compare the final days of the estate to a "lingering death" (185) and its inhabitants to nomads who "drag out their days in wretchedness" (186). They show all of the clan's survivors to be in new "rounds" of life. The Khrushchevs are huddled like animals in small icy rooms; they are lost "in dreams and in wrangles and worries about their daily bread" (186). Tonia has drifted from being a bride of Christ to being a "Siberian shaman" (186)—a regressive comment on her sexuality, Scythianism, and spiritual beliefs. Natal'ia's dark eyes and whispers are sepulchral; her wasted body sleeps, corpselike, on a cold stone ledge. Petr's son, the most recent Khrushchev meld of master and man, is a railway conductor: a lord of apocalyptic machines and chainlike tracks. It is with a sense of righteousness that "my sister and I" condemn the clan as "a whole class [of people] degenerate and insane" (185), and as victims of rapid rebirth, "having vanished from the earth in as little as half a century" (185).

"My sister and I," though, do not become angry or bitter; they do not espouse codes, resist change, and take refuge in roles, fantasies, and dreams. Instead, they distill the good from the past. Their stance toward Natal'ia is their point of departure. The siblings observe that, though Natal'ia has been a willing victim to chain, she does not seek death for others or herself; nor

Self as Lord

does she, like Aunt Tonia, spend her final days screeching and fluttering like a bird. As presented by the siblings, Natal'ia regains her dignity by confessing her wrongs; by allowing time and distance to soothe her hurt; by moving from a self-possessed "nun" to a selfless caregiver to the youthful siblings; by seeing her "love" for Uncle Petr as an infatuation; and, most important, by calling upon memory, even acting as its "voice," to present Dry Valley with forgiveness and love. In other words, when the Khrushchev duo tell the story of *Dry Valley*, they have focused upon an individual who has suffered for her sins but who has also delayed rebirth by acknowledging the duplicity of desire and by making amends for a self-driven life. In this sense, Natal'ia dramatizes the conflict and hard-won hope of an "enlightened" person who stands apart from the downward spiraling, unregenerate Khrushchev clan. The voice of the clan's memories, Natal'ia is a mentor who teaches the siblings—and Bunin's readers—by extension.

"My sister and I" also disclose their own enlightenment. Going back through time, they have discerned the pitfalls of ego and the blessings of memory. In Natal'ia's company, they put sufficient distance between themselves and history so that they, too, can interpret the Dry Valley in terms of recollections and legend. Temperately, and with inner freedom, the sibling narrators reiterate that they have become "more and more estranged from the actual world of Dry Valley" (185) and that they "are left not with the life of the estate, but only with the memory of it" (185). Sometimes, in fact, they even wonder "if the family ever really lived at all" (186).

When they submit Dry Valley to the interpretive power of the past, "my sister and I" temper their harsh judgments of the estate and clan. Even though they censure the family homestead, they can also rejoice that it has "held on as if by miracle" (185). Even though they censure the most recent Khrushchevs as wastrels, they also see their ancestors as pillars of "patriarchal" Russia: "men of ancient lineage, governors, commanders, eminent men, and the close associates and even relatives of tsars" (185).

The narrators move the clan forward to "modern" life by retracing the path of memory. Although the siblings do not know precisely where family members are buried, they sense an "eerie closeness" (186) to the clan, their appointed comrades in the joys and sorrows of life. Touring the family cemetery, the Khrushchevs unite themselves in spirit with the Khrushchevs of all places and times in relishing the blue sky, the cool afternoon, and the spreading trees. Like the generations before them, brother and sister Khrushchev accept suffering, death, and karma as facts of life; but they are not seduced or overwhelmed by these entities. They gaze calmly upon sultry fields, gilded crosses, and a "jaded mare with a thin greenish forelock and pink battered hoofs" (187).

Privy to Gautama's Truth, the last of the Khrushchevs conclude *Dry Valley*, knowing who they are and how they wish to live their lives. They have lived close to the Paths of Egression and Return. They know the workings of ego, Mara, and chain, and the idiosyncrasies of the Khrushchev karma. They know that time and space are illusions and that, through Memory, what seems so "infinitely far" can "suddenly be made so close" (187). Finally, "my sister and I" know that, by telling the story of *Dry Valley*, they have left for posterity a cultural monument that details but safeguards the memory of the estate and the clan forever. But that is not all. Indeed, it is in the presenting of Dry Valley as a phenomenon of the modern world that "my sister and I," the last of the Khrushchevs, defy regression and rebirth and truly rise to the stature of "enlightened" beings in contemporary life.

CONCLUSION

In *Dry Valley,* Bunin portrayed gentry masters with much the same realism and detail as he did peasant men in *The Village,* as individuals caught in the struggle with self and chain. As a student of the Buddha, though, Bunin did not limit his call for liberation to Russia alone; rather, he saw that all humankind was in need of his message. It was in his next major piece, *The Gentleman from San Francisco,* that Bunin expanded both his insights and his goal: to bring enlightenment to the world.

Chapter Four

Self as Entrepreneur:
The Gentleman from San Francisco

THE CONTEXT

In August 1914, Nicholas II mobilized troops along the Austro-Hungarian border and precipitated World War I. What Bunin had feared for decades had come true. Russia was on the brink of samsara. It was entering its most cataclysmic cycle of reaction, upheaval, and reform; it was losing all semblance of stability.

Bunin cared little that he had been right about modern life, but he did follow the war closely and bemoan the "abyss" and the "apocalypse" that he believed were engulfing civilization.[1] He did not despair because he hoped that the struggle among nations might renew the world. For instance, five months after the outbreak of war, Bunin wrote to a friend: "I am firmly convinced that this Christmas will not be the last bloody one, for I know that people are beasts. . . . But there are thousands of 'buts' which are joyful and comforting: the voice of the human heart."[2] Bunin ended his letter with two visions of a new society. In one, a "great idol" seemingly protects humankind from harm; in the other, the Lamb of God bids his subjects to "to rise up and look around."[3]

This dichotomous vision—the choice between God and a demagogue—Bunin took directly into his next great work, *The Gentleman from San Francisco,* published in 1915. That Bunin could hope for "buts" amidst world turmoil—the "voice of the heart," the love of God, and the potential for world renewal—speaks eloquently of his faith in life and the possibility of enlightenment for all. Bunin's faith, though, tells only half the story; his time on the island of Capri, a key setting in *The Gentleman,* tells the other.

BUNIN AT CAPRI

For four years beginning in 1909, Bunin regularly visited Capri, and undoubtedly, his time there was the happiest period of his life. The reasons for this were straightforward. For instance, Capri, to Bunin, was the ideal haven for modern man: an outpost on the sea, apart from civilization and yet close to it, joined by ferries to Naples and Sorrento. Capri was small and spartan, a rock of roughly four square miles rising about two thousand feet to Monte Soliaro, a height from which Bunin could contemplate his universe and be at one with his world.

Capri also sparkled with history. The island had been the summer home of Emperors Augustus and Tiberius; it had two medieval castles, and it bore the marks of Greek antiquity, pirate raids, and struggles among the French, British, and Italians for possession of the tiny isle. The natural and historical riches of Capri thrilled Bunin in much the same way that Ceylon had several years before. At Capri, he again had experiences of "paradise," Nirvana: a situation in which life was what Bunin thought it should be.

SOURCES OF THE NOVEL

The years immediately following the publication of *Dry Valley* were among the most productive in Bunin's career. His success as a writer of Russian village life spurred him to seek more encompassing settings for his Buddhist-based themes because Bunin now saw rebirth and chain not only as Russia's dilemma, but also as humankind's. In 1915, five years after *The Village* and four after *Dry Valley,* Bunin scaled a third mountain of truth with *The Gentleman from San Francisco,* one of his best loved and, to Western readers, most famous works.

The Gentleman from San Francisco has many sources. Many of the people and events in the work were taken from Bunin's own experiences at Naples and Capri—for example, Lorenzo the servant, Luigi the boatman, the Abruzzian mountaineers, and the hired dancers aboard the ship *Atlantis.* Bunin's earlier poetry and prose were also seedbeds for the piece. The eschatological theme of *The Gentleman* had partial roots in his writing of the 1890s and early 1900s. The image of a boat as a "dark, midnight coffin" (1:100) appeared in a poem in 1896; the scene of the hero's fatal struggle with a collar stud echoed a similar incident in Bunin's story "Small World Landowners" (1891).

The international setting in *The Gentleman* Bunin drew both from his extensive travels abroad and from his fictional cycle *The Shadow of a Bird* (1907–11). A poem in this cycle entitled "The Call" (1911) reads like a catalog of the images in *The Gentleman:* a ship likewise named *The Atlantis,* a godlike Captain, sailors fettered by nets and cables, and a passenger who, responding to memory, crosses the sea "abyss" to new lands (1:333). Moreover, Bunin had already explored the ostensible theme of *The Gentleman*—the disparity between the colonizing rich and the native poor—in "The Brothers" (1914; see chapter 1). He was also editing an anthology of the verse of Rudyard Kipling at this time.

Beyond actual people and events and select motifs of his pre-1915 poetry and verse, an additional source for *The Gentleman from San Francisco* was Bunin's view of modern life as apocalypse. Bunin was haunted by the Book of Revelation and its prophecy of universal conflagration. He later recalled: "The terrible words of the Apocalypse—'Woe to you, Babylon, mighty city!'—resounded persistently in my heart when I was writing *The Gentleman from San Francisco,* for I foresaw unheard-of horrors and downfalls hidden in our culture."[4] In its fuller context, the precise passage (Revelation 17–18) contains the spirit and several key images that Bunin would use: lustful kings and merchants, "captains and seafaring men," devils' haunts, and sudden execution for the sinful city.

Finally, Bunin's plan for *The Gentleman* can be traced to three seemingly random ideas. The first was the 1914 translation into Russian of Konrad Gunther's study *Ceylon. An Introduction to the World of the Tropics.* The work, an amalgam of nature descriptions, lyrical digressions, and reminiscences of Gunther's childhood and youth, so delighted Bunin that he modeled several of the scenes in *The Gentleman* after one of its chapters, "Life aboard Ship," a portrayal of Gunther's fellow travelers aboard the ship *Prince Ludwig.*

The second idea was a letter from Gor'kii to Bunin, written in August 1912, in which he described a woman who had clawed her way through life only to die of a heart attack at a party. "Now there's the twentieth century for you!" Gor'kii pronounced grimly to his friend.[5]

The third idea germinated within Bunin himself. Bunin had spotted a copy of Thomas Mann's *Death in Venice* in a Moscow bookstore in the summer of 1915, and when, in October of that same year, he recalled that an American had died suddenly in a hotel at Capri the winter before, he decided to write a story entitled "Death in Capri." Mindful of literary influences (and of critics' labels and tags), Bunin insisted that he had not read *Death in Venice* until *after* he had finished *The Gentleman.* To be safe, though, Bunin changed his title after writing the first line of the piece.[6]

PREFATORY REMARKS

The Gentleman from San Francisco resounds motifs from *The Village* and *Dry Valley.* Like Tikhon Krasov, the hero of *The Gentleman* is a self-made man who feels restless and rootless. Like the Khrushchev siblings, the hero leaves familiar surroundings and has opportunities to find roots in the past. *The Gentleman from San Francisco* differs, though, from its fictional antecedents, and the structure of the tale is a major point of departure. If the narrators of *The Village* and *Dry Valley* built their works about vast and complex chronicles of village and family life, the teller of *The Gentleman* offers his work as a parable, as a simple, short lesson without relativity or doubt. The story has a recognizable beginning, middle, and end, and moves swiftly from problem to resolution. It also features explicit contrasts. Rich and poor move between land and sea, storms and sun, old worlds and new. They do so, moreover, within a framework that is taut and trim ("masculine and severe," one critic said)[7] and under the aegis of a single, detached speaker in full control of the tale. Finally, *The Gentleman from San Francisco* appears as conventional allegory: the odyssey of a pilgrim.

The simplicity of *The Gentleman* is deceptive, however. In this work, Bunin expanded an earlier theme from *The Village* and *Dry Valley*. That is, in *The Gentleman*, he explored the nature and consequences of the "false" pilgrimage: the mock journey of the ego to worlds, present and past.

THE GENTLEMAN AT DOCK

The narrator uses an epigraph from the Book of Revelation to set the theme of *The Gentleman from San Francisco*. The great ancient city of Babylon is doomed to sudden execution in one hour. Against such a dark backdrop, the narrator introduces his unnamed hero, the Gentleman from San Francisco. As has been noted, the Gentleman recalls Tikhon Krasov. He, too, is a "first category" individual, a journeyman on the Path of Egression.

The Gentleman from San Francisco, though, reveals a stronger and more rapacious sense of self than did the hero of *The Village*. Tikhon was a peasant in the provinces, but the Gentleman hails from the urban upper class. Tikhon controlled the locals of a village, but the Gentleman has had "thousands of Chinese"[8] as employees. Tikhon greatly feared the future, but the Gentleman has centered "all his hopes on the days to come" (308). Also, the Gentleman has been spared Tikhon's worry about posterity because, unlike Tikhon, he has a child, a daughter. Indeed, given the Gentleman's robust sense of self, it is not surprising that he does not confront inner disquiet until he is fifty-eight, almost twenty years later than the forty-year-old Tikhon, and that he senses this discomfort only dimly and without the searing angst that destroyed the lord of Durnovka.

The Gentleman from San Francisco, though, pays a higher price for his illusions and desires than Tikhon did. In spite of his economic successes, he has "not really lived, but merely existed" (308). He has repressed the desire for change in numbing custom and routine. In so doing, he has harmed not only himself but others. His wife is vacuous and dull; his unmarried daughter is "no longer young and rather sickly" (308).

In his focus on the future, the Gentleman from San Francisco typifies Bunin's view of modern man. For instance, the Gentleman lacks all personal memory. He never recalls his family, his home, or his climb to the top. Also, the Gentleman's here and now has been a contest with other selves, as a race that lacks a finish line and that also marks him as an eternal "second" in life. In truth, the Gentleman has not had his eye on the future as much as on the backs of those who have bested him in his career. As the narrator ironically notes, he "had almost come up to the level of those whom he had once set up as an example to himself" (308).

Most tellingly, the Gentleman is a candidate for new "rounds" of life. For instance, as an unnamed "Gentleman," the hero possesses spiritual ties to Bunin's Uncle Petr and Voitkevich in *Dry Valley*. He, too, falls somewhere between an identifiable personality and a regressed "he"; he, too, clings to role poses and codes of etiquette in a desperate effort to forestall dissolution. Moreover, that the Gentleman is from San Francisco further suggests that he is one of the damned. He hails from a New World Babylon that had only recently been destroyed. The Gentleman is thus, figuratively, doomed to undergo swift destruction even before he starts his journey.

SURFACE RIGHTS, INNER WRONGS

Upon first glance, the Gentleman appears earnest about renewal. He realizes, for instance, that it would be good for him to rest and, more tantalizingly in a Buddhistic vein, "to catch his breath" (308). The Gentleman also seems to be heeding Gautama's prescription for enlightenment. That is, he is leaving the land of samsara (San Francisco) to cross the "restless ocean of suffering" and to reach "the harbor of refuge," "the cool cave," and "the farther shore." Indeed, the Gentleman fashions an itinerary that affords countless opportunities for Nirvana, for encounters with ancestry, culture, and primordial existence. He will begin his journey between the months of December and January, metaphorically on the cusp of old and new lives. Furthermore, the hero has allotted a full two years for travel, and high points in his journey include fountainheads of memory that contrast markedly with his New World. The Gentleman first plans to visit southern Italy to "bask in the sun . . . to see the ancient sites . . . and to hear the wandering singers" (309). He then will go on to the Near and Far East, to more ancient and unspoiled lands of contemplation and enlightenment. The Gentleman also takes his wife and daughter with him on his wisdom quest; he wants them to share in the joy of wandering.

As he plans his pilgrimage, the Gentleman styles himself a "philosopher," a traveler on the Path of Return, even a spiritual brother to Saint Francis, the namesake of his native city and a Bunin hero who escaped samsara and lived in harmony with God and life. His time frame is no longer future but present and past; his locus of operation is no longer a modern-day Babylon but the big wide world. His modus vivendi is no longer work but rest; his goal is no longer power and money but the sun, sites, and singers in the cradles of civilization.

In truth, the Gentleman from San Francisco is nowhere close to enlightenment because he is still living his old life. Specifically, he has not confronted the sudden threats to existence that impelled the masters and men of *The Village* and *Dry Valley* to catastrophe. The Gentleman is very much the master of his personal universe. His family respects him; his fortune and property are secure; his laborers do not threaten his life. His pilgrimage is thus false, for he has neither renounced desire nor given his wandering the blessings of mind and heart. Furthermore, when the Gentleman maps out his travels, he corrupts any pilgrim status with fantasies about "light flirtation" (308) and trysts with Neapolitan girls. He also schemes, almost subconsciously, that he might marry off his spinster daughter to a prince or millionaire aboard ship. Additionally, the Gentleman from San Francisco looks to pilgrimage primarily as a custom of his social station: a status-seeking rite performed by the "class of men to which he belongs . . . when they too are ready to enjoy life" (308). He understands travel only in terms of "reward" and "pleasure," of "holiday" and "carnival" (308–9).

For the Gentleman from San Francisco to view travel as carnival is consistent with the self-minded righteousness with which he has conducted the rest of his life. The Gentleman is "firmly convinced" (308) that he is "entitled" (308) to fun and games while gadding about the globe. Resolutely, therefore, he embraces the very activities of select society that will spell his ruin both in this life and in the next. The salvific promise that could be associated with his measured, linear trek back through time is derailed by activities of chance, speed, and death and by suggestions of circular rebirth and chain. The Gentleman looks forward to roulette wheels and automobile and yacht races. He anticipates shuffleboard—to slide orbs into chain squares—and he aspires to rifle practice and to bring soaring pigeons downward, like "golf balls" (309).

The spirit of carnival and the rounds of activities that make up the Gentleman's trip give both a macro- and a microview of his coming tragedy. In both dimensions, he is caught in a samsaric loop. On one hand, any real progress is surely canceled by the fact that he is circumnavigating the world and that he intends to return to the exact place (physical and metaphysical) from which he started. On the other hand, as the Gentleman moves along in his journey, his world will constrict into increasingly smaller circles that will cause him to whirl about, dervishlike, grasping for a hold on life. Like young Kuz'ma in *The Village*, only on a much wider scale, the hero will travel without any discrimination or discernment. He plans to embrace good and bad with abandon: "the *Miserere* in Rome . . . bullfighting in Seville, bathing in the British isles . . . Athens, Constantinople, Palestine, Egypt, and even Japan—on the way back, of course" (309). The Gentleman from San Francisco travels physically but is stymied spiritually. Advance will be to samsara, not to enlightenment.

LEAVING SHORE: LIFE ABOARD THE *ATLANTIS*

Oblivious to the tragedy that awaits him, the Gentleman from San Francisco begins his voyage in grand style. If the heroes of *The Village* and *Dry Valley* wandered Russia on horses or in carts, the Gentleman crosses the Atlantic on an ocean liner, appropriately named the *Atlantis*. As the mythological allusion suggests, the *Atlantis* appears to be a powerful and prosperous island, a civilized home to an imperious ego that wishes to conquer the world. The *Atlantis* also represents the worst of *modern* times, the handiwork of a society that worships power and greed.

The *Atlantis* assuages all "new age" needs, such as the dread of the challenges and complexities of life. As was the case with the estate in *Dry Valley*, the protective insularity of the *Atlantis* appeals to escapists. An all-night bar and Turkish baths swathe frazzled individuals in hazes that are watery, smoky, or alcoholic; a newspaper published aboard ship edits out real life. All things, in fact, are orchestrated to screen false pilgrims from reality. More revealing, the serenity on the *Atlantis* has for the Gentleman and his fellow travelers a quasi-religious quality. The ship offers a mock-spiritual retreat in which they shed personal responsibility and find renewal in the prescribed routine of life on board.

The narrator in *The Gentleman* presents the ship as any Shangri-La. For instance, he surrounds the Gentleman with passengers from the narrow gamut of power and wealth. These passengers, too—a famous author, a celebrated beauty, even a prince—are egressive types. Along with the Gentleman, they follow a quasi-monastic way of life in which they don habitlike pajamas; they parody a "liturgy of the hours" with the periods established for meals, rest, and socializing; and they turn their lives over to a captain who resembles a Buddha and who functions as a god: "a man of monstrous size and corpulence who always looked sleepy, who resembled an enormous idol . . . and who very seldom emerged from his secret chambers to be among the passengers" (310).

Aboard the *Atlantis*, the passengers punctuate periods of exercise, reading, and rest with gluttony. As the main activity aboard ship, eating functions like the divine office to mark the passage of the day, but this ritual feeds the body, not the soul. Upon rising, the Gentleman and his fellow travelers sip coffee or cocoa; after bathing, they sit down to an ample breakfast; at eleven, they fortify themselves with sandwiches; at midday, they enjoy a grand lunch; between the hours of four and five, they are served snacks; and at seven, they promenade to dinner, a two-hour meal that is "the main purpose and the crowning glory" of each day (310).

If You See the Buddha

Ironically, the narrator describes dinner on the *Atlantis* with details and undertones that suggest a high mass. The wealthy entourage enter a large marble room that is like a huge church, resplendent with light and warmth. They are met by the captain-idol and by clergymen waiters who escort them to altar tables, adorned with candles, wine, and flowers. Also, the guests dine to splendid music and amidst "clouds of aromatic smoke" (311).

Liturgy in *The Gentleman from San Francisco* serves a different function, though, than it did in *The Village* and *Dry Valley*. In these works, the lords and peasants accepted ritual cosmically, as a means to ward off the devil, apocalypse, and death; the passengers aboard the *Atlantis*, however, pervert liturgy to erect a barrier between themselves and life, to impose order on their superficial world, and to disavow the supernatural and embrace idols in its stead. They ensure apocalypse. Using "liturgy" as a buffer between self and reality, the characters in *The Gentleman from San Francisco* will fail to negotiate the good and bad that lie ahead. They will miss chances for enlightenment surely and routinely, and they will fail to perceive warnings of samsara and chain.

CRUISING TO REBIRTH

The liturgies aboard the *Atlantis* seem to work wonders, physical and spiritual. At the dinner mass, the Gentleman could remind a Bunin reader of the youthful Tikhon Krasov. As portrayed by the narrator, the hero has an "excess of life and vigor . . . lean, well-knit . . . and looking much younger than he actually is" (310). The Gentleman's family mirrors his good fortune. If, earlier, his daughter had been described as "no longer young and rather sickly" (308–9), now she enjoys the attention of a prince.

In fact, though, the well-being observable in the Gentleman and his family aboard ship is deceptive. While the boat makes passage to Europe, the three advance, actually, to rebirth. The Gentleman is part Scythian, part shackled corpse; his head is like "old ivory"; his face is "yellowish" and "Mongolian"; his moustache is "silver"; the fillings in his chainlike "large teeth" are "gold" (311). The Gentleman's daughter also shows a corrosive touch. She lacks a name, she has dotlike pimples and noxious breath, and her diaphanous gown and powdered shoulders suggest that she is like a "ghost." Regression, as the narrator makes clear, strikes young and old alike.

In their move toward new life, the Gentleman and his family are constantly in the company of people and things that intimate fettered life. The captain-idol has a black coat trimmed with gold braid; the headwaiter wears a chain about his neck. It is the figure of the Asian prince, though, that most clearly dramatizes the pull of samsara on the passengers' lives. Initially, the prince stands apart from his traveling companions in bearing and demeanor. If the other travelers are conspicuously nouveau riche, the prince has the "blood of ancient Asian kings" (312). The prince is uncomfortable with his hereditary status and with the obligations of his birthright. He does not wish to act upon the wisdom of his ancestors and become a teacher for his nation. Aboard the *Atlantis,* therefore, the prince assimilates to the crowd. He does not challenge the captain-idol, censure the dinner mass, or teach his comrades the wisdom of the East. Rather, like the Krasovs who spurned the land and the Khrushchevs who declined the duties of caste, the prince rejects his roots by traveling incognito and by taking part in the ritualized hedonism on ship. In Bunin, though, one pays dearly for such inertia or cowardice.

As a result of his negations, the prince finds himself adrift in a sea of modernity and, simultaneously, a victim of regression. He is not a mysterious, dashing figure, but rather, a "nice, simple, and unpresumptuous man" and "a very short . . . little boy who is quite odd and unprepossessing." Descriptive details include that he is a skewed circle-and-line figure with gold-rimmed glasses, "slim" hands, and a "horsehair" moustache that is "stringy and coarse like that of a corpse" (312). Additionally, the prince's "plain but neat" (312) English overcoat and bowler hat also makes clear that he has rejected the spiritual heritage of the Orient—his Old World—and that he has embraced the arbitrary, conforming mores of the West or the New World. He has a spiritual kinship with Voitkevich, the renegade Buddhist-Kalmyck officer in *Dry Valley.* In *The Gentleman from San Francisco,* the narrator suggests that the prince is yet another lifeless idol, a second fetish-Buddha, for the passengers of the *Atlantis* to worship and revere. The prince is "perfectly wooden, broad-faced, and narrow-eyed"; his skin is "thin, olive-colored . . . and stretched tightly across his flat face . . . as if thinly coated with varnish" (312).

OF SHIELDS AND SELVES

Given the cast of regressed characters aboard ship, it is not surprising that for all the superficial luxury, the *Atlantis* alternately exudes a deathlike stillness. During the rest periods after lunch, the voyagers are like corpses, "wrapped in rugs" (310) and "sprawled out in chairs with legs flung carelessly . . . and with feet up" (311). During other activities, the passengers, though mobile, seem frozen in time and space, immobilized by the "pearly golden halo" (310) of the banquet hall that functions as a magnet holding them firmly in the chain. Such statuesque pictures conform to the theme of the tale because the passengers aboard the *Atlantis* are appendages to events, not initiators or individually active participants in them. Ritualized eating and other sense-numbing activities focus the attention of the Gentleman and his company on their own bodies, their own egos.

The Gentleman and his family epitomize this isolation. In contrast to the Krasovs and Khrushchevs, who struggle with their clans, the Gentleman and his family have relatively little to do with one another or with any other passengers. Father, mother, and daughter have separate rooms. They are seen in the group, but the three, wooden and erect, scarcely ever talk, mingle, or dance.

The dalliances of the Gentleman and his daughter also show self in its unwillingness to relinquish its shield. Aboard ship, the Gentleman is taken by a famous beauty, but the flirtation is empty and coarse. Both persons suggest "manacled" decay: the Gentleman wears "gray spats"; the woman has "painted eyes" and keeps a pet dog that is "tiny, humpbacked, hairless, and kept on a thin silver chain" (313). Also, though the Gentleman and the beauty stand next to each other at the dinner mass and ball, no relationship beyond an occasional, suggestive glance develops between them.

The relationship between the Gentleman's daughter and the prince is more charged emotionally but follows the pattern of her father's with the beauty. The Gentleman's daughter is "vaguely discomforted" (313) by her father's flirtation, but when the girl meets the prince, she exhibits the classical symptoms of "first romantic" love. She is not taken by the prince's "wealth, fame, or an illustrious name" (314), as much as she is seized by her own needs. Therein lies the problem, for, as the Buddha taught, romantic attraction is morally inappropriate because it inflates the self and shackles the lover to the illusory object of his or her love. The conduct of the Gentleman's daughter bears out the wisdom of Gautama's teaching. When she is with the prince, she is "strangely enraptured" (312); she "does not understand a word that the Prince is saying"; she "only pretends to follow his finger . . . as he explains something to her hastily and softly" (312).

The rituals aboard the *Atlantis* make a shambles of all human affection. Love is just another item to be bought and sold. One of the ironies in *The Gentleman from San Francisco* is that the Gentleman and his daughter venture more than any of the others to explore a relationship beyond self. Their fellow travelers gaze dully upon two dancers who are long-standing employees of the ship. Unknown to the patrons, they are paid "a handsome wage to perform [the task of love] so charmingly and exquisitely" (311). In so doing, they, like the captain and his staff, do for the travelers, vicariously, what the travelers should be doing for themselves.

THE CREW OF THE *ATLANTIS*

The regression that informs the Gentleman, his family, and the other holiday seekers aboard the *Atlantis* also claims the employees of the ship. The ship's employees are guilty of wrongdoing on two counts. First, the captain and his crew labor to make the luxury life of the *Atlantis* impregnable: truth and constancy cannot be allowed to penetrate the world of pleasure and delusion. The captain and his company work round the clock to keep the fantasy on the *Atlantis* in good working order. They "feed and wait on the Gentleman from morning till night, forestall his slightest wish, keep him immaculate, and safeguard his peace" (313).

Second, the employees of the *Atlantis* do not join in the liturgical etiquette that has, ironically, been entrusted to their care. The staff of the *Atlantis* is without the amenities that shield the passengers from modern life; as a result, they suffer greatly from the very chaos they attempt to disguise from the wealthy travelers. Sailors in the crow's nest wrestle with "sodden, heavy rigging" (311) (for Bunin, a variation on the shacklelike shawl that weighed down Aunt Tonia in *Dry Valley*); they "freeze in the cold" and "reel from unbearable strain" (311). Waiters have "dot" eyeballs that bulge like "shelled, hard-boiled eggs" (311). Chinese boys stand bowlegged, have "thick maidenly eyelashes" (312), speak only in whispers, and have "chains" of plaited hair hanging down to their heels. The stokers of the ship's fires live in the "abyss of hell" (311): a Dantesque "ninth circle" (311) in which they look purple in front of the flames, while the furnaces "roar with laughter" and chomp their "blazing maws" (311). Such characterizations move the *Atlantis* backwards in time until it appears to be a sightless behemoth that "gapes into the darkness" despite "its countless, blazing eyes" (310). The long-held contention, therefore, that *The Gentleman from San Francisco* is a work about social injustice, an expose of capitalist rich exploiting the proletariat poor, is inaccurate. Both classes are victims of duplicity; both conspire, circumstantially, to bring about world ruin.

SIGNS OF DOOM

Graphic as the impressions of the ship and its crew are, Bunin's narrator uses the ocean to give a context for the passengers' precarious lot. Metaphorically, the *Atlantis* sails through the same wintry present that besieged *The Village* and *Dry Valley*. Icy fogs and wet snow spray the scene with "dots." "Rolling" seas, "frothy" waves, and the "gray-green" (310) expanse of the sea bespeak the onset of a Great Flood, the stasis of chain, and the samsaric instability of life. The *Atlantis* is buffeted by a storm—recalling the tidal wave that destroyed its legendary island namesake. Waves heave against the ship like "black mountains," making it "shudder" and "shake"; their "rippling mass swirls in a froth and flings high its foamy tails" (311).

Revealingly, the regressed *Atlantis* reports the mortal danger surrounding it. The ship's siren rivals the cacophony, the funeral sounds of *The Village* and *Dry Valley*. The siren "wails with infernal gloom . . . squeals in frantic fury . . . and moans in mortal agony" (310 and 311). The captain and his crew, though, weave a magic cloak over the ship's angst, drowning out the siren's music with bugles that keep the ship "on course" (309) by day and with the music of the stringed orchestras at night. Such efforts do not conceal the threat of "circular" return from the sensitive ear or eye, however. Bunin has the narrator carefully describe the bugles as rending the peace with their "shrill" (309) playing. The waltzes and tangoes are asyncopatic with the movements of samsara. They "sway" and "swirl" (311), moving the couples either in circles or in back-and-forth movements, at variance with the forward progress of their travels. Also, the music of the dances is "voluptuous, shameless, and sad" (311). Forgetfulness of the ocean outside and of the harsh labor from rigging to stokehold is the agenda set for the magnificent crowd aboard the *Atlantis*. All classes contribute to the pretense; the underlying turmoil of their lives, suggested by the wintry realities of the storm at sea, is ignored, despite all signals of danger.

APPROACHING NAPLES

However empty the "liturgical" life aboard the *Atlantis,* the ship triumphs over the elements and reaches the Old World. There the Gentleman is called to enlightenment. When, for example, the *Atlantis* sails in the "brilliant light of a perfectly clear day" (313); or when it stops at Gibraltar, where the environs are bathed by the sun and the feeling of an early spring prevails; or when the ship reaches Naples and the travelers are greeted with "warm smiles" (313) from the sun and with sweeping vistas of mountains and seas, the Gentleman and his fellows are being invited to liberation, to see truth in life.

As did the Krasovs and the Khrushchevs, however, the Gentleman and his company regard scenes of beauty and quiet merely as interludes in their stormy lives. The travelers fall back into grayness and instability (winter chills, horizons wrapped in mist, and land that dissolves like "lumps of sugar" (311) in the distance); they then advance in samsara. In response to the sudden changes in climate, the passengers don fur coats, thereby making themselves appear as animals in rebirth.

The return of hostile climate, the fur trappings, and the approach of the *Atlantis* to a strange land convince the passengers that they must rouse ego and exert it against the new milieu. Earlier, the *Atlantis* was tossed by winds and seas, but now it moves regally into the calm harbor. Previously, the ship's siren could, many times, have been sounding a requiem for its passengers, but now the band seems to congratulate each of them, individually, with a "deafening and triumphant march" (313). The burst of noise proclaims that the self of the New World has arrived; and, the captain, usually hidden from his passengers at sea, appears on deck, for all to see, a "gigantic and gracious heathen god" (311) who has led the people to their first destination.

Such theatrics, while impressive, fail on several accounts. The pageantry that attends the arrival of the *Atlantis* does not invigorate the passengers so much as it implies their captivity. Crossing the Atlantic, the Gentleman

Self as Entrepreneur

and his colleagues accepted their lot passively. They spent their days eating and drinking, wrapped in rugs, or looking out numbly at the empty horizon. Now, with land in sight, they resemble the regressed animal herds in *The Village*. They wish to break free. They cluster at rails, grasp the "clattering chains" of gangplanks, and swirl among porters with "gold braids" in their caps (311). Despite their power and wealth, the passengers of the *Atlantis* do not impose themselves flamboyantly on their new milieu. They do not bark orders, vie for comforts, treat people like animals, or buy and sell favors, sexual or otherwise. Rather, the Gentleman and the other voyagers only wish to seek in the Old World the very rituals of comfort and security that they have known in their passage from the New. They believe, simplistically, that "as it had been on board ship, so it had to be in Naples" (313).

ON LAND

At first, life in Naples mirrors that of the ship. The Gentleman and his family again observe a "liturgy of the hours," a "clockwork regularity" (313) behind which they find refuge from life. The evening meal is still celebrated with the pomp of a high mass, and is the high point in the daily merrymaking.

Yet the activities in Naples differ from those aboard the *Atlantis* in quality and degree. On land, the Gentleman and his family follow a schedule that is more frenetic as well as more constricted than the one on board. Touring Naples, they must dash through museums and churches without time for reflection upon what they are seeing. The environments are desolate and clogged and give only the illusion of reality. As rendered by Bunin's narrator, the buildings and byways of Naples resemble the family manor in *Dry Valley*. Streets are "corridors" (314) dark, narrow, and damp; dining rooms are "gloomy" (311); thresholds and doorways are blocked by crowds. Generally, rooms have heavy curtains, thick carpeting, tall windows, and mirrored walls, all of which facilitate a sense of insularity from life outside.

Moreover, the Gentleman and his family do not make even token visits to the mountains and the seas that beckon to them from afar. Instead, they stay within the dreary confines of the city, listless captives of modernity. As a result, the cultural and religious monuments of Naples cannot enlighten them. Museums seem "funereally stark and snow-white bleak" (314). Churches are likewise vast, empty, and cold and subtly augur the damnation of humankind. A seven-branched candelabrum "flickering redly in the depths" (314) conjures up the red Seven-headed Dragon in Revelation; altars are covered with shacklelike lace; floors are studded with slippery gravestones; the pews seem to lock an old woman in a grid; and pictures show a battered Christ being taken down from the Cross.

Elsewhere, too, the Gentleman and his family confront a civilization that resembles the Russia of Bunin's village works. Naples is experiencing trauma. The Gentleman and his family see "toy soldiers" and "tiny donkeys harnessed to dogcarts" (313); they observe "metallic" trees, "pearly silver" bays, and "awful" chainlike tramway lines (314). They look without appreciation at betraying skies that move from rosy silver in the morning to slate gray in the afternoon. Finally, the relatively nondescript persons of the father, mother, and daughter are dissolved in the "dot"-like mist and rain, in "shimmering vapors" and "frothing" water (313 and 314).

The modern Sturm und Drang that infects the Gentleman and his family in Naples exacts the same regressive toll of the local citizens. Like the crew aboard the *Atlantis,* the people of Naples, who must provide service to paying guests, lack rituals to forestall decay in their own lives. The predictable result is that they are more regressed than the "master" visitors they serve. As portrayed by Bunin's narrator, the people of Naples appear to the Gentleman to be like prehistoric creatures. Many workers bear a caricatured likeness to pterodactyls. Rotund cabbies chomp on beaklike cigars and wear "rubber capes that flap in the wind like wings" (315); women have "black heads" and "disgustingly short legs" (315). Also, and as was the situation in *The Village* and *Dry Valley,* the folk in *The Gentleman* intuit that the world is destined for ruin. Porters routinely mumble apologies for the unseemly weather. They raise their shoulders "guiltily" and mutter that "something awful is happening all over the world" (314): cold and snow in Athens and Palermo, primordial storms and rains on the Riviera, and an eerie glow around Mount Etna.

The regressive aura of Naples soon infects the Gentleman and his family. For the first time since leaving the New World, they endure discomfort and pain. The Gentleman is laid low by excessive drinking. He and his wife quarrel frequently; their daughter has headaches and looks wan. The application of hot-water bottles to their stomachs does not help them digest the wine and food so much as it momentarily keeps the three from succumbing to the malady that plagued the Krasovs: freezing from within.

OFF TO CAPRI

The distress that the Gentleman and his family undergo in Naples is seen by Bunin's narrator not only as punishment for their degenerate lives but also as a possible occasion of enlightenment. Being physically and spiritually ill, the Gentleman and his family make a potentially sound decision: they opt not to return home, to San Francisco, but to go on to Capri and to resume their pilgrimage.

It is interesting to note that when the Gentleman and his family plan for Capri, they ignore the rituals and routines that have engaged and pampered them so far. They now seek to discover the Azure Grotto, the ruined palace of Tiberius, and the Abruzzian mountaineers singing praises to the

Virgin Mary and her newborn son. Simply put, they step gingerly onto the Path of Return. Seeking rest, the Gentleman and his family have traveled first from the New World to the Old and then from Naples to Capri. Symbolically, they have been traveling back through time and history, and such a journey could help them find meaning in life.

Paralleling the ill-fated travels that many of the characters made in *The Village* and *Dry Valley*, the Gentleman and his family attempt the passage to enlightenment in their move to Capri; but there are difficulties. For instance, they travel on a ship that is smaller ("regressed") in size and without the amenities that made the illusion of peace possible on the *Atlantis*. There are no steam rooms, dance orchestras, or solicitous staff; the ship is "poor"; the saloon is "wretched" (315); and the maids impudently mock passengers' seasickness.

Furthermore, images of shackles and samsara assault the senses mercilessly. The vision of the Gentleman and his family is clouded by raindrops that seep through weak spots in the cabin and by the fog that hangs in chain-like gray clouds to merge with the "leaden surface of the sea" (315). Capri is obscured "as though it never existed at all" (315). The discordance of rattling windows, howling winds, and cries of a boy who, like a harbinger of doom, "screams shrilly, with a speech defect, and without a moment's pause" (316) besiege their hearing. And, like the drunken Tikhon in *The Village* and the crazed Petr in *Dry Valley*, the three regularly lose their balance in samsara-like arcs: swells that make the shore "fly up and down as though on swings" (316).

The Gentleman and his family edge toward the brink of disintegration. The Gentleman gradually comes to resemble a corpse. His face is dark, his mustache is white, his jaws are clenched, and his body is shrouded by a loose overcoat and cap. The Gentleman's spouse is preoccupied by the fear of death; his daughter's face, because of a slice of lemon she clamps between her teeth, becomes like a half-moon. All three lie prone on sofas, wrapped in rugs. Their eyes are closed because of nausea; their heads ache; their bodies are chilled by illness and rain.

ON LAND AGAIN: DASHED HOPES, NEW CARNIVALS

As the Gentleman and his family approach Capri, under the power of their own inner narrowness, they see the isle only as home to a new round of life. Capri appears almost as desolate as a prison outpost, a mass of black rock speckled with red lights and flecked with silvers and golds; it resembles a modern Eden where "golden snakes glide away from the lampposts on the quay" and trees have "brightly colored fruit" and "thick, shiny leaves" (316). Also, Capri bears a striking resemblance to a carnival fair such as the one that tormented Tikhon in *The Village*. The narrator convenes an international gathering of the dregs of humanity amidst the sights, sounds, and smells of new rounds of life. Italians are "garlic-stinking little wretches" (316); Russians have collars that obscure their faces; Germans are "long-legged" and "round-skulled" (316). Together with the Gentleman and his family, these groups move along the lines of fish nets, the dots of lights and mold, and the circles of tin cans, clattering chains, and crumbling stone houses and walls.

For the Gentleman from San Francisco, the longed-for Capri brings boredom and despair. He has the sudden, painful realization that he has grown very old. Predictably, the Gentleman yearns for the routines of the *Atlantis*. He desires to "eat, drink, smoke" (317)—to find renewed sanctuary for his ego, which the Old World has made more vulnerable than it was during all his years of unwearied toil in the New.

The natives of Capri surpass the crew on the *Atlantis* or the people of Naples in responding to the wealthy Gentleman with gusto. The rubrical schedule that parodied the divine office and high mass are outdone as the natives fashion celebrations modeled on biblical texts. The natives of Capri regale the Gentleman with a people's Palm Sunday, a folk rendition of Christ's entry into Jerusalem immediately prior to his death. It is intriguing to note that of all the regressed arrivals to Capri, the islanders "mark" (317) the wealthy Gentleman as a modern Son of Man. They parade the hero to the center of the city. Women and children, carrying luggage, not palms, surround the Gentleman; men push forward to show him the way.

Unlike Christ's reception in Jerusalem or of the colorful merrymaking in the scenes aboard ship, though, the frivolity at Capri is starkly monochromatic. Backdrops of glaring stagelight and dark foreboding contrast sharply. The people move Modern Man to center stage, and the Gentleman himself willingly participates in the calculated spectacle. He enters the town square as "though making a stage entrance" (317), glad for the attention and acclaim. The town square is like an "opera set" (317); the hotel entrance is "brilliantly lit" (317); a "globe of light" (317) takes the place of the sun and the moon.

The festivities at Capri do not attune the Gentleman to new realities, but, going full circle, they point him to a self-protective world similar to those on the *Atlantis* and in Naples. The carnivality revives his flagging sense of power, wealth, even infallibility. The owner of the hotel installs him in the royal suite; the best waitresses and valets are appointed to cater to his every need; the maître d'hôtel regales him with a list of choice food, echoes his wishes, and, by his every tone and gesture, assures the Gentleman that "the rightness of the Gentleman's wishes could not be doubted, and that everything would be carried out to the letter" (318–19).

Revealingly, the Gentleman is not comforted by the lavish, flawed spectacle. He is still off balance. Even on land, he feels "the floor heaving beneath his feet" (318); he is also visited by dreams, including one about the hotel owner the day *before* their actual meeting. The hotel owner is dressed in a "roundly cut" coat, and his hair has a "mirror-like gloss" (318). The hotel owner, enticing the Gentleman with the sham of modern life, is also like the ferryman Charon at the River Styx because he assists the Gentleman in the final lap or crossing of his journey to the nether and regressed worlds.

Beyond dreams, the Gentleman encounters the regressed surroundings and people of Capri. Close inspection reveals that archways, like the halo magnet on ship, grip the populace in circular return. The locals bang their clogs on cobblestone streets; urchins turn somersaults and break into "birdlike whistling" (317). At the hotel, maids recall the serrated Tikhon in *The Village* with their caps that look like "small tooth crowns" (318). The staff sounds a "dot" Chinese gong, thereby summoning the Gentleman not only to a gloomy dining room but also to samsara.

ROUSING SELF A FINAL TIME

The attention given the Gentleman because of his wealth, combined with the sense of frailty he experiences from seasickness, rouses him to assert himself. For the first time since he planned his itinerary, the Gentleman attempts to control his situation. For instance, he responds to the seduction of his regal quarters in a kingly way: he issues orders with "unhurried precision" (318), he dismisses staff with a nod, and he responds to questions with answers that are measured and "sneeringly polite" (319). Also, the Gentleman becomes aroused at the very thought of the woman dancer to be featured that night, and he dresses for dinner "as if he were preparing for his wedding" (319).

For the first time in the story, also, the Gentleman actively blocks all stimuli to enlightenment. He shrugs off the dream or prevision of the hotel owner; in so doing, he "cleanses himself to the last mustard seed" (318) of belief in other realities. Like Grandfather Petr just before his demise in *Dry Valley*, the Gentleman seals himself off from his world. He shuts the windows of his quarters and closes out the smell of the flowers below; he orders that his table in the dining room be placed far away from the doors. The hero turns up the lights in his room, "flooding all the mirrors with brilliance and glitter" (319), thereby recreating not only the "theater" of his approach to the village but also the unforgiving glare of his flawed life.

Furthermore, the Gentleman does not succeed in dominating his environs. When he closes the windows, he is "clumsy" (318); he answers questions of the staff with silence and gesturing. The Gentleman's interest when he hears the name of the dancer stems from having seen her picture on a postcard—a flat and mass-produced image of seduction. By the time he has reached Capri, the Gentleman does not command the true respect of his subordinates much more than the "masters" elicited respect from the "men" in Bunin's village pieces. Among themselves, the servants make no effort to conceal their contempt for the Gentleman. In particular, the valet, Luigi, recalls Gervas'ka in *Dry Valley* in that he, too, is "dotted" and dark (e.g., black hair, fiery eyes, and round knuckles), and also in that, while he serves the hero competently, he does so only with "feigned humility" (319).

The Gentleman from San Francisco controls his milieu. Instead of waiting complacently for liturgies of food and drink, he now dreams of "nothing but . . . a first spoonful of soup, a first sip of wine" (319). The Gentleman was "somewhat flurried as he performed his customary ritual of dressing for dinner, so he had no time for thought or feeling" (320).

DEATH BY COLLAR STUD

Badly affected by the rough crossing, easily exhausted, and still feeling as if the floor were heaving, the Gentleman attempts to confine mounting chaos with conventional codes. In retrospect, however, the scene will assume an eschatological cast and can be understood as the last rites of a man preparing for death.

Skillfully, at this point in the tale, Bunin's narrator sketches the Gentleman as a tangle of curves and angles, daubed with colors ranging from off-whites and golds to browns and blacks. The Gentleman's head is dark and yellow, but his hair is "pearly white" (320). His fingers are gout-hardened with "almondlike nails" (320); the skin at his Adam's apple sags; his body bows out at the middle.

The scene of the Gentleman's preparing for dinner has an additional ironic twist. As the Gentleman readies for dinner, the effort exhausts him. The Gentleman is "pinched" (319) by a collar stud and thereby marked for circular return. His eyes shine from exertion, his face grows livid from the tight collar, and his body begins to feel, again, that the ground is moving beneath him.

The Gentleman looks, again, at the multiple images of himself in the mirrors of his room and reiterates "Oh, it's awful!" (320). Though the Gentleman does not try to understand his own words, the words contain an acknowledgment of his wasted years, as well as the realities that he is rejecting: decline, age, and death. This admission of existential horror echoes that of Tolstoi's Ivan Ilych, but the Gentleman does not advance toward enlightenment or peace as Ivan Ilych did. Instead, the Gentleman responds—almost in a Pavlovian way and in regression, surely—to a gong announcing dinner. He approaches the "heathen temple" (320) for a final time, preoccupied with thoughts of Carmella, the evening's dancer.

It is testimony to the enduring perversity of ego that the Gentleman rouses a dying body to stand erect, to stride briskly past servants who flatten themselves against the wall to let him pass, and even to retain ideas of a pos-

Self as Entrepreneur

sible tryst. Intent, he ignores signs of warning and bypasses people and things in transit to a lower life. He ignores a German with gray hair, insane eyes, and silver-rimmed spectacles; he outpaces an elderly lady who wears a gray gown and walks "like an old hen" (321). Furthermore, the Gentleman takes only casual note of things that could, symbolically, call him to salvation: an open window, the "steady wash of the sea" (321), and a tree that he imagines "spreads its gigantic-looking branches from star to star" (321).

The Gentleman's final acts bespeak his surrender to the chain. He dons spectacles and "disappears entirely behind a newspaper" (312), engulfed by news of war until the lines of the story, like the mirrors of his room, "glaze up in glassy brilliance" (321) before him. His collar is choking him. The death of the Gentleman is a cruel and grotesque *Todestanz,* or "dance of death," performed by a body of skewed lines, angles, and dots. The hero's neck strains forward; his head arches back; his shirt juts out. His eyes bulge; his jaw sags open; his mouth shows the chainlike gold fillings in his teeth. The narrator makes it clear that the Gentleman's death dance is not being performed alone. He comments editorially that the Gentleman is in "desperate struggle with someone" (321) and that when the hero actually dies, "he was no longer the Gentleman from San Francisco—he was no more—it was someone else" (323)—in other words a self that has passed into another round of life. The selective details leave no doubt as to the hero's fate. The Gentleman is now a cold gray mass; he is carried to a cryptlike room, where he is laid on an iron bed; the only illumination is a single, circular lightbulb.

MORE VICTIMS

The tragedy of the Gentleman's end is compounded by the fact that no one learns anything from the episode. For instance, the Gentleman's family members are sketched in lines and dots. The mother's mouth is "rounded with horror" (322); the daughter's hair flares out wildly and her bare bosom is "uplifted by corsets" (322). The two attempt to reverse the Gentleman's fate by demanding that the corpse be returned to his quarters—to the protection of the regal suite he had occupied. When their word is ignored, they realize that they have shrunk in the estimation of the hotel personnel. The death has been a gross inconvenience, but it can in no way be allowed to depreciate the future money value of the regal suite.

The other guests at the hotel are even more nonaccepting of the Gentleman's death than his family is. They respond to his untimely demise like the caged animals that they, too, will ultimately become. They "stampede" (322) from the scene, screaming and overturning tables. Like the family, the Gentleman's fellow travelers also seek to reestablish life as it had been only minutes before. They return to dinner or the bar, hoping to restore the ritual barriers breached by the passing of one of their own. The guests at Capri

If You See the Buddha

suppress the Gentleman's death and other warnings of their own impending end: the cryptlike dining room, a ticking clock, and a caged parrot, which, "muttering woodenly," has "one claw flung ridiculously over the perch" (322).

In this crisis, the owner of the hotel becomes like the captain on the *Atlantis*. He fully understands the significance of the Gentleman's passing, but, rather than help his clientele to understand life, he removes the catalyst to enlightenment. To do otherwise, he shrewdly realizes, would diminish his livelihood, so he handles the *skandal* of the Gentleman's death with efficiency and boldness. First, he soothes the crowd and then has the corpse removed from their sight. Without waiting for a coffin, he orders that the body be packed in a box that had contained bottles of soda water (more dots) and be whisked off the island at dawn.

The hotel's staff comply willingly. Servants and porters spirit the dead Gentleman and his family away from the hotel. With mocking nonchalance, Luigi, the servant, orchestrates the body's removal as if he were a conductor announcing a departing train (recall the chain trains in Bunin's village pieces). Maids enjoy the spectacle as a farce. Such bravado does not completely conceal the pain and dread, though. Orders are shrill and anxious; laughter is "choking" and "soundless" (324); the box holding the Gentleman weighs heavily upon its carriers. When Luigi imitates the hero's voice, thereby passing him off as alive and well, his throat is constricted, his jaw juts forward, and his voice is "rasping, drawling, and sad" (324).

The people of Capri also assist in the subterfuge. As the Gentleman is literally carted from the island, there is again a parade, but this time the spectacle is a modern funeral, rife with shackled and samsaric images. The horse that pulls the cab is decked out in metal and circles: clamoring bells, red pom-poms, and copper trim. The cabbie is alone and silent, a man with a flabby body and bloodshot eyes, preoccupied with gambling and drink. Also, the driver does not heed either the beauty of his world or images of his own impending end. Thinking only of the money that he will receive for the task, he is unaware that the dead Gentleman "rolls his dead head" (325), one of the details the narrator uses to suggest the circles of rebirth.

Beyond the physical death of the hero, there are two other tragedies in *The Gentleman from San Francisco*. One is that the Gentleman and his family have come very close to the vision of Nirvana they subconsciously desired but have missed it. The other is that the people the Gentleman leaves behind forge new shackles in the chain of their lives. They seek satiety in food and sleep. Even though their liturgy includes a visit outside the city, to cultural landmarks atop a mountain, they follow the path of their fallen comrade. They do not have enlightenment as their goal; in fact, their "express purpose" (325) is to visit the manor of Emperor Tiberius, a "Gentleman" who ruled in the time of Christ but who, like twentieth-century counterparts, worshipped self, not the Savior. To underscore these tragedies, motifs of circular return are used along the way. The guests ride upon "strings of little mouse-gray donkeys led by ragged women with gnarled hands" (325). They travel up "rocky paths" (325) and view the "stone remnants" (325) of a long-defunct empire. Predictably, the trip ends not in discovery or freedom but in ruins perched precariously over a cliff: a fitting metaphor for the visitors' own yearning-filled lives.

Contributing to the inevitability of their tragedy, the pilgrims do not visit Mount Soliaro. As a result, they miss meeting poignant examples of liberation: people who have actually broken with desire and who now lead lives of faith, hope, and love. For instance, the travelers do not meet the carefree Lorenzo. Ironically, Lorenzo is a boatman, but, unlike the crew of the *Atlantis*, he has been, at every stage of his life, a model for painters. The pilgrims to Capri also do not make the acquaintance of the Abruzzian mountaineers whom the Gentleman and his family had wished to see. The consequences of this omission are particularly regrettable. That is, by missing the mountaineers, the travelers also miss a pristine example of simple souls negotiating their world. The mountaineers, on the way down from Tiberio, pass a statue of the Virgin Mary that has "plaster robes and a rusty crown" (326), but, in their faith, they move beyond the sham and samsara implicit in these details and sing praises to the "Immaculate Intercessor for all who suffer in this wicked and beautiful world" (326).

By choosing Tiberio over Solario and by missing Lorenzo and the mountaineers, the Gentleman's comrades also miss the opportunity to weaken old habits and attitudes and to catch a glimmer of new life. They remain convinced that the world is cold, dark, and threatening, the province of angry seas and of wicked men. They do not give credence to a world beauty that "rises toward the East" (325) or to a love that emanates from the givers of life: the sun, the newly born Christ, and his Immaculate Mother. Also, the false pilgrims do not discern that life is a struggle between good and evil and that they have the power to choose between the two, and must do so.

NOTHING VENTURED, NOTHING GAINED

Like the dead Gentleman, the travelers to Mount Tiberio have come full circle. They have been confronted by the mortality of man and the impermanence of power, wealth, and pleasure; still, they continue to choose decadence over simplicity, idols over God, self over the world. The old securities, though, do begin to pale. Cozy apartments, idol-captains, and glittering ballrooms now bring disquiet. There is no sense of carnival; the rites and rituals on the return trip do not supply the previous sense of well-deserved rest and frivolity. The pace of activities has actually been stepped up, with the voyagers attending balls nightly. The lights of the final scenes in *The Gentleman* sear with truth, though, rendering fragmentation as reality. At the balls, Bunin's narrator reduces the crowd to impermanent egos, to "aggregates": "silks, diamonds, and naked shoulders" (328). It is, however, the hired couple that best dramatize the travelers' inner turmoil and their separation from the world. The routine assigned to the couple is not one of love or even eros so much as it is a dance of "sham bliss" (328). Like the snakes that they will soon become, the couple "writhe sinisterly" and "cling convulsively" (328) to each other.

The narrator of *The Gentleman* also strikes at the *Atlantis*. The ship is reduced to lines and dots. The planes of its tiers complement the circular funnels of its stacks; its blazing eyes are barely visible in the snow. Within, the *Atlantis* carries the seeds of its own destruction. Not only does the vessel harbor the dead Gentleman below deck, but its depths take on new affinities to hell. Fire, hissing steam, and the dotlike dripping of boiling water and oil evoke a caldron that is frightening in its heat and noise. Moreover, chainlike vaults and tunnels house a "colossal shaft" that, akin to the snake of Eden or an "elongated monster" (327), rotates, samsara-like, "with a dauntlessness that was crushing to a man's soul" (327).

The chaos infecting the *Atlantis* does not spare the captain and crew of the ship. The outwardly confident captain is often roused from sleep by the howling storm. He is reassured, however, by the presence of the radio operator in a nearby cabin. The latter is even more regressed than his superior. The operator works in a control room that is "ironclad" (327) and is filled with a "mysterious roar and the flickering and sputtering of blue lights" (327). Also, this individual is framed by a metallic headpiece, an image that recalls the halo magnet of the ball and the archways of Capri and like the portrait of Mercurius in *Dry Valley,* suggests that the operator is a "modern" icon stationary in rebirth.

The *Atlantis* also faces ruin from without. For instance, the ship passes the Devil himself, who watches from Gibraltar, "the stony gateway between the two worlds" (327). In contrast to the demon in *Dry Valley,* the Devil in *The Gentleman* does not take on a human form, pronounce doom, summon up evil, debauch the passengers, or show them their place in hell. Rather, the Devil sits passively, secure in the knowledge that humankind can create its own serpents and hells. Moreover, the *Atlantis* sails into a night storm that portends the onset of death. The tempest "drones like a dirge and rolls in mountains that are like a funeral pall, black and edged with a silver fringe" (327). Against such a background, one wonders if the *Atlantis* will reach the New World and if its passengers will be returned to their old comforts and values. One thing, though, is certain. The *Atlantis,* as a key motif of *The Gentleman from San Francisco,* is destined to live. Like its island counterpart, it has entered world-memory as a symbol of self, as a legend for future generations to regard with sadness and disgust.

CONCLUSION

In *The Gentleman from San Francisco,* Bunin universalized his views on ego and enlightenment. His hero did not ascend from serfdom or inherit a decaying manorial estate; he was not a provincial magnate but an American millionaire. His setting was not the Russian village but the world at large. Bunin's message, though, remained the same. Humankind—"master" or "man," Russian or otherwise—craves self. His next major work, *Mitia's Love,* coming on the heels of revolution, war, and exile, demonstrates even more dramatically than *The Gentleman* the theme that ego alone is valued and sought in the modern world.

Chapter Five

Self as Youth: *Mitia's Love*

INTRODUCTION

On 26 January 1920, Bunin left Russia forever. For the moment, he was the Gentleman from San Francisco come to life: caught between two worlds and on the border between life and death. The chaos of revolution and war had exceeded Bunin's fears; exile could be equally brutal. As an émigré, though, Bunin valued life in a way that he could not have done in his native land. Indeed, one could argue that it was only in emigration that Bunin truly rose to the stature of Gautama's disciple, one who understood the illusion of permanency, self, and craving, as well as the value of enlightenment for all.

FIRST LOVE

As an émigré, Bunin was like many of his fictional characters in that he also used his past to reestablish personal identity and truth. One episode from Bunin's life, though, stands out in bold relief: his "first love" for Varvara Pashchenko.

Varvara Vladimirovna Pashchenko was born in 1870, the daughter of a doctor and an actress. Varvara and Bunin were classmates in Elets in the early 1880s. They met again in the summer of 1889 and married or, more likely, began living together in 1891. (Reportedly, Varvara opposed a formal marriage "on principle.")[1] Three years later, Varvara left Bunin to marry Arsenii Nikolaevich Bibikov, a writer-director and, ironically, a friend of Bunin's whom the latter had often helped in his career. Varvara died of tuberculosis in 1918 at the age of forty-eight and was buried at the Novodevichii Convent in Moscow.

Critics have tended to portray the union between Bunin and Pashchenko as poetic and pure. Nothing could be further from the truth. The relationship was troubled from the beginning. Varvara's family regarded Bunin as a ne'er-do-well and vowed to end the affair. Also, Varvara and Bunin were two incompatible egos, each bent on having its own way. Bunin was brash and insecure, a "poet" who loved Varvara as an ideal and expected her to be part of his fantasy world. Varvara, though, refused to be imprisoned by her lover's reveries. As an emancipated woman, Varvara demanded the freedom to do as she pleased, embarking on an active social life and, one surmises, on a liberated sexual life; yet when she and Bunin were apart, she punctuated long periods of silence with letters of reproach and rebuke.

It is a measure of Bunin's early sensitivity to self that he recognized that "egoism" and "egotistical love"[2]—his own and Varvara's—were preventing their happiness and blinding them to life. He wrote to Pashchenko in 1891: "Almost all the tormenting abnormalities of everyday life arise from the fact that we are unable to be simple and open, to look around us with clear eyes."[3]

Bunin did not act on his insight. He became increasingly secretive, suspicious, and fearfully anxious that he would lose Varvara. His fears were justified. Pressure from Varvara's family either to break off or to legitimize the union fed Varvara's own doubts as to her lover's stability and commitment. Her coldness provoked Bunin to frenzy, depression, and thoughts of suicide. In fact, the breakup between the two drove Bunin to such despair that his family and friends feared for his life.

In time, Bunin came to see that his liaison with Pashchenko had been a mistake. His union with Vera Muromtseva-Bunina in 1907 (they were formally married in 1922) filled the void that Varvara had left. Emotionally, though, Bunin never got over his first love, and he often recreated his affair with Varvara in his fiction, most notably in *Mitia's Love* (1924), his fourth major study on the workings of craving and self.

PREFATORY REMARKS

Writing *Mitia's Love,* Bunin revived many of the themes and motifs of his key pre-1917 fiction. From *The Village,* he borrowed such samsaric images as a ringed sun, a flushed wench, and a father corpse. From *Dry Valley,* he appropriated pictures of gentry youths, family museum estates, human borzois, wailing owls, devil spirits, and fantasy gardens. From *The Gentleman from San Francisco,* Bunin took the contrasts between city and country, Old World and New. Like the Gentleman, Mitia is exemplar of a "breed of men";[4] and he, like the Gentleman, lacks a last name.

From all three pieces, Bunin repeated the scheme of a narrator who tells the story of a character who, oppressed by craving and "roles," journeys back to simpler times but misuses memory and misses occasions for enlightenment. Also, as did Bunin's pre-1917 narrators, the teller of the *Mitia* tale begins his story as a chronicle, filled with darkness and foreboding. He writes: "Mitia's last happy day in Moscow was March 9th. Or, at least, that's how it seemed to him" (5:181).

Mitia's Love, though, moves beyond its literary predecessors in several ways. For instance, the hero is remarkably free of constraints. He is a student, "unfettered" by family or business, estate or codes, Russia or the world. Mitia has not been tested by life; he is just now beginning to experience and to explore its joys and sorrows. Also, Mitia is a young male in love—that is, he is fired by passions that are both obsessive and possessive and that consume mind, body, and soul.

SPRINGTIME IN MOSCOW

The opening setting of *Mitia's Love* counterpoints the ominous first sentence of the piece. In Bunin's pre-1917 works, "master," "man," and "businessman" confronted a wintry present, rife with execution and death. By contrast, *Mitia's Love* opens on the cusp of an early spring. Indeed, in Bunin's established symbolism, enlightenment almost seems to be Mitia's for the taking. Nature and culture stand ready to support him. For instance, sensing the imminent breakup of winter, yardkeepers sweep away ice and snow, and people anticipate the return of larks to the city. The sky is clear, and it is "almost hot in the sun" (181). Civilization itself seems to pulsate with new life. Ancient Moscow greets Mitia graciously, and the famous statue of Pushkin has a benevolent air. Even the Deity seems to care. The monastery in the scene is radiant, and March ninth begins Passion Week—the final days of memorial penitence before Easter, the feast of Christ's resurrection.

On the human plane, Mitia is in love with a seemingly model heroine. Katia is at the ideal age between child and adult. She is shy, warm, and trusting. She is also devoted to history and culture. She is studying the arts, and, as an enthusiast of the Renaissance, she champions individual dignity and resolve. Together, Mitia and Katia make a handsome couple. They are committed to learning and to each other.

Close inspection, though, reveals that the apparently auspicious beginning in *Mitia's Love* bears a corrosive touch. Ambiguity and motifs of suffering, execution, and death abound. For instance, the monastery is named "the Passion." This name calls attention not only to Christ's suffering at the hands of men, but also—at a different semantic level—to the desires that bring humankind to ruin.

Other details also demand a second look. The snow that is being shoveled is sticky, as if reluctant to be displaced, the statue of Pushkin towers over the horizon, and the larks that return to Moscow are not birds at all but birdlike buns baked for the feast of the Forty Martyrs of Sebastea. The latter detail is particularly rich in implication. The holiday complements the image of the monastery in that it continues to shift the mood from Easter to Holy Week, from resurrection to martyrdom. More specifically, the feast celebrates a group of young soldiers who chose to die for their faith and were forced to stand naked on a pond of ice but within sight of seductive fires and hot baths. The martyrs' tale has an even grimmer note, but one that is crucial to the story at hand. One soldier reportedly apostatized but, half frozen, died immediately from the intense heat of the baths.

Mitia and Katia, though so promising and comparable, also show flaws. In order to study, Mitia is living in a city far from family and soil. He exemplifies unwitting disregard for Gautama's counsel on the pitfalls of romantic love. Specifically, the attraction that Mitia has for Katia not only inflates his being but also binds him to the illusory object of his love. With Katia at his side, Mitia is like a butterfly but one that subverts the Easter symbolism associated with that image. Mitia flits "arrogantly" (181) ahead of his love. The analogy is only partially successful, though, because, figuratively speaking, Mitia is still more caterpillar than butterfly. As Katia takes care to point out, his mouth is stretched and his eyes are Byzantine; in short, he retains a regressed, Scythian linearity. Also, Mitia resembles Uncle Petr in his boyish ways: he is grasping, insecure, and childishly possessive. Not free himself, he does not wish to share Katia with the world but craves her totally for himself.

Additionally, and at the crux of the story, Mitia wishes to encase select individuals in a mythos of his own self-making. To his end, Mitia is obsessed by the desire to transform Katia into an unsullied ideal, a heroine who epitomizes innocence and naïveté—until, of course, she is alone with him. Throughout *Mitia's Love*, therefore, Katia is shown only as perceived by Mitia, as a projection of his mind and as a measure of his morbidity and derangement.

Katia does not sustain Mitia's initial impressions of her innocence and naïveté. She falls far short partially because she is a devotee of modernity. For instance, Katia loves the music of Scriabin, delights in midnight suppers with bohemian artists and actors, and takes pride in the fact that she has been asked by them to be sculpted naked. Moreover, Katia wants no part of Mitia's restrictive world. More like Bunin's early love, Varvara, in real life, she demands the freedom or, more accurately, the license, to be and do as she pleases.

Given these complications—Mitia's idealization of Katia and her resistance to that idealization—it comes as little surprise that the two fight more than they fondle. Conceivably, the intense jab-and-parry by which one partner cites the other's failings could initiate enlightenment for either or both. Just the opposite is the case, though, for when Mitia and Katia do battle, they have opposite and well-defined agendas. Mitia demands possession of Katia; Katia desires autonomy and a career in art. The struggle for dominance and control is mutual. Each travels the Path of Egression; each forges shieldlike roles to protect ego and to deflect the other's blows.

RECOURSE TO THEATRICS

The role playing in *Mitia's Love* far exceeds the posturing that took place in Bunin's pre-1917 pieces. If Tikhon tried to function as an entrepreneur, Natal'ia as a princess, and Uncle Petr as a lord, they did so in response to their rapidly changing situation. By contrast, Mitia and Katia live in an ostensibly bright and stable setting, making their playacting exclusively self-referential.

If You See the Buddha

Mitia is well aware that Katia is no paragon. He suspects that Katia is "secretly and corruptly experienced" (182) and that her avowals of devotion to him have a hollow ring. Mitia also realizes that the theater, not he, is Katia's first love. Nonetheless, and as if to assuage the jealousy and hurt that Katia's clinging to art has caused him, Mitia egotistically assumes the role of Katia's protector, the one who, ostensibly, will rescue her from evil. Actually, he wishes to capture her as the crowning glory of his own inner world. Simply put, Mitia selects Katia to augment his own inner worship and admiration.

Katia neither wants nor needs Mitia's solicitude. She spurns his possessiveness and the prisonlike aura of his dream world. For instance, Katia berates Mitia for desiring to sever her from her Bohemian crowd and to ensconce her in a "tower" (182) away from modern life. She also does not wish to be his ideal. Indeed, she responds to his "role" of protector-savior with assertive guises of her own.

At times, Katia seems to comply with Mitia's possessive fantasies. She plays the part of a soon-to-be housewife and talks to Mitia of betrothal. At other times, she acts as a siren who brings her lover to the brink of madness. Her strategy is simple and destructive. Katia keeps Mitia off balance by modulating her gestures and voice and by punctuating her discourse with such words as "but," "perhaps," "anyway," and "nevertheless" (182–83). She first entices Mitia with "conscious seductiveness" (182) but then tells him of other lovers. She gazes into his eyes but then avoids his glance altogether. She professes love for him but then calls him an Othello and a disciple of the *Domostroi*, Russia's harsh medieval code of "patriarchal" family life. She rebukes him for his jealousy but then claims that her first loyalty is to her art. She castigates him for his suspicions but then admits her wickedness and demands that Mitia accept her evildoing.

In her playacting, though, Katia unwittingly confesses to Mitia the true nature of their bond. She recites a lyric passage in which one lover gives a ring to the other. That is, under the guise of romantic "ideals," Katia evokes the image of a samsaric loop that, like handcuffs, locks two beings in rebirth.

A DOOMED PERFORMANCE

Mitia and Katia fail as lovers not only because they are intent upon their own way but also because they are too weak to sustain the roles they have chosen. Indeed, if the two dramatize anything, it is the pain of self in naked insecurity.

As Bunin's narrator makes clear, Katia is doomed on several counts. For instance, unlike Mitia, Katia is an urbanite: frenetic, rootless, and, most tragic, ignorant of the riches of primordial existence and, in particular, of "estate" Russia. Katia's links to ancestry are short and tenuous. Her father has long been absent with another family; her mother is alone and regressed.

Self as Youth

The mother's face is rouged; her hair is raspberry pink; her hands are flabby and soft. Moreover, Katia's mother grants her daughter a "strange freedom" (183) to develop herself at odds with the world.

Like many characters in Bunin's pre-1917 pieces, Katia accedes to family karma. For instance, rather than seek peace and quiet—prerequisites to enlightenment—Katia seeks an accelerating whirlwind of activity. She breaks loose from Mitia's world to fill her own waking hours dashing about Moscow. If Katia is not at classes or rehearsals, then she is seen at concerts, literary evenings, or fittings at the dressmaker's.

Like all her counterparts in Bunin's earlier fiction, though, Katia pays a high price for her pandemonium. For instance, whereas the Gentleman from San Francisco sought refuge from inner chaos in incessant rounds of food and drink, Katia seeks oblivion in constant sexual activity. To Mitia's consternation, she often appears at his room dazed and "heavily drugged from kissing" (183). Essentially, she is willing to gratify others' lusts in order to satisfy her own.

RIGHT INTUITIONS, WRONG RESPONSE

Mitia grasps that Katia is slipping from him. At first, he senses her physical absence: something magnetlike is "drawing Katia away from him" (185). Also, he frets that Katia is becoming more distracted and withdrawn: "she is changing more and more" (188), "she is living in secret from him" (185), and "she belongs wholly to the public" (186). He believes that she can no longer be trusted, and that their trysts are now "rewards for his silly torments" (189), little more than a kiss and a parting wiggle of her hips.

As would any of Bunin's self-censuring heroes, Mitia first responds to change by upholding the status quo and by laying a veneer of normalcy over his situation. Beginning a course of action that he will actively pursue later when he is at his home in the country, Mitia attempts to rationalize Katia's behavior. He tries to see life "as usual" (183) and to dismiss her frenzy as "feminine worries" (184).

Actually, though, Mitia grasps that his difficulties with Katia have moved from a lovers' quarrel to "something that is terribly wrong . . . and too appalling even to contemplate" (183, 185). For instance, he sees that Katia can no longer distinguish between theater and life. Progressively, she is playing roles both on stage and off. Katia now parrots "someone else's theatrical words" (185, 187), or she resorts to hackneyed lines from drama, such as "You love only my body, not my soul" (187) and "Go away, yes, go away, I can't stand it any more!" (189).

Furthermore, Mitia begins to realize, however dimly, that Katia is moving toward regression and death. For instance, he notes that Katia now comes to him enshrouded. An umbrella and hat cover her head; a veil and silk

If You See the Buddha

stockings enmesh her face and feet. Mitia also sees that Katia "never goes on foot" (188) but that she takes cabs, thereby facilitating the frenzied pace at which she is living. Also, he takes umbrage at the fact that Katia has been asked to pose as a "dying sea wave" (182)—a symbolic circular return to rebirth.

Most revealing, Mitia is deeply troubled by the fact that Katia takes her mounting sense of chaos to the stage. Ironically, when Katia performs as a virgin bride in a local theater, she scores a triumph; the public applauds her as an angel, "touching and sweet" (186). Mitia, by contrast, discerns something radically different: her passage to samsara. Horrified, he sees Katia's imperfection: she runs out of breath; her face is "flushed" (187); her voice breaks; and her lines exude "cheap melodiousness . . . sickening languid passion, and immoderate, unreasonably insistent entreaty" (186–87).

Possessively, Mitia regards every spectator as a potential rival. He is outraged that front-row spectators look up Katia's very short dress. He regards Katia's director as a "self-satisfied" (186) debauchee. Indeed, Mitia is convinced that the relationship between the two is "sinful and dirty" (186) and that her mentor seeks a summer tryst with her.

In the familiar move of Bunin's pre-1917 heroes, Mitia seeks to save someone else's soul, not his own. Rather than see Katia's failings as a clouded mirror image of his own fettered life and rather than release her so that he can take a giant step toward inner peace, Mitia lets Katia's instability feed his own.

It will be to Mitia's eternal regret that he does not heed Katia's charge that he is an "Othello"—that, like the unfortunate hero in Shakespeare's play, he "has loved not wisely but too well."[5] It will also cause Mitia endless grief that, though his intuitions about Katia are correct, they bring him to lacerate mind and heart with highly charged, conflicting emotions. For instance, after Katia's performance, Mitia feels "sharpened closeness" (187) to his intended mate and "pride" (187) that she is his alone. Paradoxically, though, he is simultaneously angered by suspicions that he is losing her to his imagined rivals. The narrator reflects on Mitia's mental state thus: "Mitia was jealous of everyone and everything. . . . It was not a simple jealousy, but a special kind. . . . Katia seemed unspeakably revolting and even perverse when Mitia thought of her with another man. He hated her violently then. Everything that *he* [the narrator's italics] did with her when they were alone was heavenly, but the moment he pictured another man in his place, the shamelessness of it made him want to strangle her . . ." (186). Katia's intuition had been correct: Mitia does resemble Othello, believing the worst about her in his fits of jealousy, his wish to strangle her.

Moreover, Mitia does not see that the samsaric Katia is actually infecting his being. Indeed, in his determination to bind Katia to himself, he uses memory to abduct Katia to a personal past beyond ancestry, culture, and primordial existence, and to situate her in a "fabulous world of love" (184). His idea would be a paradise, without rivals and other complications of "modern" life.

WARNINGS, INSIDE AND OUT, LOUD AND CLEAR

Like many of the heroes and heroines of Bunin's earlier pieces, Mitia receives ample warnings that something is wrong in his life. For instance, Mitia agonizes over thoughts and feelings that raise only questions, never answers. He sees his love for Katia as a "tormenting insoluble problem" (187). He does not know precisely "what he loves Katia for . . . or even what he wants from her" (187). He is bewildered not only by the "mounting strength and increasing demands" (187) of his love, but also by the to-death struggle that he believes he must wage against some phantom enemy, "against someone or something because of her" (187). Also, Mitia spends many waking hours trying to define love philosophically. Is it "incorporeal love" (188), passion-sensuality, a mixture of the two, or something different, his alone?

The power of ego prevents Mitia from discerning that "romantic" love energizes regression and that the answer to his many affective questions is literally right before his eyes. For instance, when Mitia tries to bring Katia into his "fantasy" past, he finds that his vision loses warmth and that he can only recollect her in a landscape that is thick with ice, and "dotted" with a sun that hangs in the sky like an "opaque red ball" (184).

Also, Mitia sees that his reminiscences of Katia are so filled with "poison" (184) that he must take radical steps to prevent his dream world from perishing altogether. Here Mitia takes an irreversible, lethal step. He fancies that there are two Katias. One is a woman in his own image and likeness, "a Katia whom he demanded and desired" (184); the other is "the authentic, ordinary girl" (184), the Katia of real life. Conceptually, Mitia knows that he is living a lie. He knows that the two Katias "fail dismally to correspond" (184), that he can neither separate nor reconcile the heady "mix of angelic purity and depravity" (187) he sees in the girl, and that he is laying himself open to "heart-rending pain" (187). Nonetheless, he preserves his image of his love.

Mitia also receives warnings from without. For instance, his fellow student, Protasov, sympathizes with Mitia's struggles, but he also mocks the hero and his dreams, calling him a pawn of the "procreative instinct" (190) and a victim of Nietzsche's will to power. In other words, Mitia, like Tikhon in *The Village*, wishes to seize both present *and* future for himself. Moreover, in his admonitions to Mitia, Protasov stereotypes Katia as "a most typical female being" (190), thereby implying that Katia can never measure up to the expectations that Mitia has of her. Also, Protasov unwittingly links

Katia to samsara. He notes that Katia "is not the only pebble on the beach" (190)—that she is only one of many "dot" stones—nothing special but surely samsaric.

Finally, Protasov underscores the potential tragedy in the affair. He points out that Mitia is not securing his suitcase so much as he is strangling it with leather belts that, ironically, Katia, in her pose of becoming a good wife, has gone with him to buy. Simply put, Mitia is acting out his murderous intentions toward Katia as well as his own wish to shackle and, ultimately, to end his life. More directly, Protasov compares Mitia to fictional and real-life casualties of love. If Katia censured Mitia as an Othello, then Protasov likens him to Goethe's Werther, to an (unnamed) cadet who attempted suicide because of an unhappy love affair, and, further down the regressive chain, to those male animals "who pay with their lives for their first and last act of love" (190).

FLIRTING WITH DEATH

Mitia does not listen to reason, his own or Protasov's. Rather, he begins to entertain thoughts of death. Like many of Bunin's pre-1917 characters, Mitia does not wish to live in a world he cannot control. Evidence abounds that Mitia is toying with death. For example, he tightens the belts on his pillow and blanket. He dwells morbidly on Protasov's warnings about Katia and the cadet, and he also fixates on the lyrics of Rubinstein's ballad "Azra," which he hears a student singing from across the yard. In certain details, the action of "Azra" is hauntingly like Mitia's own. Mohammed, a black slave, who loves a sultan's daughter, proclaims in an "exultantly tragic shriek" that "once we have loved, we die!" (191).

Mitia has begun to decline physically and psychically. Physically, he falls prey to "utter exhaustion" (189) and knows that he is "gravely ill" (189). Psychically, Mitia is beginning to be torn apart by his own dichotomies. He knows that his suffering is "unbearable" but "groundless" (190); he lives in a "state of strange intoxication" (190); he is both "morbidly happy" and "morbidly, drunkenly unhappy" (190). Indeed, the mere thought of Katia now drives Mitia to the "point of fainting, of dying in an agony of bliss" (188).

Despite such warnings, Mitia does not relinquish his fantasy world. He does take a positive step toward enlightenment, however, when he decides to break from Katia temporarily and to seek rest at his familial home in the country. At this juncture, like so many of Bunin's characters before him, he wishes to exchange the Path of Regression for the Path of Return.

Seeking his roots—for the riches of ancestry, estate culture, and primordial existence—Mitia experiences relief, "sudden lightness" (192), and even the hope that he will begin life anew. From the very beginning of his travels homeward, though, Mitia wards off any inner knowledge that such a trip might afford. During his final days in Moscow, he begins a pattern of behavior that he will follow at the family estate. He is so obsessed by fantasy, jealousy, and doubt—by unrealities and exaggerations of every sort—that he takes no note of springlike scents and poplars in leaf. Instead, he fixates on the unreal dream of life with Katia. He represses the "horror" (189) that he has lost Katia, and he imagines that she has recommitted to him in the present and that, in the future, the two will know "the sweetness of a prospective rendezvous in the Crimea where nothing would stand in their way any more, and where everything would come true (though what he meant by 'everything,' Mitia really did not know)" (190).

Mitia thus launches his visit to the country as a willing captive of craving. As a result, he becomes increasingly constricted and unbalanced, suicidal and regressed. For instance, on his way to the train station, Mitia squeezes into a lopsided cab, where he "holds his breath" and believes that "a stretch of his life is finished—forever" (192). Additionally, Mitia sets in motion a second pattern of behavior that he will also pursue when he reaches the estate. He projects his cravings upon his milieu, but he does not take stock of the warnings that result from such actions. For instance, leaving Moscow, Mitia finds that "everything speaks to him of the bitterness of separation" (190). He encounters, but remains unmoved by, the hallmarks of enshacklement that graced Bunin's pre-1917 pieces, such as leaden skies, husky-voiced crows, and wet cobblestones "that gleam darkly like iron" (192).

At the station, Katia comes to see Mitia off, but, in reality, just the opposite takes place: Mitia bids farewell to a Katia in samsara. To the gaunt, awkward Mitia, Katia again appears as an "ideal," pretty and pure. The truth is, though, that she is only moments away from a new round of life. Alongside a "long and heavy" train (193), Katia wears a dark gray suit and a jaunty hat that rounds her face with a broad, curving brim and that recalls her commitment to pose as a "dying wave." Revealingly, Katia and Mitia seem to realize that they will be parting forever. They do not talk about forgiveness or love; they are even silent about their upcoming rendezvous in the Crimea. Indeed, all that Mitia does at the departure is to kiss Katia's gloved hand and to wave his cap to her in "frenzied rapture" (193). Beyond this, Mitia helplessly watches his loss; against the roar of the train—"relentless, brazen, and menacing" (193)—Katia "sails faster and faster" (193) back to the platform and is "swept away" (193) altogether.

IN THE COUNTRY

A detail in Mitia's preparations for departure suggests why Mitia does not join Katia in rebirth. Hurrying for the journey homeward, Mitia buckles the belts on his packing "carelessly" (191); symbolically, he unwittingly leaves open a chance for freedom and escape.

Mitia's journey home has curative powers, since he, on the Path of Return to his roots, delights in his surroundings. Mitia finds that in the "open country" (193) he is no longer constricted physically. For the first time in the tale, he takes stock of the burgeoning "chaste" (195) spring. The gentle rain, the calm breezes, and the "profound silence of the earth" (194) interact to improve Mitia's health; they cool his fevered brow and bring him long-needed sleep. Each homeward mile also helps to restore Mitia's inner balance. His surroundings cause him to "find his bearings" (195), to see life in a "new and different light" (193), and, most important, to distinguish between a genuine and a false past. Repeatedly, Mitia recognizes that his native roots are "simple, serene, and familiar" (194), a marked contrast to the "Moscow world and the fabulous past with Katia . . . so lonely and so pathetic at its center" (194).

Furthering the healing efforts of spring in the country, Mitia's family and estate home also offer him salutary help. His mother, for instance, facilitates his long-overdue entrance into adulthood; she "treats him in a new way . . . as a grownup" (196). Moreover, and like the Khrushchev siblings in *Dry Valley*, Mitia is able to browse around the museumlike ancestral manor alone and to relish its peacefulness, simplicity, and the bright light that comes from its "eastern exposure" (196). For the moment at least, Mitia basks in the light from the East and also in its wisdom. With Katia physically out of the picture, he can let go his roles as savior and protector. He can rediscover his own roots and assume a more selfless but rightful position as a child of the universe, of nature.

REMEMBERING THE WOMEN OF CHILDHOOD

Mitia's ego does not easily tolerate this new flood of potential blessings from family, estate culture, and primordial existence. Even on his way home, Mitia's "entire being is aflame with piercing fire" (193). Katia's lingering perfume and the increasing distance from Moscow subtly influence Mitia not only to recast his love into an ideal but also to experience new torment. On the train, despite long periods of restorative sleep, he "feels terribly tired" (194), and new questions about life and love are accompanied by "anguish and ineffable joy" (194).

At this point, Mitia has embarked on a "false" voyage similar to those that engaged young Kuz'ma in *The Village*, Natal'ia in *Dry Valley*, and the businessman in *The Gentleman from San Francisco*. Mitia delights in samsaric markers in his travels homeward. He regards a semaphore in the forest as "especially charming" (194), even though the sole purpose of the green dot light of the mechanism is to guide the passage of the chain-train into the country. He is enchanted by such regressed images as wretched villages and the "strange figure of a man who might have come from ancient times: barefooted, wearing a ragged cloth caftan and a sheepskin hat on his long straight hair" (195).

As Mitia merges images of good and bad into an unstable, explosive compound, his inner world becomes morally more ambivalent. Driven by Eros, Mitia's fantasy jumbles and equates earthy and erotic images and scents: "Katia, the village girls, the night, the spring, the smell of rain, the smell of horse sweat, the smell of earth, ploughed up and waiting to be sewn, and the smell of Katia's kid glove" (195). Given the nature of his "false" trek homeward and his recent experience in Moscow, however, it should not be unexpected that, when Mitia arrives at the family estate and begins to recall his early years there, he is not immediately absorbed into the memory of ancestry, culture, or primordial existence. What he does recollect are the women of his childhood and youth.

The women of Mitia's childhood and youth shed light on the samsaric nature of his painful cravings for affection. Through his recollections about these women, it becomes clear why "his entire being secretly yearned for love since childhood, since boyhood" (196). Like Katia, the women of Mitia's childhood and youth are "aggregates." For instance, although Mitia recalls his nanny only as a face, a sarafan, and an ample bosom, he remembers a "heavenly light" (197) and a "hot wave" (197) permeating his being. Mitia can recall his nanny "aggregate" only as if in a dream, but the reader grasps that the image and experience of the woman have left him incapable of distinguishing eros from ideal, illusion from reality.

Mitia's response to his nanny brings him to react to members of the opposite sex with "secret, devouring curiosity" (197). Subsequent encounters become more conscious and painful but also more mysterious and dreamlike: curiosity, infatuation, and rapture; moping, crying, and languor; longing, premonitions, and anticipations of the heart. For instance, Mitia recollects the girls of his boyhood birthday parties as "small, enchanting creatures" (197), as "shards" of dresses, hats, and ribbons. He recalls a "sportive" (197) schoolgirl as a Katia prototype, a regressed individual who, perched in a tree like a bird, wears a round comb in her hair and engages in shrill shouting and laughter. The schoolgirl had lured Mitia into fantasy, into "magic" (197), but afterwards, he "moped . . . sometimes even cried . . . seized by a gnawing longing" (197).

NATURE AS LOVER

In addition to his nanny and the girls of his childhood and youth, Mitia recollects yet another "first" love: a very memorable spring that had occurred at his home two years before. Unlike the fragmented flashbacks to his childhood friends, Mitia's recollections of that spring are raw and sexual. He remembers, for example, that the field was ploughed for oats, that the trees glistened with moisture, that snow dripped from roofs, and that there was "something primordially indomitable in the black, pungent earth that lay upturned in clods" (198). Also, Mitia recalls his horse as a type of alter ego, a male animal at the height of his physical prowess. The animal "breathes nosily through inflated nostrils" (198); it "emits a growl from its depths with magnificent, savage strength" (198).

Mitia's remembrances of his past emphasize his penchant to view love as an emotion that is "objectless and incorporeal (198)," chronic and all-inclusive: spring, schoolgirls, wenches—"someone or something all day and every day" (198). Mitia's recollections of people and times gone by also show his proclivity to ignore nature as a catalyst to enlightenment. Mitia responds to nature as a sexual lover might, as to something he can desire and capture for himself alone.

Finally, in their selective nature and ardor, Mitia's memories of his prestudent years at home cause him to violate Gautama's counsel to accept life as constant change and view stability and permanence as illusory. Since Mitia is overwhelmed by the amorphous and shifting details of schoolgirls and of earth's annual renewal, he locks in on Katia as a single, fixed point of reference, an immutable object of desire: "someone who embodied the entire world and who triumphed over this world" (198).

A WENCH, AN OWL, AND A CORPSE

Roused by his sensuous responses to his past and to the perennial attraction of spring, Mitia reaches out for the first woman he meets, the housemaid, Parasha. Parasha recalls the regressed Youngbride in *The Village*, for Parasha, too, is a line-and-curve humanoid made up of aggregates soldered together by heated sensuality and brazenness. Parasha has a sweaty, flushed face, freckles, and a sturdy body that, snakelike, stretches and curves at will. She carries scalding samovars and washes floors with hot, steamy water; she dramatizes her rebirth by appearing as a frenetic "bluishly remote" (196) shadow in the reflections of the windows that she cleans.

Though aroused, Mitia does not seduce Parasha or entertain thoughts of later trysts. His is not the angst of Tikhon Krasov in *The Village*, who seeks to cheat death and to perpetuate self. Rather, for Mitia, Parasha only underscores his ideal of the Katia of his ego dream. Parasha's earthiness helps him downplay "the ordinary Katia who, in Moscow, had so frequently and so hurtfully failed to become one with the Katia of his wishful thinking" (196).

However specious the strength Mitia draws from Parasha, it enables him to withstand two explicit challenges to his wrongdoing: a wailing owl and a vision of his father. Stepping out into the night, Mitia hears an owl engaged in mating. Entranced, he listens to "wild, fearful hooting that rises to a yelp," "a soul-shattering wail," "perverted laughter as if it were being tickled or tortured," and "a shriek of mortal ecstasy" (199).

Mitia is repelled by the owl's actions. (Recall the regressed owl that so unnerves Natal'ia in *Dry Valley*.) He senses that much of the animal's sexual hysteria echoes his own emotional tumult and, in particular, his immature confusion about his desires. The owl also "whimpers piteously, imploringly like a child" (196). The owl produces in Mitia an encounter with samsara. Mitia "shudders" and "freezes with fear" (199). (Bunin's narrator uses the verb *otsepenet'*, which has as its root *tsep'*, or "chain.") Mitia sees the owl as the Devil himself; it personifies the darkness that "seems to be watching him hostilely from all around" (199). Reflecting upon the bird's "mating horrors" (199), Mitia thinks of love with abhorrence—as a nightmare, not a dream. Subsequently, his sleep is disturbed by "morbid and revolting thoughts and feelings about what his love had come to in Moscow that March" (199).

Mitia also has a recollection of the wake of his dead father. As was the case with Il'ia Mironovich, the father of Tikhon Krasov in *The Village,* Mitia's father is the quintessential soul in chain. He lies unattended, a monochromatic amalgam of triangles and lines. The hands of the corpse are pale and folded; the chest is raised beneath a full-dress coat. The beard is sparse and very black, the nose white. The body is heavily shackled by a huge coffin lid that is covered with gold brocade. If as a reaction to the Devil owl Mitia had a profound, metaphysical sense of evil, when he remembers his father's corpse, he has an eschatological view of reality. Mitia "suddenly feels death in the world" (200); he believes that "the end of the world is near" (200). His surroundings correspond to intimation of death: pale, eerily quiet, and suffused with a "nauseating and sweetish" (200) funereal smell that lingers, despite repeated efforts to air and scrub the house. (Recall Katia's persistent perfume.)

The images of the Devil owl and the father's corpse invade Mitia's fantasy world but do not rouse him to move toward enlightenment. Instead, he meditates upon a photograph of Katia and writes her a letter "full of faith in their love" (200). Progressively, he deludes himself into feeling Katia's "constant love and radiant presence in everything he lives by and delights in" (200).

In these newest acts, Mitia prejudices himself further against reality. He also misses the fact that Katia's picture is flat, two-dimensional. It presents his love as an iconic "image" (200) with an "almost round" (201) (samsaric) face, and it incites him to new delusions. Just as the Gentleman from San Francisco ogled the postcard of the dancer, Mitia uses the photograph of Katia to fan the flame of desires. Imperceptibly, it also serves as a fetish against evils of change and death. Mitia thinks that Katia's love will be "unlike any other" (200) and that, with her, he can weave a "spell of quite another order"

(200). Mitia thus drifts into an increasingly fragile dream world made up of Katia's image, near delusions of her presence, the impermanence of springlike nature, and a youthful, passionate, first love.

AN UNNATURAL SPRING

A key paradox in *Mitia's Love* is the hero's drawing of increasing strength from an expanding void. Katia, as the narrator reveals through Mitia's consciousness, is no longer a person in her own right or an individual advancing to chain or even a pretty picture for him to admire. Rather, by this time, Katia has passed into abstraction: a creation of her lover's fevered imagination. Earlier, in her own right, Katia exhibited dramatic presence and vulgar sensuality; now, recast by Mitia's idealization, she is represented by Bunin's narrator as "nonexistent" (200–201), an entity devoid of grammatical person, animacy, and gender. She is marked by the neuter pronoun "something" and modified by the adjective "extraneous" (*eto postoronnee*, 200).

Despite compelling evidence of Katia's samsaric state, Mitia continues to experience her as "immaculate" and "beautiful" (201). When he receives his first—long delayed—letter from Katia, he responds to it in much the same way that Natal'ia regarded Uncle Petr's mirror in *Dry Valley*. That is, he becomes so engrossed—even obsessed—that he further loses contact with reality and moves straight toward death and rebirth. Like a (regressed) animal carrying off its prey, Mitia clutches the letter, moves to the most remote part of the garden, looks about furtively, and tears it open. Katia's letter, though, only stirs new confusion, yearning, and warnings of death. "Dazzled and frightened" (202), Mitia does not even understand the letter until he has read it five times. Katia's missive does not bring Mitia to sexual climax, as the mirror did Natal'ia, but it rouses him to "incessant sensation" (200) and to expect more letters from Moscow. Katia's note with its theatrical lines— "My beloved one, my one and only" (202), rendered in a "familiar, pathetic handwriting" (202)—hastens Mitia's realization of his end. In contrast to the resurgence of life in nature, Mitia experiences a chill running through his head, blood recedes from his face, and "the earth swims out from under his feet" (202).

Katia's missive extends ego power over its host. During his first weeks at home, the burgeoning "paradise" (205) that greets Mitia is the stuff of enlightenment: the hot sun, blue sky, and lush verdure lustily rescue the earth from wintry regression. Mitia's experiences of earthly renewal, though, cause him to imagine that "everything was Katia" (201), that "Katia's image did not retreat or get lost among the [springlike] changes . . . but that she participated in them, lending herself and her beauty . . . to the flowering spring . . ." (202).

Self as Youth

The many scenes of awakening nature in *Mitia's Love* recall and augment the ambivalence of the introductory setting in Moscow. For instance, when nature stands objectively apart from Mitia, Bunin's narrator shows that the youth is conscious of it as charming, robust, and life affirming. Spring, when undefiled, creates a "holiday" (203) atmosphere. It gives Mitia peace and joy, and it impresses upon him that he is at one with the world.

When nature must progressively bear the onus of Mitia's self-projections, though, it is a witness to regressive life. Mitia selects more and more for discordant sounds and noxious smells, skewed angles and arcs, and colors that are pallid and penitential, plastic and metallic. For instance, the air is "slate black" (219); there are smells of manure and decay; and land "rolls" uneasily in wavelike hills and depressions. Also, the spring sky appears as a "void" (231) that is "speckled" with a sun that is white, crimson, or red, and a moon that "glitters like silver" (231). Most of nature, in fact, is "flecked" with dust, sunspots, "rusty" raindrops (234), flies that trace "magic circles" (232) in the sky, woodpeckers that drill dots into trees, and (regressed) butterflies that, still shackled by desire, travel about in pairs (214).

In this particular spring—now a projection of Katia—the verdure, in particular, seems threatening. For instance, trees multiply, rise higher, and advance threateningly on the home. They "sift" (228) out the light of day; they "slant" (213) scenes with separable rays of sun. They also block walks and alleys, cast menacing shadows, peer into the windows of Mitia's home, and regress the estate, making it seem—even feel—smaller than it is. Other aspects of the verdure add to the dark and sinister impression. Budding branches and boughs form chainlike "nets" and leafy "lace" (202, 203, 205), and are heavy with dotlike apples and the sexually symbolic pears.

The last item is particularly apt, since the aroused Mitia often sees the environs of the estate as a seductive bride, eager for his taking. For instance, nature "dresses itself" (201, 203) in "bridal whiteness" (203), "black velvet" (201), and "silvery-gray fur" (225). Nature entices Mitia with a "soothing, silky rustle" (230) and brushes his face with a "feminine touch" (205); it wears blossoms that are strongly scented, like Katia's glove.

SENTIMENTAL VERSE AND
A PROPHETIC CUCKOO

The menace lurking in Katia's letter "aggregate" and in the samsaric spring is intensified by the fact that there are no more letters from Mitia's love. Mitia becomes increasingly moody and irrational. He worries incessantly that he has lost Katia and that his "reasoning" (203) will no longer be able to sustain his dream much longer. Retreating to his behavior in Moscow, Mitia does not relinquish desire or seek enlightenment. Rather, he does what a wounded self would do: he withdraws further from reality. Specifically, he buries himself in the family library and devours books of outmoded, sentimental verse.

In the serene, Old World atmosphere of the library, Mitia's poetic readings are not only "self-inflicted torture" (204) but also a type of "incantation" (204) in which, like Natal'ia in *Dry Valley*, he implores the elements to help consummate his love. For hours on end, he repeats certain lines as if they were "magic" (204). At first, this exercise is so exhilarating that Mitia deludes himself into thinking that he is a poet: loving, triumphant, and poised for the "bliss of consummation" (204). Since his efforts to conjure up Katia now so "silent and sparkling . . . alien and remote" (204) do not elicit even a second letter from her, Mitia regresses dispiritedly from poet to sorcerer—with closed eyes, cold heart, and wrathful mood.

The increasingly manic Mitia is attracted to the other village lasses at his estate. The peasant women who now entice Mitia display the same regressive "attributes" that characterized Katia, Parasha, and the girls of his childhood and youth. For example, Son'ka is skinny, sportive, and coarse, but she is also highly intuitive and senses that Mitia is obsessed with desire, that he is in "love." Son'ka herself is smitten by the hero; sitting aloft in pear trees, she flirts with Mitia by making allusions to sleep, inflamed flesh, and horseback riding. She even invites him to a tryst, going so far as to stretch her legs into a "triangle." Also, like Katia, Son'ka seeks to keep Mitia off balance. She baffles him with eyes that are passionate one moment but cold and hostile the next. She torments him with her admission of other lovers, even of her upcoming marriage to a shepherd. Even more disquieting, Son'ka's actions and bold remarks clearly suggest Mitia's impending fate. She compares his hair to horsehair, she covers his face with a cap, and she likens the hero to a calf that appears on the scene, love starved and topped with a curly white fringe (recall the "lace" of the blossoming trees in the samsaric spring). Pathetically, the calf nibbles at the chainlike flounce of her dress.

Calflike, Mitia craves Son'ka's attention, but he does so more from instability than from active desire. At this point in the narrative, Mitia is not enjoying life so much as he is merely existing. He is emotionally paralyzed by the "secret anguish in his heart" (208)—his endless waiting for a new letter from Katia and the "impossibility of confiding the secret of his love and his torments to anyone" (208). Aroused by poems extolling a "world of love" and "unfolding rose petals, moistened with dew" (208), Mitia responds to Son'ka as a "secret participant in his life" (208), a heady "substitute for Katia" (208).

Mitia's feint at intimacy with Son'ka is, though, just new evidence of the pair's regressive fates. What might have become a liaison is merely a play of aggregates, a kaleidoscope of bodily parts and smells. Mitia's consciousness is penetrated by the scents of Son'ka's skirt and blouse; he rests his head on her knees, legs, and stomach. Bunin's narrator is careful to mention that, as Mitia lies there, his face is dappled with sunlight, and his smile remains characteristically awkward and wide: angular. Once again, a bird—this time a cuckoo, a conventional symbol of cuckoldry, egoism, betrayal, and unrequited love—breaks into the hero's reverie with a cry that "cleaves the earth to its very bowels" (208). With "terrible clarity" (208), the cuckoo's cry tells Mitia what he has refused to admit: despite his desire for Katia and for "superhuman happiness" (209), there would be no more letters from Moscow, and he "was done for, finished" (209).

NEW ATTENDANTS TO CHAIN

Opportunities for enlightenment seem to have faded, and Mitia seems to be destined for a new round of life. Looking into a mirror, he sees the self that both Katia and Son'ka had caricatured: eyes that are insane and Byzantine, hair that is curly but sparse, and a face and torso that are gaunt, bony, and crude. Mitia does not draw any illumination from this portrait, however. Rather, he allows family and home to edge him even further to ruin.

For example, like Katia, Mitia does not have a father. His brother and sister are away, and his mother has put the home in second place so that she can go out into the fields and, from there, manage the estate from morning to night. Revealingly, Mitia's mother does comprehend his struggles; she is too preoccupied with her own doomed lot to alleviate her son's distress. She is forging her own shackles in samsara. A circle-and-line figure (lean and wearing spectacles), Mitia's mother crochets a chainlike piece with grim determination; she "digs" (210) into her needlework as if preparing for her grave and for her next round of life. The woman does not possess the sensibility to grasp that her son would attain inner peace by relinquishing romantic love; instead, she actually deepens his dilemma when she suggests that he visit a neighboring household that has several eligible girls.

More than just the mother, the whole ancestral estate shows a corrosive, samsaric touch. If earlier it was the exterior of the house that seemed to contract from the pulsating pressure of the Katia-filled spring, now the interior also begins to show decay. For example, Mitia is conscious that the table is bespeckled with sunspots, the mirrors are oval and elongated, and the air is shadowed and dotted with wasps. Also, the more time Mitia spends at home, the less equanimity and peace he has. Instead, he paces like a caged animal, seeking release, but he is also brooding and sullen because he does not know what he must do or why.

Under these pressures, Mitia moves slowly and relentlessly toward dementia. His thoughts and actions conflict. Emotions and memories lacerate his heart. He is caught in a "magic circle" (215). Katia has by now become a "genuine obsession" (211). Mitia senses her "presence in everything . . . to the point of absurdity" (211)—even though he knows that "Katia no longer existed for him" (211). Also, Mitia is once again victimized by jealousy. He is firmly convinced, but with no concrete evidence, that Katia is "in someone else's power" (211), that she is "giving her love to someone else" (211), and that "everything in the world is unnecessary and tormenting" (211).

Round and round Mitia goes: trips to the post office; rambling letters to Katia; emotional cycles of indifference, resignation, desperation and hope; recurrent outbreaks of volatility and paranoia, morbidity and secretiveness; spiraling yearnings both to escape and to cling to his love; roundabout reflection as to the motives and nature of his affections; kaleidoscopic images of past and present, springs and summers, city and country, family and friends, photographs and trains, suns and cuckoos, Russia and abroad. These images and preoccupations engulf Mitia in a swirling vortex that takes him downward, drives him to exhaustion and sickness, and, ultimately, to madness and death.

Mitia enters rebirth, totally. Physically, he sleeps days and is awake nights, further emerging as an egressive soul, as an "I" isolated from the "All." He shudders when he thinks of a ribbon of Katia's, the only "attribute" of hers that he actually has in his possession beyond her photo and her short missive to him. Like everything else in *Mitia's Love,* Mitia's body also breaks into aggregates with each part raked raw by rapture and torment. Mitia's head and breast feel "sharp pain" (211–12); his body trembles as if with fever; his mind becomes "befuddled . . . blind to everything . . . as though he were gravely ill . . . or mad" (211–12).

Mitia also steps into rebirth spiritually. From the past, for instance, Mitia recalls two ominous visions of his love. First, he recollects his farewell to Katia at the train station in Moscow, that time at which Katia herself actually entered rebirth. Second, Mitia conjures up Katia in a more elaborate, "theatrical" setting—an evening when the two attended the Bolshoi. The vision features the famed hall as a samsaric "abyss" (212), filled with a faceless crowd, "aggregate" finery, and the circular pearly glow of chandeliers. The ominous mood of the scene is heightened by the music of Gounod's *Faust.* The music—first "thunderous and demonic," then "infinitely tender and sad" (212)—not only echoes Mitia's emotional tumult but also portrays a story not totally unlike Mitia's own. Faust, too, toys with death in his love for the peasant girl, Marguerite.

In the present, Mitia's vision of Katia contains such elusive details as milky gardens and pitifully sporadic pleas to God that Katia come into bed with him "if only in a dream" (212). It is indicative of something tragic and unnatural that, in his vision, Mitia sees Katia in an uninhabited estate that is surrounded by black firs and pine needles that are slippery, rusty-colored, and tinged with "golden glints" (213).

It is Mitia's vision of Katia in the future, though, that tells most dramatically what lies in store for him. Here Katia stands in a highly charged atmosphere: a red sun, white-hot highways, and burning sands. Characteristically, Katia is all smiles and sparkle, but she is also rounded by a parasol, pebbles, and waves.

Mitia's visions of Katia return him to the same destructive patterns as before: Mitia again identifies Katia with vibrant nature. To his disordered mind, the sun shines with Katia's youth, the garden exudes her freshness, and the church bells echo her grace. Even the wallpaper in his bedroom "demands that Katia should share with him the dearness of this old country world" (215).

Mitia also resumes his habit of seeing women as aggregates and of breaking Katia into shardlike parts. Every girl he meets immediately brings to his mind the hat, hips, gloves, veil, and diminutive stature of his Moscow love. Finally, Mitia recommences gazing into Katia's photograph and falling into a "stupor" (215) every time he sees her image. Every time he does this, Mitia distances himself further from reality and keeps the healing effects of earth's renewal at bay.

These visions of Katia bring Mitia's yearnings for death to an inflamed state. As before, Mitia knows that his dream world is terrifyingly hollow and contradictory. He knows, moreover, that the happiness he experiences from his visions of Katia is not his but "someone else's and long ago" (213) and that this happiness "lacks the most essential something" (215): the genuine love of a genuine person. Mitia also senses that the "circle" in which he has hidden from life is no longer "magical" but "vicious" (215). That is, he senses that "he is coming to the limit of what he can suffer" (213) because he has reached a "state of extreme exhaustion" (216). His only outlet is to seek solace again in reading and to yearn for his end. "What will be, will be" (217), Mitia thinks fatalistically.

Mitia's dalliance with suicide begins with an idle resolve. "I'll shoot myself" (214), he blurts out after his vision of Katia at the ruined estate. The idea has more vitality than Mitia could have dreamed or intended. Rather quickly, he is mesmerized by the thought. On one hand, he knows that there is "nothing crazier" (214) than suicide. On the other hand, though, Mitia takes perverse delight in lurid fantasies of "shooting himself, shattering his skull, abruptly stopping the beating of his healthy young heart, stopping thought and feeling, going deaf and blind, and vanishing from the ineffably beautiful world" (214–15).

The actual form this death wish takes at first, however, is only for Mitia to sequester himself further from life than the library permitted. He now spends whole days in the woods, and he ceases to visit the post office, to write letters, or even to think about his love. But this seclusion and lethargy are short-lived. With the lack of resolve that characterized the passive "lords" in *Dry Valley,* Mitia allows the folk to break through his isolation and to rekindle his desires. This rekindling is all that Mitia needs to hasten his entry into rebirth.

THE FINAL FALL:
THE STEWARD, ALENKA

The steward of the estate and the peasant girl, Alenka, are Mitia's final attendants to the chain. The steward brings Mitia to new imbalance; specifically, he chides Mitia for his passivity and isolation. Mitia has, for example, increased his fantasy readings, his monkish moping, and his hopes for letters from Katia.

The steward deepens Mitia's sense of withdrawal, though, when he drunkenly drives Mitia in a rough cart. Short as the trip is, the "jumps" and "jolts," "bumps" and "bounces" (217, 219, and 225) of the journey make the overly sensitive Mitia think of life as plagued by earthquakes and other natural disasters. In his disordered view, for instance, he feels that fields "tremble" and "jump up" (229) before him.

The steward is detrimental to Mitia spiritually also. For instance, it is he who brings the unhappy hero to articulate, a second time, that he will shoot himself. Worse, the steward titillates Mitia with references to "wives and wenches" (217) and by proposing to Mitia that he take the peasant girl, Alenka, for his delight.

Alenka resembles many of the regressed men and women in *Mitia's Love.* Like Katia, Alenka is small, lively, and mocking, at once womanly and childish. Like the steward, she chides Mitia for his seclusion, recommends various lasses to him, and teases him for loving Katia and about his lack of letters from her. Alenka, too, is defined in circular warp. She wears a polka-dot blouse and can, at any given moment, roll her eyes, round her arms, "wiggle her rump" (124), and shake the "dark ringlets" (221) of her hair. Like Parasha, Alenka unnerves Mitia as if she were a shapeless ghostlike spirit—a pronominalized "dark something that rolls over to him" (*eto temnoe katitsia na nego,* 232) in the woods. Like Son'ka, Alenka wears chainlike flounces on her dress; like Mitia's mother, she embroiders. Her many circles finally are complemented by triangles: pointed breasts.

Mitia realizes, subconsciously, that Alenka will spell his ruin. The steward tells him plainly that she is "poison" (218), and Mitia himself resists meeting Alenka at church. It is almost as if fearing a fatal explosion of his long, pent-up desires that Mitia agrees to a tryst at all, "against his will" (218). An encounter between the two happens amidst surroundings and entities that, like the semaphore in the forest, mark sexual arousal and regression—either among "young oaks" (225) or in a stone gully. Also, when Mitia has consented to visit Alenka, he encounters a headstrong stallion that recalls the train in Moscow, dogs that wag their tales in arcs, and peasants who bow low to him, calling him a Tatar and a borzoi. These chance incidents heighten his uneasiness. (One of the peasants, Trifon, is a beekeeper—that is, an overseer of the multiple dots that invade the scene.)

Driven by desire, though, Mitia is selectively unaware of these omens. For example, he is so consumed by "feverish eagerness" (218) that he imagines the (triangular) belfry of his childhood church "thrusting itself up from behind the tops of trees" (218)—a symbol of his sudden rush of sexual prowess. Moreover, once Mitia consents to an assignation with Alenka, new signs of regression make a mark on him. His face is gaunt, accentuated by his sparse, curly beard; his eyes are black and "permanently dilated" (219). Internally, Mitia's soul is beset by new doubts and qualms about love: befuddlement over Alenka, musings about Katia, and yearnings to resume his compulsive visits to the post office. He is nearly overcome by darker intuitions that "everything in Moscow was finished for him forever" (224).

Meanwhile, the samsaric spring continues to reduce to a trancelike state, further sealing him off from everyday life. For example, rain swishes monotonously on roofs; the garden exudes a "pale but sweepingly and fantastically beautiful light" (223). The air is, typically, hot, sultry, and sensual, and the redolence of flowers, earth, and manure merges with the resonance of birds and bees "digging the whole of their . . . bodies into flowers" (223).

Mitia's encounter with the samsaric spring has this unexpected result, however; it is so potent that it drives him to seek solace in the past, in memories of his childhood and youth. Once again Mitia undertakes a journey back through time that could be potentially salvific. He takes such positive stock of his early years that he believes that "it is possible to live in this world without Katia" (223). This moment is one of true enlightenment, but a fleeting one. The mere sight of Alenka returns Mitia to his old ways, to his trance, to the abyss, to samsara. Bunin's narrator describes Mitia's consciousness thus: "Mitia felt like a sleepwalker who, dominated by someone else's will, was walking faster and faster toward a fatal but irresistibly luring abyss" (226).

Given Mitia's hypnotic state, it comes as little surprise that his tryst with Alenka moves forward without either the intensity or the violence that urged Tikhon to Youngbride in *The Village* and Iushka to Natal'ia in *Dry Valley*. Two additional reasons explain why everything surrounding Mitia's tryst with Alenka augurs failure. First, his desire is less for the peasant girl than for whatever object will still or sate the craving within himself. He is in no condition to give or receive love. Mitia is so self-centered that he is bored (his days drag on), bitter ("poetic love" [230] now irritates him), high-strung (ordinary sounds distress him), noncomprehending (verse readings have left him cold and confused), humiliated (even servant women taunt and tease), and vengeful (he is angry with Katia). Mitia is at a total impasse. It is a desperate belief on his part to think that sex with Alenka will somehow resolve his sense of being traumatized and lead to his "liberation" (223).

Second, Mitia is on a cusp between old and new lives. Immediately prior to the assignation, Mitia is preoccupied with earthly finality. For instance, he walks—a final time—through the "frighteningly empty" (231) rooms of his home and "bids farewell to the estate" (231). He repeats—less empty now—his desire to shoot himself, and he makes the sign of the cross over his abdominal region, a generalized symbol of his devouring desires for women. In addition, sounds of hoofs, bells, wheels, and snapping branches reinforce the "indifferent, alien, and hostile" (230) in life, and new dreams of *Faust* recast the theater-abyss as even "more bottomless, golden and crowded" (229) than he had thought just weeks before.

Just moments before the tryst, portents of Mitia's death and rebirth abound. As before, the blood recedes from his face, but this time his head also spins, his teeth chatter, and his body is alternately as "rigid as iron" (233) or convulses in tremors and fits. Unaware of what he is dramatizing, Mitia resumes his earlier animal-like actions: this time as an animal stalking its prey. Waiting for Alenka, he crouches low in the bushes, "strains his senses to the utmost" (232), and charges into the distance. For all his idealizations and fantasies, Mitia's desire for sex lacks all that is mature or spiritual. Since this desire is exclusively physical, "the excitement seizes only his body, not his soul" (232). Also, and consistent with his relationships with women—urban and rural, present and past—Mitia experiences neither closure nor climax with Alenka. His desires do not end in bliss but in gnawing disappointment.

FINAL MOMENTS

Already perched precariously over the abyss, Mitia disintegrates utterly. Externally, he now falls somewhere between a "modern" tangle of circles and triangles colored with decadent hues and a "ghost," a fitting complement to Katia, Parasha, Son'ka, Alenka, and the other spectral women in his life. For instance, Mitia has blue hands, purple lips, a mauve face, and eyes that are swollen and insane. His arms are folded in angles behind his head; his mud-splattered legs are crossed. Mitia's cap is shapeless and dark gray, and his jacket is black. (Compare Tikhon's and Kuz'ma's muddy arms and legs, as well as their shroudlike clothes in *The Village*.)

Tortured internally also, Mitia "hears" Katia's voice one last time—a letter disavowing their "love." He crushes the missive into a dot ball and is forced to realize irrevocably that "everything between them is finished forever" (235). In total despair, Mitia takes a first step into rebirth. In nature, the scenes are "ten times more violent than before" (235)—he also endures spasms of fevers and chills and rehearsals for death (Mitia collapses on his bed)—and bring him to "narcosis" (235), to "another world" (235), to an experience of "new" life.

In his final moments on earth, Mitia has a two-part vision. On the one hand, he dreams that he is safe in his room at home and in hearing distance of members of his family. On the other hand, Mitia is in "return." He begins as a (regressed) baby who is "rocked" (235), samsara-like, by a nanny; but he ends as an "invisible spirit" (236) who, voyeurlike, watches the intimacies of a couple in their own pilgrimage to rebirth. Like Mitia, the pair is drawn as inscribed circles, painted in monochromatic and decadent tones. The woman has rounded hips, braided hair, and milky-blue breasts with pink nipples. The man is bloodless, with curly black hair. Mitia can only participate vicariously in his dream. For one thing, he does not know the nanny or the couple in question. For another thing, Mitia is spirit, not body. He imagines himself in a kind of ménage à trois with the couple, but, characteristically, he experiences only lust, terror, and revulsion at his own thoughts—that is, sensations that speed regression and even preclude return to human form. To his horror, Mitia imagines that the woman of his vision has hidden his baby self in a drawer.

Even more terrifying, when Mitia awakens from his dream, he finds himself in a present that he deems worse than hell. His body is covered with dot sweat, convulsed with fever, and assaulted by the sounds of splashing rain and laughing voices. Also, Mitia is consumed by new horror and pain. He believes that he is permanently estranged from his family, that Katia has been "crushed" (236) for her own failings; and, finally, that he is akin to a "modern" Adam expelled from his self-made "paradise" (236), and for whom there will be "no salvation, no return to the divine vision" (236) that has sustained him for so long. Mitia's fevered state and raging desire even leave him unclear about his actual sexual preferences. Tormented all his life by women and girls, in the closing moments of the narrative, he is repelled by the horror that, possibly, he has engaged in "monstrous unnaturalness of human copulation" (236) with the *man,* not the woman of his dream.

Seeking release only from his anguish, Mitia rushes to rebirth. He again searches through his drawer, but this time, fatalistically, he does not retrieve Katia's picture or even the baby self that the woman of his dream has tried to hide. Rather, Mitia takes out a revolver. Feverishly, he puts the round, phallic barrel of the "cold, heavy lump" (237) into the wide, dotlike orifice of his mouth and presses the trigger. In one last orgasm, he passes from this world only to enter, chained, into the next.

CONCLUSION

In *Mitia's Love,* Bunin explored the dynamics of the young male ego in love. He envisioned a hero who, by virtue of his station in life, is unfettered and

If You See the Buddha

free but who becomes so seized by desire that he—like his predecessors in *The Village, Dry Valley,* and *The Gentleman from San Francisco*—enters into rebirth. At this point, one wonders if Bunin thought that regression and samsara were the lot of all humankind. The answer is no. In *The Elagin Affair,* his next great work, Bunin again sketched a couple in love, but they are a pair who struggle with desire and rebirth. The heroine, Sosnovskaia, fails miserably, but her lover, Elagin, comes away from the encounter sadder, wiser, and most important, enlightened as to workings of self and chain in life.

Chapter Six

Self as Actor: *The Elagin Affair*

INTRODUCTION

In summer 1890, Warsaw was rocked by a scandal of love and death when, on 19 July, a young Russian officer, Alexander Bartenev, shot and killed a Polish actress, Maria Visnovska. The personae were Bartenev, a nobleman with bright prospects for a military career, but a profligate, given to bouts of temper and drinking, and Visnovska, a commoner who was older than Bartenev and whose life in the theater was so jaded that she wanted to die. Differences in the couple's religious and social backgrounds, though, created an unbearable strain on the relationship and precluded any hope of marriage; and Visnovska often fantasized about her death, surrounding herself with funereal objects and rehearsing a final farewell with her young lover.

The actual circumstances of Visnovska's murder were intriguing—and bizarre. Bartenev admitted his guilt to friends and freely handed himself over to the authorities. Investigators found Visnovska's body in a wakelike setting, a dimly lit room strewn with flowers, and she had left behind a note, intended to absolve Bartenev of his crime. "The man who is killing me," she wrote, "is acting honorably. He is my justice."[1]

Visnovska's murder by Bartenev occasioned a sensational courtroom trial that was held in Warsaw in February 1891, and reported by newspapers throughout Russia. (Chekhov was moved by the accounts to comment that Visnovska's life had been "so complex and absurd that only Dostoevsky could make sense of it.")[2] At the trial, the counsel for the defense, Fedor Nikiforovich Plevako, contended that the liaison between Bartenev and Visnovska had been highly theatrical, that the couple had been the victims of their fantasies, and, finally, that they had entered a pact according to which Bartenev was to murder Visnovska at the latter's request.[3] Despite Plevako's eloquent defense, Bartenev was found guilty and sentenced to eight years of hard labor. (There was no jury.) Family and friends had the sentence commuted, but Bartenev was demoted to a footman in the infantry. He continued to lead an unstable life, finishing his days as a homeless wanderer who, like Dostoevsky's Raskol'nikov, was often found near the scene of the crime. Bartenev died on 12 December 1916 either on a backstreet in Warsaw or at his family estate in Tambov (accounts differ).[4]

BUNIN AND *THE ELAGIN AFFAIR*

When Bartenev murdered Visnovska (1890), Bunin was only twenty years old, but the incident affected him greatly, and thirty-five years later he used the liaison as a subject for a story. Although the affair between Visnovska and Bartenev was tawdry and macabre, thinking about it deepened Bunin's stance as Gautama's disciple. Specifically, in *The Elagin Affair,* Bunin expanded many of the images and ideas of *Mitia's Love* to probe the relationship between a jaded actress, Sosnovskaia, and a young officer, Elagin. The young couple, driven by desire like characters in Bunin's previous works, stand on the cusp between "old" and "new" lives. Unlike their fictional predecessors, though, they seem open to enlightenment. They are aware of the reasons for their unhappiness, and they also make an abortive attempt to be liberated, to quit this world and to enter into nonexistence.

Sosnovskaia and Elagin fail in their quest, though, and for a straightforward reason. They do not pursue enlightenment so much as they pretend to it: what they actually seek is "not to be." Consumed by their tempestuous desire, they prefer to leave this life and to enter oblivion. On the other hand, the pair also seeks "to be." Each is taken with the things of this world; each forges masks and roles to energize ego; each seeks to still cravings and to manipulate events in order to gain power and control.

Pursuing a way fraught with ambiguity and artifice, Sosnovskaia and Elagin posture. They vacillate wildly between slavery and freedom, self and non-self, life and death; but what they imagine to be high theater is, in reality, melodrama, even farce. Their erratic behavior ends not in the quiet of Nirvana, but in "rebirth," another round of life on this earth.[5]

PREFATORY REMARKS: THE NARRATOR

The Elagin Affair complements *Mitia's Love* on several accounts. In both works, a couple is roused by desire and moving from love to death. Elagin resembles Mitia, an inexperienced youth, in the throes of sexual awakening. Sosnovskaia is a more advanced form of Katia, an actress better versed in the ways of the world than her inexperienced lover.

The Elagin Affair differs from *Mitia's Love* in many ways, though, with the most critical one being the role of the narrator. Like the teller of *Mitia's Love,* the narrator of *The Elagin Affair* espouses enlightenment, but, unlike any of Bunin's speakers discussed thus far, he does not present the case of Elagin and Sosnovskaia from a unilateral, cohesive point of view. That is, Bunin's narrator in *The Elagin Affair* reviews the testimony and evidence, leading both himself and the readers through a maze of conflicting ideas and opinions. He prevents readers from drawing any conclusions about the couple until all the facets of the "affair" have been tested for authenticity and fit. In so doing, the narrator draws his readers into the work—as the jury that was absent in the real-life Bartenev-Visnovska case. By this narrative method, also, the readers do not see the tragedy of Elagin and Sosnovskaia as a conventional story of love and death but as the tangled quest that it is: two ill-fated beings destroyed for freedom and peace.

On first glance, the narrator of *The Elagin Affair* resembles "my sister and I," the *Ich-Erzählung* speakers for the Khrushchev clan in *Dry Valley*. Like them, he seeks to penetrate the surface realities of scandal, murder, and death, and to discern the workings of desire and liberation in life. Also as "my sister and I" did, the narrator of *The Elagin Affair* acts as an investigator who meticulously gathers the "facts" of the affair, but without relinquishing control of the narrative. He incorporates multiple views, but as integrator of evidence, his voice" is the sole reference point for the other speakers in the piece.

The teller of *The Elagin Affair*, though, differs from the last of the Khrushchevs in many ways. Whereas "my sister and I" strove to use memory to weave a thematic unity, the narrator of *Elagin* keeps unraveling the threads of a neatly quilted pattern for close scrutiny. Also, the "polyphony" of Elagin's tale is more extensive and penetrating than anything the Khrushchevs could have attempted. For example, "my sister and I" relied almost solely on their own observations and those of the servant, Natal'ia. By contrast, the narrator of *The Elagin Affair* measures his own opinions against the speeches of the prosecuting attorney and the counsel for the defense, the testimonies of Elagin and the evidence of witnesses, the rumors and gossip in the town in which the murder occurs, and, most intriguing, the notes, cards, and diary excerpts that Sosnovskaia leaves behind. The result is both the "polyphony" of the tale and its tense, disturbing plot line.

In a crucial way, the narrator in *The Elagin Affair* departs from Bunin's *Dry Valley* by rejecting linearity and closure—physical and philosophical. The *Elagin* tale is one of the most radical of Bunin's pieces. Opacity, contradiction, and ambivalence are in; clarity, certainty, and system are out. The story is "complex"[6]: fluid, open, and sustaining a discourse that embraces diverse times, places, and opinions.

For example, though the *Elagin* narrator examines each piece of evidence with precise references to time and space, he also mixes and matches many of the episodes by replaying several of them from different angles and points of view. He breaks many of the scenes into "aggregates" and reassembles them into new and more intriguing configurations, but there is no indisputable beginning, middle, or end. Patterns of image and idea dominate those of plot and plan, and the story goes in samsara-like "circles" or takes "sharp turns" (285), baffling to the readers.

The narrator of *The Elagin Affair* uses few of the images and motifs that informed *Dry Valley* or other stories in Bunin's long fiction, such as ancestral estates, masters and men, flashes of memory, journeys back through time, and scenes of apocalypse and ruin. Even motifs of chain and rebirth appear but intermittently in the work, and the doom that typically attends recalcitrant selves in Bunin is absent altogether.

Additionally, the narrator of the *Elagin* tale avoids epistemological and moral absolutes. He does not judge Elagin and Sosnovskaia against some conventional precept or standard. Rather, the narrator balances the couple's strengths and weaknesses while maintaining that he himself is a relativist with singular views on love and marriage, sickness and health. For instance, he is unwilling to draw the line between sanity and madness (269). He is even more diffident about affairs of the heart: "Are love and marriage so very closely bound together?" he asks, "Would Elagin have found peace . . . by marrying Sosnovskaia? Is it not well known that every strong love . . . has a peculiar tendency . . . to shun wedlock?" (269–70). Indeed, it is the narrator's openness to philosophical and moral issues in *The Elagin Affair* that allows him to draw scenes as "simple pictures" (261), so that he and others can engage in intense debate on Elagin and Sosnovskaia, their innocence or guilt, their bondage or liberation.

Further, unlike the undiscerning young Khrushchevs in *Dry Valley*, and as corollary to his disavowal of certainty and closure, the narrator in *The Elagin Affair* invariably qualifies whatever people tell him, asserting that there are different ways to look at things, different truths to discover. The narrator has, nevertheless, made it clear from the very first line of the tale that the "affair" is "horrible," just as it is also "strange, enigmatic, unsolvable" (260).

It is the narrator's opening stance that most clearly signals that *The Elagin Affair* will be different from previous Bunin works. Whereas earlier narrative voices presented their characters and immediately foretold their dismal outcomes, the narrator in *The Elagin Affair* presents his own quandary—the apparent insolvability of some affair—followed by the voice of the counsel for the defense arguing for his client. It is not until three pages later that the reader learns who the accused is or what the nature of his crime is.

Finally, the teller of the *Elagin* tale differs from "my sister and I" and other speakers in Bunin's long fiction in that he structures the work as an ongoing puzzle—a literary Rubik's cube, so to speak—by which he challenges his readers to follow closely as he twists and turns a chain of discrete pieces of information in the hope that they will establish a pattern of the innocence or guilt of the characters.

As proof of a commitment both to his readers and to the truth, the narrator often intrudes directly into the narrative, moving from a sympathetic bystander to an intimate witness of events. He continually reviews the evidence or challenges public opinion, identifies enemies and friends, and, most important, corrects erroneous inferences derived from testimony or gossip. The narrator, together with the council for the defense, acts as Elagin's "defender" (271). As needed, he uses such metadiscourse as "I repeat" (270), "I think" (275), "I would have asked" (271), "I listened" (272), and "I did not understand" (272).

Despite these interventions, the narrator is careful to sustain interest and intrigue. On one level, *The Elagin Affair* is a story of sex and violence, the stuff of tabloids, melodrama, and detective novels. The work has a peculiar logic, and readers encounter a series of narrative highpoints: Elagin's confession in the barracks, the scene of the murder, the trial. They see the couple first separately and then together. Finally, they hear the reconstructions of the actual murder and hear the moral of the tale.

Also, the narrator keeps encouraging readers to function as jurors. When he bids his characters to have patience, or when he has them trying different keys and locks or scraping dark walls searching for switches to turn on lights, his readers are drawn along. The readers fashion hypotheses, learn from their mistakes, and try to make sense of the contradictions. The narrator also makes clear that those who persist and crack the riddle of *The Elagin Affair* will come away from the piece enlightened. They will be instructed in masks and poses, the injustice of prejudicial verdicts, and sham ideas of release. Simply put, they will have had vicarious experiences of many of the obstacles that impede genuine liberation.

Finally, the narrator in *The Elagin Affair* differs from the tellers of *Dry Valley* in self-conscious artistry. Bunin's earlier tellers presented themselves as teachers and as arbiters of good and evil, but the speaker in *The Elagin Affair* seeks to transmute the murk of life into art. He realizes that *The Elagin Affair* draws from the mindlessly sordid and simplistic material that could be the basis for a "dime novel" (260); yet he also realizes that the affair between this soldier and actress can be transformed into beauty—the "creation of a profound and artistic work of fiction" (260). Shown in its complexity, the "affair" could transcend the ravages of time and serve as a model, artistic and philosophical, for readers of generations to come. The aesthetics of *The Elagin Affair* thus engage the narrator's attention as much as do its philosophical and moral aspects. He is as intrigued with the "drama" (262, 269, 271) of souls wrestling with desire as he is with the "tragedy" (271) of their lives.

SEEKING AN ALLY:
THE COUNSEL FOR THE DEFENSE

At the outset, the narrator of *The Elagin Affair* makes clear that the counsel for the defense, Elagin's advocate, is the narrator's ally. He is an individual who speaks "justly" (260) about Elagin. As the first voice in the tale, just

If You See the Buddha

after the narrator's own, the counsel for the defense is a shrewd, fascinating figure who sustains the mood of enigma and relativity set by the narrator in the first sentence. His method is to pose thesis and counterthesis, seeking a balanced view. Initially, the counsel concedes that the murder of Sosnovskaia by Elagin seems cut-and-dried and "unworthy of any special philosophizing" (260). The facts compel belief. The defendant has pleaded guilty; both the couple and the crime are inane and drab.

The counsel then summarizes the concluding argument of the prosecuting attorney and, by implication, the sentiment of the town. Elagin is regarded as "regressed," a "criminal wolf" (261). The counsel immediately objects to these epithets, though, and begins to adjust the parameters he himself has apparently just set. "But all this is not at all so," he contends, "all this is so only in appearance; there is plenty to disagree over—the grounds for dispute and deliberations are many." (260).

Elagin's counsel refuses to take the readily available option of presenting the best in the accused, requesting leniency, and hoping for clemency. Rather, he fights vigorously for his client, seizing upon Elagin's refusal to admit wrongdoing for his crime—his disturbing claim that he murdered Sosnovskaia without "conscious evil will" (261)—as the pivotal point of his defense. Also, the counsel states that Elagin's affair is atypical; it has no precedent in traditional law. He thus appeals to the judge, and in a larger context, to his jury readers, for openmindedness and understanding. Like the narrator, the counsel for the defense does not accept simple answers to complex questions. "No lawmaker," he contends, "has indicated by what, precisely, judges must be guided in cases such as ours; a great latitude has been left for the exercise of their understanding, conscience, and insight" (260).

Mindful of his difficult task, Elagin's lawyer goes to great lengths to establish his own professionalism. Every detail he reports has received his personal, scrupulous attention and is, he submits, credible. He admits that the data reveal an intriguing dichotomy, both a deep and surface structure, so to speak. This dual structure demands a new, fresh look at the "affair," something that no one has, thus far, been willing to give. Elagin's lawyer asks: "But what do we see in this case of ours? Why, precisely this—that there seems to be not a single trait, not a single detail in it, which the prosecution and I could regard as alike or on which we could agree.... Every minute I am forced to say to the opposing counsel: 'Everything is so—and yet it isn't so!' But that's the most important thing; the fact that everything 'isn't so' is the very core of this case!" (261).

THE FACTS OF THE CASE

The counsel's support of relativity and mystery opens the way for the narrator of *The Elagin Affair* to recap the facts of the case. From his own meticulous fact finding, he reconstructs a series of scenes as if he had been an intimate observer. In the first picture, Count Elagin bursts in on members of his regiment and tells them that he has murdered Sosnovskaia, an actress. When he also tells where her body is, some of his disbelieving colleagues rush off to the site.

Many of the details in this scene can be recognized as stock devices from Bunin's Buddhist-based repertoire. Before Elagin's arrival, the air is stuffy, dry, and still. The officers are young but sprawled out lifelessly, their faces "sleep-laden and bewildered" (262). Into this setting, Elagin enters as a whirlwind of chaos and confusion. Like other Bunin heroes, Elagin loves the grand display. He is intentionally noisy, familiar, and audacious, speaking in a "deliberately raised voice" (261); he jangles bells, clinks his spurs, and clatters his boots. Not surprisingly, Elagin also has the hallmarks of regression. He is a puny, line-and-circle figure, freckled, and carroty-colored; his legs are "bowed and unusually thin" (262). Despite his inelegance, though, Elagin is a dandy, a host to a "weakness" (162) that links him to Bunin's Tikhon Krasov in *The Village* and Uncle Petr Khrushchev in *Dry Valley*. After confessing his crime, Elagin becomes even more samsaric in appearance. He joins his supine colleagues first by slumping on a sofa and then by stretching his body and flinging his hands in "triangles" behind his head. To all appearances, he has entered a ghostly realm. His face has a "supernatural pallor" (263); his eyes reveal "something not human" (263).

The narrator accepts the counsel's view that everything in Elagin's affair cuts two ways. He immediately, therefore, puts forth details that the prosecuting attorney and the hero's associates overlook or ignore—items that not only counter the image of an Elagin in rebirth but even hint that perhaps he has achieved a measure of liberation. It is understandable that many critics of *The Elagin Affair* believe that Elagin has actually attained enlightenment, for much of what the young officer does in this scene differs sharply from the thoughts and deeds of earlier heroes in Bunin's long fiction. For instance, previous characters had committed crimes against backdrops of eerie nights and winter storms, but Elagin greets his fellow officers in the serene hours of a bright summer morning (a fact that the narrator reiterates later). Other regressed souls hid their decay in layers of clothing, but Elagin sheds his coat and suspenders before announcing his wrongdoing. Former Bunin heroes writhed and shuddered in transit to new lives, instilling fear and loathing in their onlookers. Elagin, by contrast, strikes his comrades as calm and controlled, stirring them to express sympathy and disbelief. Revealingly, no one condemns Elagin or places him under arrest; rather, the Captain is ready to "howl" (263) over him, and his fellow soldiers suspect that something momentous has actually happened. Even more unusual for a Bunin story, though, Elagin's comrades do not fear the dead but are "drawn irresistibly" (264) to look at Sosnovskaia's corpse.

Many of the details of Elagin's initial portrait become increasingly ambiguous. For example, his supernatural pallor and nonhuman eyes, which could suggest regression, could also indicate that he has entered a realm of grace and peace. Also, with no subterfuge, Elagin presents his comrades with the key to the apartment that harbors the corpse of Sosnovskaia, a key that, symbolically, may unlock the mystery surrounding the couple.

Sosnovskaia, when reconsidered, also shows the same pervasive duality that characterized Elagin. She is a meld of bondage and liberation. For instance, the setting in which her body is eventually found features many images of samsara and chain. The "love nest" of Elagin and Sosnovskaia is located in a old, uninviting building behind iron bars. Elagin's colleagues open "a most mysterious door" (264) and make their way down an "utterly dark" (264) corridor. They arrive at a "narrow and somber place" (264) that recalls the sites for the wakes of Ilya Krasov, Tikhon's father in *The Village*, the businessman in *The Gentleman from San Francisco*, and Mitia's father in *Mitia's Love*.

Additionally, the room in which Elagin's colleagues find Sosnovskaia is like a tomb. There are no outlets except for a single window that has been draped in black. In this pervasive darkness, a lone small lantern gives the room a "sepulchral" (264) cast. Black bunting covers the walls. Arranged in (samsaric) curves, it looks like an "enormous parasol" (264) or, more regressively, a huge "bird of prey with spreading webbed wings" (264).

Amid such accoutrements, what Elagin's colleagues and the police find is Sosnovskaia lying in state, and, one might add, in apparent rebirth. Sosnovskaia is "gleaming white" (264), an aggregate or pattern of circles, lines, and angles. Her head inclines on her breasts; her arms extend straight along her body; her feet are slightly apart in an abstract triangle. Sosnovskaia also seems shackled. Her clothes are iron-colored and made of "chainlike" material; for example, her peignoir, chemise, and cape have lace collars and are made from gray gauze and silk embossed with a "pearly" sheen (265).

Sosnovskaia is also apparently a victim of explicit (sexual) desire. Resting at her feet is a Hussar sabre that "looks exceedingly crude by the side of their feminine nakedness" (265). Lest the sword, with its phallic implications, be overlooked, the narrator remarks that a police sergeant prevents one of Elagin's colleagues from picking up the sword and removing it from its scabbard to examine it for blood, an act that, he says, would be "unlawful" (265) handling of evidence.

After viewing the corpse, readers who sense the Buddhist mythos underlying Bunin's tales may profess "cynicism and horror" (262) at the crime and agree with the prosecuting attorney and the town gossips that Elagin is guilty. The dead Sosnovskaia, though, is markedly different from the corpses in other Bunin works: she does not show the ravages of death. There are neither blood, stains, traces of crime or struggle, nor signs of suffering or death agony. (The doctor later reports that her demise was instantaneous.) Also, Sosnovskaia's face and torso are not a discolored yellow, black, and blue. She is not prematurely old, nor does she bear comparison to humanoids, animals, or ghosts. Rather, the narrator casts Sosnovskaia as a "very young woman of rare beauty" (264)—one whom the investigators regard with amazement and fear.

SOSNOVSKAIA: LIFE AFTER DEATH?

It is the narrator's attention to the paradoxes surrounding the dead Sosnovskaia that serves as the pivotal, if most enigmatic, aspect of the piece. The positive qualities of Sosnovskaia's corpse mitigate, if they do not completely erase, negative, regressive ones. For example, as was the case with Lorenzo, the ego-free boatman in *The Gentleman from San Francisco*, Sosnovskaia satisfies the exacting demands of artists for "ideal" (264–65) women. She is literally perfect, fulfilling "every requisite" (265) for beauty. She has a small and regular face, tiny and unblemished feet, and perfectly coiffed hair. Her eyes are fixed and half-open; her lips are childlike, simple-hearted, and charming.

More intriguing than the corpse itself, however, are several notes and cards that Sosnovskaia has left behind. These lend credibility to her "blessed" state by doing two things. First, they grant Sosnovskaia a posthumous voice. Second, they tell much about the last moments of her life and suggest that she has, perhaps, been on the path to salvation. For example, the notes and cards underscore what the narrator had asserted earlier—that she and Elagin were in a "tragic situation" (266) from which there was no escape, and that the murder was at her request—implying that Elagin has acted "justly" (266) in killing her. Sosnovskaia neither asks pardon for her crime nor thinks that she has done anything immoral. Quite the opposite, she repeatedly asks for God's help and even expresses belief that someday she will see her mother in heaven.

Seemingly, Sosnovskaia dies divorced from ego. Singular among Bunin characters, she clearly sees the "abyss" (267) before her, but she does not fight death or brood over its finality. Rather, she thanks her friends for their fellowship, reaffirms her commitment to "sacred art" (267), and tries to secure her mother's economic well-being. Most telling, Sosnovskaia states that she is dying "not of her own will" (*ne po sobstvennoi vole,* 267). Indeed, she seems to have freed herself from the ego's need for "system" and its blindness to the inner workings of life. Although she is educated, she writes her notes with "wretchedly spelled" words (266), and she intimates a sense of stability. One of her cards reads: *Quand même pour toujours* ("Always the same thing").

The narrator in *The Elagin Affair* omits to say whether he thinks Sosnovskaia has been "saved"—that is, whether she has attained enlightenment and whether her life is a model for all. Such a claim, he senses, would not only be didactic, too much like the prosecuting attorney's; it would also destroy the sense of relativity and "isn't so" that he has so carefully crafted into his work. Instead, at this point, the narrator explores the possibility that Sosnovskaia may not have been "liberated." He adds negative details to her portrait, too, suggesting that she may be neither liberated nor condemned but suspended between old and new lives.

In truth, the question of Sosnovskaia as salvific is problematic. In her final pose, which is dissonant with both her regressed body and manacled surrounding, her corpse is too proper and stylized to be taken seriously. Earthly fashion, not transcendent Nirvana, attracts her. On an ordinary day, her coiffure "could grace any ball" (255), and her torso appeals to "fashionable" (255) painters. Even in death, therefore, Sosnovskaia seems to be performing. Metaphorically, she is again on stage, regaling onlookers—Elagin's comrades—with a heart-stopping rendition of her being.

Bunin's narrator in *The Elagin Affair* calls attention, subtly, to Sosnovskaia's flaws by intimating that, for all her posthumous beauty, she has not gained in inner knowledge. For instance, in death, she retains a "puzzled expression" (265) on her face, suggesting that the mystery encountered at the portal between life and death has confounded her. This look of perplexity is not surprising when one takes a closer look at her predeath notes. Though mute, Sosnovskaia, like the famed Shakespearean character, is a lady who protests too much. She complains about fate, last hours, the abyss awaiting her—but her complaints enhance her posturing, contributing an aura of melodrama. Moreover, several of the notes are found on the two raised circles and dots of Sosnovskaia's bosom, casting symbolic doubt about their credibility. Most unassailable of all the circumstantial evidence, though, is the fact that Sosnovskaia's beauty has begun to fade: more precisely, it has "turned to stone" (265).

Sosnovskaia's death pose prepares the way for the dots and inscribed circles that begin to appear both on and in what is—only apparently—her unblemished body. Proceeding with an autopsy, the doctor discovers a wadded-up handkerchief stanching a small, round wound. The postmortem also reveals that Sosnovskaia has tuberculosis (inner "dots") and that she has attempted release, probably not by asceticism or sustained meditation, but surely by champagne, sexual relations, and drugs. (The vial near her body bears the inscription "OP.PULV" "OPIUM PULVIS," or "opium dust") (266).

Just as the narrator has declined to indicate whether he thinks Sosnovskaia has been saved, so he refuses to imply unequivocally that she has succumbed to samsara. In death Sosnovskaia does not regress completely, become a ghost, or fade from public view. Rather, she seemingly reasserts her dramatic presence by becoming "still more awesome" (265) in her beauty. Again, questions outnumber answers; contradictions engulf consistencies.

Indeed, *The Elagin Affair* draws readers into the puzzlement and confusion that surround the heroine. They, too, are suspended between right and wrong, Nirvana and chain, old and new lives—unable to judge.

ELAGIN—SINNER OR SAINT?

The narrator also presents conflicting evidence and tentative reflections about Elagin. Sosnovskaia and Elagin defy typical or logical modes of behavior; they exhibit features of both the released and regressed; in sum, they elude the categories of legal or societal judgment. The narrator continues to show that what seems "true" about the couple is, upon closer analysis, "not true," and that what seems "so" about them is "not so."

The narrator considers Elagin's plight first by attending to the voice of Elagin's adversary, the prosecuting attorney (and, by implication, that of the citizens of the town). The prosecutor employs the same method of scrutiny that the narrator used at the beginning of the tale. He asks a series of close, rhetorical questions to help himself and his listeners frame an account of the affair. Unlike the narrator, though, the prosecutor must try to establish the guilt of the couple beyond a reasonable doubt, a prejudicial approach that the narrator of the *Elagin* tale has opposed. Indeed, when juxtaposed with the eerie, conflicting details of Sosnovskaia's wake, the prosecutor's line of reasoning is simplistic and hollow. For example, he reiterates his contention that Elagin is a "wolf" (267) who has killed Sosnovskaia with "malicious and premeditated intent" (267). The prosecutor also rejects social, psychological, and otherworldly explanations for Elagin's behavior. He does not accept the notion that the officer is a victim of unfortunate circumstances, or that he could have acted from drunkenness, insanity, or despair. The prosecutor closes his eyes, too, to the "mystery" surrounding Sosnovskaia's wake, dismissing it as dull and mundane. Although he admits that the setting of the murder is the stuff of "witches' spells" (269), he focuses on the "extremely prosaic" (269) details of the scene: scraps of supper and Elagin's use of the chamberpot. The prosecuting attorney attaches scarcely any significance to the haunting ambiguity of Sosnovskaia's statement that "she is not dying of her own will" (269). Rather, he applies it pragmatically to support his claim that Elagin is regressed, a "congenital enemy of society and the social order" (268), and an individual "bestialized by an idle and unbridled mode of living" (269).

For his part, the narrator rejects many of the prosecutor's observations and seeks, more and more, to formulate his intuitions that something unusual, even momentous, has happened to Elagin. He dismisses the prosecutor's speech as a "tirade" (268), one that is "unusually strange" (268). This rejection contrasts sharply with his earlier acceptance of the counsel's defense as just. The narrator takes particular issue with the idea that Elagin

If You See the Buddha

is a wolf and an enemy of society. In his view, other causes have motivated the affair.

In making a case for Elagin, the narrator next seeks to do what the prosecuting attorney has not done—put together a complex picture of the young officer, drawing data from the voices of others. Specifically, the narrator analyzes the speeches of the prosecutor, the testimony of witnesses, and his own observations about the defendant. He reconstructs the accounts of Elagin's behavior immediately after the murder and his confession at the barracks, and he reconsiders Elagin's conduct in the courtroom.

Initially, the narrator speaks as if the young officer could, in fact, have been enlightened. Far from being a criminal wolf, Elagin strikes the narrator as someone who has "suddenly awakened from the stupor of misfortune" (271) and who now wishes to present both his and Sosnovskaia's lives as a lesson for all. Elagin always seems to do the right thing. Not only does he seek to secure Sosnovskaia's "blessed" state, but, after he has murdered the actress, Elagin does not appear concerned about self. He is not frightened, flustered, or anxious to escape (as a criminal wolf or any of Bunin's regressed characters might be). In fact, Elagin does not leave the scene of the crime. Rather, he remains there "for a long time" (268), taking scrupulous care to present himself, his lover, and the room in a favorable light. He put himself in "order" (267) and the dead woman to "rights" (267). Even more tellingly, Elagin does not destroy evidence that could be incriminating but actually displays it prominently, including the card on which Sosnovskaia affirms that she is "not dying of her own will" (267). Finally, Elagin takes care to guard the "nest" from intruders until he has confessed his crime. He locks the door to the place "meticulously" and "carefully" (270), making it clear that he values the corpse and its effects and that it is he who holds the clue—the key—to what he and Sosnovskaia have experienced.

Elagin shows similar restraint and dispassion at the barracks. His comrades venture the opinion that the young officer must have been in a trance, another world, since they recall pleading with him to "come to his senses" (270). Also, doctors and comrades both note Elagin's recollected state throughout the time of the confession and the trial.

To the narrator, Elagin's deportment at the trial suggests still further evidence of his liberation. Under the harsh interrogations and insinuations of the prosecuting attorney and the people of the town, Elagin conducts himself in a manner "by no means ordinary" (268). He is serene and possessed. He does not plead for mercy, act in his own defense, snarl at the judge, or display defiance (as had Tikhon's brash ancestor in *The Village*). In a manner reminiscent of his behavior in the barracks, Elagin seems strangely uninvolved with the proceedings and indifferent to the verdict of the judge.

Just as Sosnovskaia's hallowed image had not withstood close scrutiny, though, some of Elagin's thoughts and actions appear flawed when closely examined. For example, his ostensibly selfless acts and otherworldly mien conflict with his bold, brash entry into the barracks at the beginning of the piece. Elagin's attention to the dead Sosnovskaia also raises doubts. If one accepts her wake as a setting in which an ego performs, then Elagin must be understood as an accomplice, an experienced stage manager, so to speak, who helps the actress achieve her sensational, posthumous pose.

Also, when Elagin is alone in the spotlight, or when his doings in the barracks and in the courtroom are under close inspection, it seems plausible that he is not enlightened or at peace, but in a zombielike, benumbed state. He does not exude the joy or excitement of an enlightened one; rather, he is unhappy, even morose. At the barracks, for instance, Elagin bursts into tears when he hears what he must surely have surmised: that he is no longer an officer. Such is not the response of a "liberated" individual. Also, in the courtroom, he answers questions "quietly, abruptly, and with a certain heart-rending timidity and sadness" (268). Elagin, in short, follows a course common to many of Bunin's male characters. He, too, pines for the very things that have caused him grief: his "former happy life" (270), his military status, and Sosnovskaia, "the woman he loved truly more than his own life" (270). Moreover, Elagin's regression has not yet come to a halt. Like Sosnovskaia, his head is tilted; it rests in his hand, screened from the public, no longer emanating a supernatural quality.

RECONSTRUCTING THE PAST (I): ELAGIN: A MISSPENT LIFE?

The teller of the *Elagin* tale rebuts the prosecutor on still another point—that the personalities and backgrounds of Elagin and Sosnovskaia have "nothing in common" (271, 275). With characteristically meticulous care, the narrator poses an opposite view: that Elagin and Sosnovskaia are both individuals who seek release from the desires and yearnings that have enthralled them.

The narrator begins this part of his discussion by reexamining several allegations advanced by the prosecutor at the trial—that Elagin is a wastrel, prone to drinking and scandal, and abusive of women. The latter charge had been substantiated by reference to Elagin's treatment of Sosnovskaia. The narrator takes issue with these allegations, as well as with the prosecutor's earlier characterization of Elagin as a beast or wolf. Glossed over earlier, this metaphorical characterization is now fleshed out in samsaric detail. That is, the attorney depicts Elagin not only as a beast and a wolf but also as a "sharply defined degenerate" (272): torso squat, shoulders stooped, mustache like an albino's, face "extremely indeterminate and vacuous" (272).

Although the narrator realizes that Elagin does suffer regression, he seeks to downplay the officer's "chained" fate. First, he criticizes the prosecutor's portrait of Elagin as "coarse . . . and cruel effrontery" (272), and second, he repudiates the earlier claim that Elagin's actions defy social and psychological explanations. He counters that Elagin is victimized by two sources: (1) a clan that is enamored with, if not shackled to, self-protecting ideas of authority, power, and restraint (generations of military forebears), and (2) a wellspring of desire, opened, at this precise age, by sexual awakening.

As regards Elagin's rootedness in the military, his own father has mindlessly conformed to an inherited norm. He is stern, morose, and intimidating. Moreover, Elagin's mother, a "passionate" (272) individual, had died when he was young and had no chance to influence his upbringing. As for his awareness of sex, the twenty-year-old Elagin, not unlike Mitia in the preceding tale, is in the throes of a life passage whose violent desires he cannot understand or control. The narrator recognizes that Elagin has entered upon "a fatal age, a dreadful period which determines what a man's entire future will be" (271). Elagin and Mitia can be compared in their delayed and disproportionate reaction to first love. Both young men encounter sexual maturation not merely as a first love, frivolous and fleeting, but as the stuff of "dramas and tragedies" (271), as "something far more profound, more complex than the agitation and torment ordinarily ascribed to the 'adoration of a beloved being'" (271). For Elagin, this maturation is a "weird blossoming, the excruciating revelation, the first sacred mass of sex" (271).

Despite the obvious parallels between Elagin and Mitia, Bunin's narrator in *The Elagin Affair* individualizes Elagin. For instance, the narrator reconsiders Elagin's "sharply defined heritage" (272) to establish that the young officer has drawn both strength and sensitivity from that background. Elagin is an "extraordinary nature" (272) gifted with remarkable physical stamina and, not unlike the young Khrushchevs, with "a particular sensitivity . . . to all that ties him to his fathers, grandfathers, and great-grandfathers" (272). If, therefore, Elagin rejects the "classical appearance of a Hussar" (272); if he is indeed a "degenerate" (273) who is spindly-shanked, freckled, and green-eyed; and, if, as a child, he showed fear and "trembling" (272) before his father and is estranged from the man now, it is not necessary to conclude that the young officer is indolent, heartless, or "cowardly" (272). Rather, Elagin's present alienation and rebellion could result from the fact that now the young officer is at least dimly aware of his regressive state, a fear that the weight of karma has entered his life.

To establish credibility for his assertions, the narrator reviews the testimony of Elagin's fellow officers with whom Elagin has shared the "greatest intimacy" (274). These comrades give the "finest reports" (273) about Elagin. Countering the prevailing low opinion of the young officer, they agree that the defendant is a complex individual, one who is essentially good, even though they admit that he is also "peculiar" (273): wild, erratic, and high-strung. Indirectly supporting the narrator's theory about Elagin's recent sexual maturation, before Elagin became involved with Sosnovskaia, he always seemed to be in nervous flight from someone or something, as if trying to stay free from some fate or ensnarement. They recall Elagin as unstable physically and emotionally. He sometimes lapsed from accepted modes of etiquette and behavior, and, at any given moment, he could be happy or sad, timid or brash, kind or cruel. His confidence about his gifts one day could be offset by despair about his fate another. Despite their general approbation of Elagin, his comrades recognized that his life was one of extremes, of existing on the edge of an abyss. The officers react to Elagin's confession of his murder of Sosnovskaia at first as if he is being hysterical—for whatever reason. His announcement mingled remorse, rebellion, and reserve; passionate weeping gave way to sardonic laughing, wild smiles, and trivial concerns for clothes. They assumed this was one of Elagin's mood swings.

Loyal and balanced, Elagin's colleagues hold mixed views similar to those of the narrator. They maintain that even if the young officer was sometimes a "sinner," he was just as often a "saint." He could be kind, gracious, and considerate, especially to members of the lower rank and file. Such observations make several inferences plausible. For example, although Elagin has awakened sexually and has become erratic in some way, he does not seem to be driven by desire for power and control. He is not like Tikhon Krasov or the Gentleman from San Francisco, devoted solely to money and career; nor is he, like Mitia, nearly obsessed to have the various women he meets. Indeed, Elagin's case seems to be confined to theatrics, to costumes and gestures that mask an ego still in an early stage of development. The onset of Elagin's sexual drives is not an animalistic thing: he does not lose his considerable artistic talent and sensitivity; he is deeply affected by drama, and he is "moved to tears" (274) whenever he hears symphonies and songs. Indeed, Elagin's "unusual" (274) musical sensibility, coupled with his "exultant nature" (273) and his rejection of mundane routine—he is always expecting "something genuine, something out of the ordinary" (274)—helps substantiate the narrator's idea that the defendant may be attuned to worlds other than this one, and that he does not regard his present reality as his last. (By contrast, one can recall how music irritated Mitia, Tikhon, and the Gentleman from San Francisco.)

The consensus of the narrator and of Elagin's soldier comrades is that Elagin is an individual of ample energy and gifts, even though he is unfocused, misdirected, and anxious to escape both the legacy of his family and the karma to which it gives rise. When the prosecutor, therefore, charges that Elagin is typical of "spoiled youth" (274) or that he has deprived Sosnovskaia of Christian burial or sought "animal enjoyment" (274) from his love, the prosecutor is being irrelevant. Tangents replace testimony as the prosecutor's case becomes shallow and he seems to rely more on public sympathies than on legal or metaphysical subtleties.

RECONSTRUCTING THE PAST (II): SOSNOVSKAIA: DEAD OR ALIVE?

As the narrator has correctly surmised, Sosnovskaia is similar to Elagin in many ways. She grew up neglected and lonely, a "stranger" (278) in a family in which order and obedience were valued over warmth and love. Like Elagin, in her upbringing, she lacked the influence of the parent of the opposite sex. Her father, a petty government clerk, committed suicide when she was three years old, and her stepfather, another clerk, died young. Sosnovskaia's mother dispatched her to a boarding school, since the mother's only concern came to be that her daughter have a strict Catholic upbringing. Sosnovskaia rejected her "lackluster" (275) origins as well as the "bourgeois" (275) life that her mother had chosen for her. From childhood on, she was, like her lover, seen as a special type: "pure-blooded" (275), artistically gifted, with a special attraction to the theater, and, most intriguing, she possessed "strange psychic traits" (275).

Despite these resemblances, Sosnovskaia differs from Elagin in several key ways. For instance, like Katia in *Mitia's Love*, Sosnovskaia is jaded, corrupt, and more experienced in the ways of the world than Elagin is. (Sosnovskaia is twenty-eight, Elagin, twenty-two.) Also as was the case with Katia, Sosnovskaia is more energetic, willful, and focused than her lover. She knows precisely what she wants in life and succeeds in her quest for it. Though Elagin passively acquiesces to his military heritage, Sosnovskaia negotiates life on her own terms and clears all obstacles from her path. Immediately upon graduating from school, she overrides the objections of her mother and pursues her dreams of acting. Sosnovskaia takes the initiative to develop her fledgling ego; she is "not at all the type," as the narrator says, "to submit to anybody whatsoever . . . succeeding . . . [in her idea] that her life could not possibly be humdrum and inglorious" (277).

Sosnovskaia's rise to stardom was meteoric. As with Mitia's Katia, though, or for that matter, any of Bunin's characters discussed thus far, Sosnovskaia's ego, a short-term asset, is a long-term liability. She pays a high price for her rapid ascent to stardom. She does not serve "sacred art"—and with the inevitable consequences. Unable to "restrain self" (278), Sosnovskaia compromises prudence and sensibility, being attracted to "regressive" people and experiences. Metaphorically speaking, she seeks to taste "all the wines in the world" (279), but her indiscretion sets her reeling. The young actress becomes "frenzied" (279) by desires for money and fame. In this state, she falls prey to a "boar-scoundrel" (277, 278), a Galician landowner who takes her on whirlwind travels, teaches her to use drugs, and imprisons her in his harem.

Essentially, Sosnovskaia yearns for love, but she tries to sate her desires by arousing the yearnings of others. To admirers and friends, Sosnovskaia becomes increasingly regressed in her appearance and behavior. Her lips—slightly open and like rosebuds—form a circle. Her gaze, somewhat like Katia's, promises "something depraved" (280). Possibly the most intimidating thing about Sosnovskaia is a certain resemblance to dangerous animals. Like Elagin, she is described as "carnivorous," "cunning," and "feral" (279). In fact, when Elagin gives Sosnovskaia a bearskin rug, she goes to the brink of rebirth, turning somersaults with the ease of an acrobat. (Recall how the regressed street urchins at Capri turned somersaults in *The Gentleman from San Francisco*.) Furthermore, continuing the animal image, Sosnovskaia does not attract admirers so much as she "ensnares" (280) them. Always the actress, she raises scandals to lure toadies and hangers-on. She drives men to "frenzy" (280) with enigmatic glances, meaningful smiles, and childlike sighs. She leaves her admirers "enraptured and amazed" (277) with those parts of her body that her peignoir or her Oriental and Greek costumes do not cover.

Sosnovskaia realizes, though, that she is losing time and not gaining total sway. Her response is typical of any character in Bunin who cannot have his or her own way: the young actress wants to die. In Sosnovskaia's case, however, the desire for death must itself have a highly theatrical cast. She lets her desire be known so that she can remain the "talk of the town" (278) and worry male friends into doing her bidding. For example, Sosnovskaia challenges her admirers to pay the price of death in exchange for a single night with her. She furnishes a room for suicide (and samsara), stocking it with poisons and circular weapons like arc- and spiral-shaped sabers and daggers. At a social gathering or rendezvous, she will suddenly hold a loaded gun to her head or put strychnine in her mouth, threatening to kill herself unless a lover kisses her lips or feet.

Gradually, Sosnovskaia falls victim to her own "playacting" (280). She suffers from nervous derangement, loss of memory, and hallucinations. She also continues her descent to rebirth. For no apparent reason, Sosnovskaia "rolls" (281) her eyes. Like Elagin, she is restless or even periodically violent, smashing tumblers and wineglasses and stopping only when her audience begs her to continue.

It should be noted here that Sosnovskaia is not as yet a totally lost being, for, though she is succumbing to desire, she is, as her diary reveals, also attempting to understand desire and the anguish it causes. Sosnovskaia's journal, divided into three sketchy parts (her years as a student, her time as a neophyte actress, and finally, her mature period), reveals much of her inner struggle and the "parable"-like (278) tale of her life. Like *The Elagin Affair* itself, it is a "scrapbook" (276) of jottings, thoughts, and utterances in which Sosnovskaia echoes the narrator's "discourse" by recording some opinions on the nature of love and life that are similar to his. Sosnovskaia's diary reveals that she has more than a passing awareness of the workings of ego and could be on her way to enlightenment. For instance, as a high school student, she shows a marked preference for such authors as Alfred de Musset (1810–57) and Zygmunt Krasinski (1812–59). They ponder key dilemmas of existence, and, from them, she cites passages on the nature of self and the dynamics of suffering, alienation, and death. She is particularly impressed by what they say about people's constant struggle to shield their souls from the world, and by their theory that, since human beings and angels are of little worth, one should strive to be either God or a nonentity.

In her own youthful jottings, Sosnovskaia reflects upon and expands such views. Even as an adolescent, she seems to fathom what most Bunin characters realize only late in life, if at all; indeed, her insights resemble a minicatalog of Buddhistic belief. For example, Sosnovskaia sees the world as "deathly wearisome" (276), as a zoo regressed to "millions of carnivorous eyes" (276). She assents that "not to be born" (276) is the greatest happiness and that one should return to "nonexistence" (276) as soon as possible. Sosnovskaia distinguishes herself still further from other chained people in Bunin in that she grasps the "enigmatic" (276) nature of love. She sees that love is a desire, both "attractive" and "charming" (276), which can, however, draw the spirit to "hell" (276). Like the narrator (and Gautama), Sosnovskaia has reservations about deep emotional attachments and resists relationships that lead to the binding commitment of marriage.

The excerpts in Sosnovskaia's diary exhibit many of the same theatrical and "haphazard" (276) flaws as her notes and cards. They are a schoolgirl's academic reflections—to which the actress may have given her mind but not her body and soul. Once again, the overall impression is that Sosnovskaia is not serious about Nirvana but merely enacting a melodramatic role. There is much evidence for this view. For instance, Sosnovskaia does not pursue enlightenment in any consistent or substantial way. She ignores her diary for months, and when she does resume writing, she interrupts her insights about life with prosaic concerns for the laundress and the dressmaker. Despite her protestations to the contrary, Sosnovskaia is very much shackled to her desires. As a result, her life abounds with contradictions. Sosnovskaia is intrigued by nonbeing, but she is more reluctant to leave this world, which, in one entry, she confesses that she loves with a passion, like one "possessed" (276).

Sosnovskaia's jottings are not presented as liberating truths but as platitudes and aphorisms. They are more like lines for one who is role playing and seized by desire. For instance, De Musset, one of Sosnovskaia's favorites, can be compared to Elagin. A Romantic in the tradition of Byron and Hugo, De Musset was initially mocking, precocious, and carefree but later became melancholic, disillusioned, and prone to sexual and alcoholic excess. Like *The Elagin Affair,* many of De Musset's stories and dramas were tragicomedies that featured bored heroes and pure-hearted debauchees who sought love in a life of excess. For instance, in his play *Rolla* (1833), he depicted a young rake who commits suicide in a final night of debauchery. Krasinski, another of Sosnovskaia's favorite authors, also fires her desire. An aristocrat dominated by his father, he dramatized the doom weighing down on the best representatives of his class.

Sosnovskaia's inner conflict causes her deep pain, as is evident in her youthful diary excerpts, which grow increasingly lonely and darkened by despair. Early on, Sosnovskaia becomes disaffected with theatrical life and complains, as Katia had to Mitia, that the public wants only her body, not her soul, and that her admirers are oblivious to the struggle raging within her. In this section of her diary, Sosnovskaia reiterates her wish to break from existence; but she does not focus on this growing need. Finally, though, burned out by her success, Sosnovskaia questions the nature of desire. She wishes to travel so that she can "love throughout the world" (277), but she also becomes increasingly intrigued with the idea of death—even suicide—as the answer to her own problems. Weary though she is of city audiences, she performs excerpts from De Musset and Krasinsky; she gazes at the sky, "so splendidly beautiful and bottomless" (277), she wishes—simultaneously or alternately—to declaim and weep, to fall in love and die. At such times, death could seem either "unnatural" (281) or "splendid" (277), but the wake she envisions could be "marvelous" (277); "How wonderful that will be!" (277) she writes. The narrator and Bunin's readers already know at this point that Sosnovskaia has so arranged matters that, at her death, there will be a white gown and a room furnished with music, flowers, and funereal drapes.

The final pages of Sosnovskaia's diary foreground the histrionic quality of her life. At the point when the entries were made, Sosnovskaia was seeking to escape the "anguish and ennui" (279, 280) of existence by reading Schopenhauer, a devotee of the Buddha. At the same time, though, she was clinging tightly to the romantic De Musset. For instance, in her journals one finds that she takes a cue from his *Ballade à la lune* (1830), although she misses his devastating parody of the cult of the moon, a favorite trope in Romantic fiction. For her own emotional binges, Sosnovskaia seeks out moonlit settings. She frequents churchyards, being "happy and joyous" (279) in the mystery of the moonlight and in the company of "thousands of the dead" (279). So rapt, she wishes "to declaim over graves . . . and then to die of exhaustion" (279). Sosnovskaia also attends the wake of a stranger and takes copious notes on the body, the chapel, the moon, and the "staggering rapturous impression" (279) that the scene makes upon her. The closer Sosnovskaia gets to the moon or to death, the more she is enticed by death. She lacks only one thing: a partner to bring her performance to an emotional peak, an eclipse to seal her fate.

ELAGIN AND SOSNOVSKAIA: DEATH OR SALVATION?

Having presented the separate case histories of Elagin and Sosnovskaia, the narrator finally examines the tightly locked mystery of the piece—the relationship and parallels between the two. As a model investigator, he compiles an exhaustive list, documenting their "feelings and attitudes" (281). As he reviews additional testimony from Elagin and the witnesses, reiterates the charges by the prosecuting attorney, and interpolates the sentiments of the town, the narrator begins to dominate the piece His voice almost obtrudes as he exhorts the readers to reflect upon valuable or illuminating images and ideas, but he justifies his intervention because many of the crucial actions either have taken place privately or have been recorded at various times and places. These pieces of evidence have been, moreover, wildly erratic and contradictory. As a result, the core narrative—the assembling and interpreting of the evidence—requires scrupulous care lest the prosecutor's charges and the public prejudice railroad the facts to an unwarranted conclusion.

The narrator looks first to Elagin's version of the affair. It is remarkably calm and clear. Despite all that Elagin has endured and stands accused of, he describes his liaison in concrete details. Furthermore, Elagin keeps his listeners riveted to his testimony by reaffirming his innocence and testifying that he murdered Sosnovskaia but only *"by her will"* (281)—an interpretation that is repeatedly challenged in the evidence.

Much of what Elagin says about his affair with Sosnovskaia recalls to a Bunin reader the ill-fated liaison between Mitia and Katia. For instance, Elagin, like Mitia, is the aggressor in the relationship. He is seeking to satisfy the youthful desires that have begun to rage within him. Meeting Sosnovskaia at a theater, he falls in love with her immediately and imagines (incorrectly) that the feeling is mutual. He begins to suffer the same "cruel pangs of jealousy" (282) that eventually drove Mitia to madness. Also like the hapless youth in *Mitia's Love,* Elagin pursues the relationship with his beloved even though this pursuit brings him sadness and anguish, not joy. For instance, he can scarcely endure separation from his love; he suffers from Sosnovskaia's indifference—real or feigned—when he professes his love for her; and he so fears rejection that he only asks permission to kiss her hand. Like Mitia also, Elagin briefly lays claim to sexual intimacy, but the "victory" is Pyrrhic: in Sosnovskaia's case, access to her body in no way guarantees possession of her soul. Elagin, however, has become so obsessed by physical desire that he cannot rest until he possesses her.

Elagin becomes bolder in his demands. He visits Sosnovskaia more frequently, expresses his ardor "more and more often" (282), and entices her with gifts that point to return: Elagin gives Sosnovskaia circular mandolins and bouquets, along with rings and bracelets studded with dot diamonds in addition to the bearskin rug that causes the actress to somersault to new life. In addition to expressing his ardor, Elagin seeks a stable relationship by appealing to Sosnovskaia on her own dramatic terms. He is an accomplished thespian, so he can enter into poses with his own melodramatic sense of theater. For instance, Elagin makes a vow of "eternal love" (283) to Sosnovskaia, swearing her as his wife in front of a cross and a Roman Catholic church—ironically, emblems of her youthful rebellion.

For her part, Sosnovskaia is intrigued by Elagin not because he is superior to the other men in her life but because, while her other paramours were content to be her audience, he assists her in her acting, playing the part of her lover offstage. Initially, Sosnovskaia treats Elagin like any other admirer and complains to him about her "fate, her strange soul" (282). Progressively she receives him in bizarre surroundings (her Japanese room), runs him through the same "game-jokes" (284, 285), allows him increasing intimacy, and presses him about his readiness to yield his life for a single night of love with her. (He replies that he would.)

Sosnovskaia is unnerved, though, by Elagin's demands for permanence. She is nowhere near willing to cede herself to another. To marry Elagin, Sosnovskaia fears, would bring about a prosaic death in life, one that would be agonizingly painful and slow, at complete odds with her own subconsciously planned "dramatic" death. In a half-articulate statement of her view, Sosnovskaia requests that Elagin give her a (circular) brooch in the form of a (regressed) skull and bearing the inscription: *Quand même pour toujours* (283). Tellingly, for one who is chained in a fully schematized death tableau—but only subconsciously so—Sosnovskaia answers Elagin's counterdemands for everlasting commitment only with sighs, silence, sadness, pensiveness, and by repeating her mysterious signature phrase, "*Quand même pour toujours.*" Sosnovskaia is so deeply moved by Elagin's avowals of love that she acquiesces to a symbolic wedding even to the point of their ordering rings. She resists permanency, however. Simply put, she is neither able nor willing to surrender her being.

In fact, Sosnovskaia responds to Elagin's vows of love by intensifying her acting out of ego. She leads Elagin through a *Todestanz,* or "dance of death," so mannered and melodramatic that it devalues the tragedy of their lives first to "comedy" (283) and then to farce. For instance, there are scenes in which the aggrieved hero is waving a revolver or threatening suicide or forcing his love to accept a key to their nest or a wedding ring to wear on her finger. The equally aggrieved heroine falls on her knees, mocks and entices her lover, hurls back the wedding ring, takes opium, breaks appointments, vanishes for short periods of time, and orders her beloved to do her bidding—to prepare a new place, according to her specifications, for their meetings. Hero and heroine manifest raw aversion and longing, jealousy and madness. They fight, reconcile, send notes, and suffer miscommunication until the almost stock denouement: a tryst ending in murder and death.

In the initial steps of the dance of death, it is Elagin who follows Sosnovskaia's erratic cues: glance for glance, note for note. His temperament can range from extremes of hot or cold, but the young officer realizes that Sosnovskaia's choreography is just a self-styled exhibition. When Elagin recognizes that there is no dance of partners, he suffers terribly. His head "swims" (284) over her antics; he has "gone crazy" (283) because of her, and he becomes "bitter and humiliated" (285) over her neglect.

Unlike Mitia, though, Elagin can and does learn a great deal from his experience. As Sosnovskaia leads Elagin into more frenetic steps in the *Todestanz*, he glimpses the life issues he had scarcely been aware of before he met Sosnovskaia. The narrator takes a solicitous view of Elagin because (unlike previous Bunin characters) Elagin takes stock of his dilemma. With a degree of clarity, Elagin articulates who he is and what he has become: he is in a "tragic situation" (282); his love for Sosnovskaia is "fatal" (282); he is "perishing" (283) in the relationship; he is on brink of madness, even suicide. One of Elagin's letters to a friend that is offered as evidence at his trial lends credibility to these ideas. In this letter, Elagin confesses that he has met "a woman quite unlike anyone else" (275) and also that he has learned a *"thing or two"* (275) about life.

As Sosnovskaia's diary jottings had been so revealing, Elagin's letter "scribblings" (274) also reveal his fragmented character, his desire to break with "system," and his craving for destruction. In general, the shreds of written evidence from Elagin appear more genuine than Sosnovskaia's; they come from the heart, not the proscenium. Whereas Sosnovskaia hides her failings behind "masks" and "roles," Elagin openly confesses that he has become something less than fully human: regressed. He is, in his own words, a "bum" (275), a "drunkard" (275), a "fool" (275) and, most self-deprecatingly, a "fly" (274) crawling out from an inkwell and speckling the world with dots. Elagin confesses that he no longer cares for the things of this world, but he says this without the vainglory that marred Sosnovskaia's similar assertion. "I've attained some sort of indifference," he writes to his friend, "Nothing—nothing!—matters. If things are right today—well, glory be to God for that! But who cares what tomorrow may bring!" (275).

In this same letter, Elagin accepts his distress as a stimulant that makes him increasingly restless and causes him to challenge the status quo. He notes that his soul is rent by conflicting emotions, tormenting his strength and frustrating his yearning for the "good and lofty" (275). (Testimony by Elagin's colleagues corroborates that it was only after he met Sosnovskaia that he became increasingly sad, listless, and enamored with death.) A further index of Elagin's detachment is that he would welcome leaving this world and experiencing other realities. Specifically, he wishes to grab hold of an "ever-elusive melody" (275) that comes faintly to him from afar. For example, during a late-night blizzard, in a behavior pattern new for Elagin, he is stirred to sudden escape. He jumps out of bed, grabs his horse, and races madly through the streets. Another sign of his changing is his new mode of signing the letter and giving his address as "Cornet Elagin, Russia" (275). By this gesture, the young officer relinquishes all pretext of being an "extraordinary being" and becomes a contemporary Everyman. Despite his generations'-long military ancestry, Elagin acts like a "modern" man, rootless and ridden by desire. He is also anxious and craves to understand the reasons for his suffering.

It is further witness to Elagin's awakening that he is willing to end his relationship with Sosnovskaia. The prosecutor makes one observation about the defendant that is beyond a "reasonable doubt": Elagin is no Othello (272)—he may not have loved either wisely or well. There is a limit to what he will suffer for love. This distinction moves Elagin even further away from Bunin's Mitia. If that hapless youth was an Othello type who clung tenaciously to Katia's things, using her portrait and the smell of her glove to kindle his dreams, Elagin seeks to escape Sosnovskaia and all the things about her that deeply stir him. Though it is painful to do so, he realizes that "everything is at an end" (284) between them. He demands that Sosnovskaia return the wedding ring to him, and he sends mementos—including her photograph and gloves—back to her house. Furthermore, whereas Mitia dismissed his friend Protasov's counsel that Katia posed a samsaric threat, Elagin heeds a similar warning from a rival, Shkliarevich, about Sosnovskaia; and he is "secretly glad" (285) for the admonition.

PUBLIC AND PEIGNOIR: GETTING A CLEAR PICTURE

The chain of events linking Elagin and Sosnovskaia strengthens dramatically when the actress almost enters into rebirth. While adding yet new circles to her image—Sosnovskaia is making "coils" in her hair with a curling iron—she accidentally sets fire to her peignoir. She screams wildly and tears off the blazing garment. Though some dismiss the incident as "trifling" (286), to the narrator it gives a "very lively sense" (286) of who the nonacting Sosnovskaia is. All along, Sosnovskaia has had some complicated yearning for death, but, like everything else, she has intended to arrange it solely on her own terms. Had she been burned by the flaming peignoir, she would have met a most undesirable end, which, however, would have been one typical of many of Bunin's chained characters. Specifically, she would have entered rebirth with her body marred by circles and dots, and she could not have ended the drama of her life in a carefully staged tableau. Realizing the horror of what a death in life it would have been if she had borne burn scars, Sosnovskaia tells her maid: "Just think, what would I have looked like if I had been burned all over? My eyes would have been just a couple of burst blisters, my lips would have puffed up. I'd have been a fright to look at. . . . My whole face would have been covered over with cotton wool" (290).

Unnerved by this accident, Sosnovskaia acts speedily and leaves nothing else to chance. She scripts her end. First she resumes her ties to Elagin. She reconciles with her abjectly faithful costar; she inspects the apartment stage and setting for her final act. She also arranges for a tryst there—not, however, without acting out the part of a crazed, spurned lover and subjecting Elagin to new rebuke and remorse. After their lives are linked anew, Sosnovskaia is silent and submissive, then cold and mocking. All the while she hints at the regression that infects them both: Elagin is not a "man" (285) but a "bowlegged puppy" (288); and she herself should be chopped into "small pieces" for her perfidy.

Less dramatically, but perhaps more tellingly, Elagin can also sense Sosnovskaia's regression. He notices the "small pieces," the aggregates that make up her being. Instead of some overwhelming impression of her beauty, he sees her tears, he smells her perfume, he hears her voice, "icy and malicious" (285). Nevertheless—and this fact is a clue to the key tragedy of *The Elagin Affair*—Elagin readily reunites himself with Sosnovskaia. Despite the misery and pain Sosnovskaia has occasioned, Elagin begs her to forgive him, to return her photographs, and to resume wearing the wedding ring. For his part, he agrees to a tryst in their sepulchral nest. Elagin returns to Sosnovskaia for a simple reason: He is still codependent and has had no healthy experiences with freedom or detachment. He needs to bind and to be bound.

MAKING A CASE: THE NARRATOR

At the point of this momentary reunion, the narrator interpolates a new voice. Just as earlier he sought to balance the prosecuting attorney's presentation—slanted against the ill-starred couple—now he introduces the judgmental voice of the public. With the people in the town, the narrator is even more piqued than he was with the prosecuting attorney. As he views the public reaction to the Elagin affair, he sees it reduced to melodrama, "scandal" (287), and "comedies of love" (287). The public resembles the thrill-seeking audience that Sosnovskaia has enthralled but repudiated throughout her theatrical career. The narrator decries the "amazing poverty of human judgment" (287). The people have not "understood or empathized" (286) with the plight of the couple; they have agreed only on the "vulgar banalities" (287) of the affair; they have "as if on purpose, severely distorted the characters of

Self as Actor

Elagin and Sosnovskaia and everything that went on between them" (287). The people have, the narrator claims, "looked, but not seen, heard but not listened" (287). Because of their uncouth approach, they have not been able to learn from the "tragedy"; nor have they applied Elagin and Sosnovskaia's dilemma of self to the struggles of humankind.

The narrator discloses these errors by reproducing significant voice excerpts from Elagin and Sosnovskaia, as well as from the townspeople themselves. The narrator shows that the people in the town are privy to many of the episodes and details involving Elagin and Sosnovskaia but that they have not wrestled with their factual knowledge to achieve comprehension or a consensus. The public accurately judges Sosnovskaia's diaries as "banal" and "naive" (289) and her churchyard visits as "unconvincing" (289), but they dismiss her and Elagin's dalliance as sensational and as unworthy of serious reflection. Betraying their own taste for the histrionic, they see Sosnovskaia merely as a "prostitute" (289) and Elagin as a drunken wastrel who cannot think beyond the "clanking of his sabre" (287). Neither is regarded as a person of feeling.

The narrator seeks to clarify these misapprehensions. First he reminds the townspeople that the murder is not what they had expected—or desired. As he points out, Elagin has had opportunity (and reason) to shoot Sosnovskaia earlier; but when he finally does kill her, he does so without the blood, gore, or struggle typical of a melodramatic liaison. Second, the narrator reminds the people that the Elagin affair is more dramatic than real. He has them recall what they know and have admitted many times—that Sosnovskaia is an "actress" (287) schooled in role playing not only from the theater but also from real life. Coupled with Sosnovskaia's background is the fact that Elagin had wanted to turn "a comedy into drama" (287, 288) and that the obsessed couple had often "played out scenes" (287) and "put on acts" (288).

Finally, the narrator resolves many of the riddles surrounding the Elagin affair by piecing together the couple's story as a moral tale. Sosnovskaia is indeed the "heroine of a great scandal" (287), but she has herself to blame, becoming and remaining the victim of a sensuality that is "sharply expressed ... and impossible to satiate" (288). "Sensuality" is conceived of broadly here as a hedonism that goes beyond debased sexuality to include a paganlike love of life, an obsession with the things of this world, and cravings that bring Sosnovskaia alternately from joy to despair. In expounding this interpretation, the narrator writes: "Sosnovskaia had everything: beauty, youth, fame, money, hundreds of admirers and she availed herself of it all with passion and intoxication. But her life was one continuous yearning, a ceaseless craving to quit this earthly vale, where everything is never quite what it seems to be" (289). It is this unreality of things' "not being so" that Sosnovskaia can no longer endure. Her escape, therefore, is a special case of an ego in distress: the actress enters into a type of hypnosis, a protective shell in which she "acts" (290) to numb the pain of her life.

Elagin is also confused about true pain and false release. He may be attuned to other worlds, but, because of "hypersensitivity" (289), Elagin cannot escape the karma of his clan and race. Like a moth to the flame, he is drawn to Sosnovskaia because he is an "atavist type" (289) whose covert desire is for destruction.

FINAL THINGS

Sosnovskaia plays out her last days in desultory ways. Brooding in bed, languishing in a lover's arms, writing notes on black-bordered stationery, burning letters and notes, and bidding prolonged farewells to family and friends, Sosnovskaia finally has her preoccupied, last encounter with Elagin. As recounted by Elagin at the trial, it is apparent that Sosnovskaia scripts, directs, and stars in this scene. Clad only in her neatly repaired peignoir, she directs Elagin's every movement. Sosnovskaia's lines in this scene disclose the modus operandi of her life. When she avers that Elagin is her "doom and fate" (294), or says that everyone is against them, or that she is a woman "without firmness" (294), or that she will be Elagin's love forever despite having usurped his soul and driven him nearly mad, she underscores not so much the tragedy of their tangled situation as her own sorry plight. Though thoroughly insincere, she copes as she knows best—her predetermined death chamber is the setting she has envisioned and has had erected, and her lines and actions depart reality for the histrionic.

Sosnovskaia's contention that she is dying not by her own will but by "the will of God" (294) speaks to the heart of her dilemma and also resolves a troubling issue in the work. However inexplicably, she believes that it is the Almighty, not Elagin, who is bringing her to death. This belief is, of course, false, but it allows the actress to exit this world exultantly and spares her either the burden of responsibility for her cravings or the arduous pursuit of Nirvana.

Although Sosnovskaia retreats into "roles" as she exits from life, Elagin understands that he is a foil in Sosnovskaia's closet drama and that he is acting under "artificial light" (293) on a cryptlike stage. He also realizes that genuine life and sunshine lie just beyond the shrouded walls, but he does not flee the Poesque unreality of the scene. Rather, long benumbed by what he has suffered at Sosnovskaia's hands, he spirals downward from "complete impotence" (293) to a state of near "coma" (294). Playing his part, Elagin accedes to Sosnovskaia's final stage directions. He resumes wearing his wedding ring and writes farewell notes; he even thinks of suicide, believing (incorrectly) that that is what she wants him to do. Finally, when Elagin advances the action by killing Sosnovskaia, the murder is markedly melodramatic. When Sosnovskaia's final lines fall on his ears, they may have sounded profound, but they are trite. They fail utterly to disclose—or even allude to—the fate awaiting her. "Farewell, farewell," Sosnovskaia says, "Better yet, greetings now and forever. . . . If we have not succeeded here, then perhaps there, above" (296).

After the unbelievably tidy killing, Elagin himself cannot leave the theater of action. He is, as it were, traumatized. He remains in the inscribed circle—both of the pool of artificial light and of his own longing and desire. He does not experience release at Sosnovskaia's death but only denial and disconnectedness—for example, first "wild unconsciousness" (296) at the moment of the murder and then "complete apathy" (296). Rather than kill himself, along with his love, Elagin arranges the corpse into a beautiful position, rearranges details of the set, and is hypnotized by the perfection of it all. By entering so fully into Sosnovskaia's staged exit, he signals his own level of regression. By surrendering himself, he consigns himself to live in "penal servitude" (296) to ego. Even if many of these actions were performed almost outside his awareness, Elagin pursues, through them, the same regressive death in life that has destroyed Sosnovskaia.

The narrator concludes *The Elagin Affair* by doing what he does so well: he asks a series of summary questions, bidding his readers, one final time, to reevaluate all that they have seen and heard. He leaves open the question of Elagin's guilt by appealing to Sosnovskaia's probable judgment of the officer. "What would she have said," he writes, "if it were in our power to make her rise from the grave?" (296). The implicit appeal in the question is the narrator's own bias: Sosnovskaia would reiterate the riddle of the key phrase: "Everything is so . . . and yet it isn't so" (261). That very paradox or enigma, as Bunin suggests, through the narrator, cannot be answered by single "voices." No one voice can be trusted, not even Sosnovskaia's or Elagin's. The fact that a civil crime has been committed cannot be denied, but the judgment of that crime is full of overtones that make reality and unreality.

CONCLUSION

In *The Elagin Affair*, Bunin focused on the plight of a young officer and a jaded actress who sense the workings of ego but who prefer to enact life rather than live it. In this, they join the Krasovs of *The Village*, the Khrushchevs of *Dry Valley*, the businessman in *The Gentleman from San Francisco*, and Mitia and Katia in *Mitia's Love* in that they, too, succumb to samsara and chain. If Bunin was unhappy with *The Elagin Affair*, it was possibly because he had again portrayed individuals who become hopeless victims to desire and fail to achieve Nirvana. Bunin's dissatisfaction must have been in the unresolvable nature of the struggle and in the near pointlessness of two young lives; it could not have been in the enormous advance he made into polyphonic technique and the power of nonclosure in truly great modern works. In his last major work, *The Life of Arsen'ev,* Bunin attempts to break the doomed circular pattern of his previous long fictions and tries, for a final time, to show his readers how to live in the world, without subjugating it to self, or self to that world.

Chapter Seven

Self as Author: *The Life of Arsen'ev*

INTRODUCTION

In 1927, when Bunin began writing *The Life of Arsen'ev,* he was in crisis. Although *Mitia's Love* and *The Elagin Affair* had convinced Bunin of his artistic growth, old devils had returned to haunt him. Soviet Russia, instead of collapsing as Bunin had hoped, was becoming a formidable presence in the world. Physically and philosophically, Bunin felt trapped. He knew that he could not return to Russia for many years—if ever. He was a "man without a country," with nowhere to turn.

In his angst, Bunin summoned memory to transport his soul from the cold captivity of the present to the warm freedom of the past. *The Life of Arsen'ev,* therefore, Bunin's last great narrative, reflects his journey back through time and his passage to enlightenment. Aleksei Arsen'ev, Bunin's narrator and alter ego, recalls the past; but, unlike other characters in Bunin's fiction, Arsen'ev learns much from "times gone by." He comes to know that suffering, loss, and death are unavoidable but also that one need not succumb to rebirth. He believes that life is worth living and that enlightenment is available to all.

THE "ADULT" NARRATOR: DISCIPLE OF THE BUDDHA

The Life of Arsen'ev can be seen as "summary text" whether one measures it against Bunin's own writings or against other Russian and world literature—for example, the fictional attempts of Leo Tolstoi and Sergei Aksakov in the nineteenth century, and of Aleksei Tolstoi and Maksim Gor'kii in the twentieth, to recapture their childhood, adolescence, and youth. It also bears some affinity to Proust's *À la recherche du temps perdu* (1913–27), in which an adult "I" recreates his early years in *fin de siècle* France and expresses love for the world, despite his considerable sufferings in it.

Themes of "family" and of "lost youth" are, of course, at the heart of Bunin's fiction. Many of the ideas and images in *The Life of Arsen'ev* echo or extend motifs in these earlier works. There are portraits of peasants and gentry, students and petty bourgeois. Bunin draws heavily on scenes of cities and estates, of wintry presents and warm pasts; he champions the healing effects of memory; he reiterates themes of faith and doubt, love and death. In *Arsen'ev*, though, there is a major innovation: the narrator is an adult protagonist at peace with the world.

The early stages of Arsen'ev's life resemble the lives of other Bunin characters, but their fates differ. Like them, Arsen'ev has led a life of self, but he also has learned from his mistakes and has matured through suffering. Analogous to Tikhon Krasov in *The Village* and the businessman in *The Gentleman from San Francisco,* Arsen'ev has done well professionally. At age fifty, he is an established and talented writer. Unlike the other two, however, Arsen'ev is also successful personally. He is essentially ego-free. He does not constantly question his achievements, hate his existence, or flee his environs; he does not need to control, vent anger, or dread the grave. Indeed, a reader notices that Arsen'ev is extraordinarily confident about life. He boldly introduces himself on the first page of the work and then proceeds to give his views on life and death. His story is encyclopedic. Living, as he believes, fully, he attempts to reconstruct a personal and national mythos to project life in the first twenty or so years of post-Emancipation Russia.

Arsen'ev also feels compelled to do what other characters in Bunin tried to do, though these usually failed—that is, he seeks sustained enlightenment. For instance, by the time Arsen'ev undertakes his narrative, he is both a worldly-wise pilgrim and a faithful disciple of the Buddha.[1] At times, Arsen'ev is so immersed in the "past," that his soul enjoys "momentary expansion" with the people, places, and things he finds there. He rejoices that he has "kith and kin" (6:8); he is a devotee of religious and cultural monuments of faith, with Saint Peter's in Rome being on a par with the pyramid of Cheops in Egypt.[2] Like the Abruzzian mountaineers in *The Gentleman,* he transcends regression to seek out settings of quiet and peace and to proclaim the "joys of earthly existence" (12).

Arsen'ev engages the world as an "I," but he is not hostile or manipulative in the way that consumed the good judgment and energies of almost every character from *The Village* through *The Elagin Affair.* Rather, Arsen'ev models an "enlightened" being who has abandoned the Path of Egression and is connected to the "All." Arsen'ev places spiritual community—a "supreme love" (40) for God and humankind—above power, money, or fame. Thus, though Arsen'ev's participation in existence is full, it is detached. He sees his environs as "maternal" and as "breathing freely," but he also realizes that life is "illusory," that the earth is "ever-deceiving" and "physically crude," and that "all human joys are poor" and the catalyst for "bitter self-pity" (16, 18, 42, 46, 54, 56). It is because of his detachment, however, that Arsen'ev does not self-destruct.

In his deepest convictions, Arsen'ev clearly shares Bunin's own reworking of Buddhistic beliefs. For instance, Arsen'ev defines himself by his ability to recollect, and to think and speak almost exclusively from memory. Furthermore, it is memory that allows Arsen'ev to integrate a host of personal and aesthetic contradictions. He can reconcile being controlled, collected, and content with being intuitive, emotive, and open to his world.

Because of memory, also, the story line that Arsen'ev weaves is a timeless web. Whenever Arsen'ev is remembering, his youthful ego may be center stage, regardless of time or place, but his adult self may also be there to know enlightenment and to interpret the workings of life. Even when his story would seem to be linear, he sometimes moves it in circles: nested recollections emphasize the moment, merge present and past, and rework key images and ideals such that the reader has a sense of return. Finally, given Arsen'ev's retrospective approach, he can detail bitterness and pain while expressing genuine forgiveness—even love—for whatever has caused him grief. Furthermore, whenever he does recall his conflicts with chain, samsara, and desire, he can also reaffirm his periodic liberation from all three.

Possibly the greatest value of memory is that it endows Arsen'ev with a positive conception of "rebirth." As Bunin himself did in some of his "enlightened" moments, Arsen'ev "remembers" present life merely as one "round" in an endless cycle of personal existences. This sense of timelessness permits him to claim innate, predestined, and otherworldly knowledge. Through feeling the appeal of other places, Arsen'ev also affirms "another, infinitely richer reality"—boundless and multiple vistas beyond "this earth or this one life" (13, 26, 75).

The fact that Arsen'ev has been reborn more than once causes him to believe that he has rejected regression and has evolved to a higher state. At the time of his narrative, in fact, Arsen'ev, a nobleman artist, has intimations that he had once been a nomad denizen of deserts and tropics and, again, that he had sojourned on earth as an "ardent Catholic" and a medieval knight in various castles in the past (35, 36, 46). Looking at pictures in a book, he states: "What sweet, bright visions, what genuine nostalgia did I experience. . . . I collected so vividly all that I had seen and absorbed . . . in my former, immemorial lives. . . . Egypt, Nubia, the tropics" (37). Such "intimations of immortality" lead Arsen'ev to accept his present situation with equanimity and to meet the future with the peace conferred by wisdom and strength.

Freed by memory from so many constricting parameters, Arsen'ev enters his "craft of letters" (7) with memory as his aide. For Arsen'ev "letters" is a life-giving avocation. It defies time and space and rescues people from obscurity by making them "animate" (7) and immortal. Acting under the amorphous shaping power of memory, Arsen'ev transcends the conventions of genre and logic. Memory selects people, places, and things at will and invests his narrative with a haunting lyricism that, like an ocean tide, rises and falls with the pull of his mood. "Life," Arsen'ev writes, is an "accumulation of impressions, pictures, and images . . . a ceaseless flow of feeling and thoughts . . . of recollections of the past . . . of anticipations of the future . . . a certain kernel, a certain meaning and purpose" (153).

Arsen'ev's pasts and presents, myths, poetry and legend, and chronicles of humankind are assembled so that they closely resemble the old photograph album that he comes across as a youth. Arsen'ev mounts "catalogs" of "faded pictures," moving from being "completely estranged" from the people, places, and things that he sees to being "intensely aware" (148) of the times in which they graced this earth.

Having appropriated key Buddhist beliefs and personalized notions of memory and rebirth as architects of his thought, Arsen'ev can present himself both as a seasoned teacher and an earnest student. He is joyful about its mastery of many things but also humble in the face of the still vaster unknown. Self-knowledge gives rise to questions that preclude facile, metaphysical closure and keep open the path toward enlightenment. Inner awareness of cycles helps Arsen'ev contend with desire, and, in particular, the craving for permanence and control. Whereas narrators of Bunin's other long tales began their stories on ominous notes, Arsen'ev opens with questions that have engaged humankind since its beginning, "What, then, is my life?" he asks. "What, in general, are 'human things and deeds'?" (6, 7).

Because Arsen'ev believes in both the eternity of life and the immortality of the soul, he contends that "we lack a sense of our beginning or end" (7). For him birth, age, and death are the accidents of life, not its essence; they are phenomena that, when understood creatively, impel one to love life, do good, and make the most of one's years on earth. In Arsen'ev's schema, only one thing can inspire dread, that the record of one's life might be condemned to "darkness," to the "sepulcher of oblivion" (7).

Arsen'ev's equanimity, wisdom, and confidence are all the more remarkable because he has suffered greater change and loss than any of the Bunin characters discussed from previous works. Tikhon and the Gentleman actually had presentiments of a world going awry, but Arsen'ev has endured revolution and civil war at home and is a permanent exile abroad. Moreover, he has confronted images of samsara and death to an extent that would have driven Tikhon and the Gentleman mad.

Arsen'ev can recognize regression everywhere. His home in Provence has a "small graveled square" and is perched on a "steep rocky ridge" amidst a "restless wintry glitter." From its windows, Arsen'ev sees "hazy mountain peaks" and fortresses that are "gray, stony, and covered with rusty scales." He also hears the "hard, long leaves" of palm trees "rustle and crackle" like "graveyard wreaths" (186, 187). Arsen'ev senses "rounded" life even in items that traditionally signify sanctity and salvation. For instance, his town's cathedral shares samsaric traits with the rusting statue of the Virgin Mary in *The Gen-*

tleman from San Francisco and the village church that rose, phalluslike, in the background of Mitia's sexual excitement in *Mitia's Love*. His cathedral is a vast gray mass; its "round" portal is girded by a chain of stone (regressed) figures, and its cross is topped by a cock, which, in Bunin, is a symbol of sexual longing, prowess, and regret.

Furthermore, while Arsen'ev believes in the immortality of the soul, he sees that humankind is "born with a sense of death" and that "there exists an entire category of people who . . . live their entire life under its sign" (7, 26). Indeed, throughout the tale, Arsen'ev confronts death and decay. As a child, adolescent, and youth, he witnesses deaths in his family and among friends; there are funerals and wakes; and before his eyes, there is the collapse of a centuries-old way of life. As an adult, Arsen'ev pays his respects to the samsaric remains of a Russian Grand Duke, with its gray head, jutting beard, and "finely carved nostrils." The corpse lies in a leaden casket "padded with ribbed velvet" and situated amidst "semicircular windows," "silver icons," and the "pearly light" of chandeliers (188, 189).

At such times, Arsen'ev does not succumb to suffering or loss; he, rather, abandons desire and professes joy over existence. Periodic suffering and loss seem to nurture in Arsen'ev a sense of purpose that other Bunin characters have lacked: one must tell his life story for posterity and point the way to enlightenment. Arsen'ev sees himself only as a "moment" in immortality and eternity, in world culture, and its throbbing, perpetuating memory.

BEGINNING THE TALE: THE PAIN OF REMEMBERING

Very early in the story, Arsen'ev thinks of his existence in generalized Buddhistic images. Already in the introduction, he refers to a "Path" or a "Way." This path is "continual and pure"; it is "the father of everyone and everything"; and it is a "doctrine" that all of humankind, including his remotest ancestors, have followed. Having rethought "rebirth," Arsen'ev also claims a joyful "connection" and "communion" with his forebears: his "fathers and brethren, friends and kinsmen" (8).

Arsen'ev's Buddhistic images come into even greater focus, though, once he acknowledges bad karma—that "evil men" (8) in his family have fouled the blood line, scorned clan codes of conduct, and deflected individuals from their quest. Conventional images of regression and rebirth are accentuated when his family crest is introduced: a tangle of circles and lines, three rapiers, topped with crosses, and a ring that the clan sees as symbol of "loyalty and eternity" (9) but that readers of *Mitia's Love* and *The Elagin Affair* recognize as a fatal link in the chain of love and death.

The enshackling images that mark Arsen'ev's family crest and ancestry are more than motifs; they pervade the very stuff of his remembering. As

Arsen'ev looks back over his early years, he is shocked to find that he has repressed his childhood, adolescence, and youth and that he can recall them only with great difficulty. His early successes produce only aggregate listings of people, places, and things that "flame brightly" in his consciousness but that are also "trivial," "disjointed," and "leaden" (14, 40, 62, 69).

If reconstructing his past is the road to enlightenment, Arsen'ev realizes that this will often be "bitter" (182) and incomplete. Sadness and loss seize him whenever he remembers that chapters of his life have closed and that their people and events are but shadows in his consciousness, a source of bittersweet affection. "Everything and everybody we love is a . . . sweet and joyful torment," he writes. "Think only of that eternal fear of losing the beloved person, the conscious frailty of losing all things!" (14). Liberation will, in fact, cost dearly.

In the process of remembering, Arsen'ev himself is overwhelmed by a sense that he, too, will someday forever depart this earth. "It often occurs to me now," he confesses, "that I will die, and that I will never again seek the sky, the trees, the birds, or the many, many other things . . . which have grown to be a part of me, and with which it will be such grief to part" (20). Arsen'ev's moments when he resists change, broods about death, and craves permanence and stability alternate with and war against the deeper recognitions of enlightenment and detachment.

Both "bright" and "somber, sharp, and cruel" (41) memories torment Arsen'ev. Not unlike the young Khrushchevs in their journey back through time in *Dry Valley*—Arsen'ev realizes that memory's power is autonomous and that it can inspire redemptive visions that assuage pain just as readily as it can trigger nightmares that are "perplexing," "miserable," and "morbidly sensitive" (9).

At times, when Arsen'ev recalls his happy childhood amid calm surroundings, he remembers the simplicity of the estate, the peace of country nights, and the "June abundance" (20) of light and life. To the Bunin reader, though, these locales parallel the regressed backdrops of earlier tales. Abundance and repose are almost always followed by catastrophic events. Almost predictably there will be "strings" (16) (aggregates) of scenes that are either too constricted or vast, too noisy or quiet, too bright or dark; they will either be "without history" (19) or, more tragically, bear the heavy imprint of history's repressive hand. Even Arsen'ev's early environs, however, feature lines and angles, circles and dots; the atmosphere is increasingly one of fear, impotence, or gloom.

For example, the country landscapes that Arsen'ev recalls have a samsaric monotony. Land moves to "slimy funnels" and "undulates . . . in ever-thickening waves"; it is "squared" into "checkered plots" and "dotted" with dew, stubble, and stones. Menacing conditions wreak havoc on the more somnolent or pastoral scene. Storms remind sinners of the loss of Eden and the advent of apocalypse. Lightning strikes like "white-heated serpents" and reveals "mountains of copper clouds" (18, 125). Autumn, curiously the dominant season in Arsen'ev's life, leads to arctic winters, gloomy springs, and fiery summers, only to reemerge as the tonal season of the piece.

Collectively, Arsen'ev's recollected pasts share certain regressive features. For instance, the sun is the most pernicious dot in Arsen'ev's universe. Aloft it scorches the earth and multiplies itself in chains of windows and signs. At its setting, the sun presses down on the earth and immerses everything in red before it abandons the world to eerie twilights and fingerlike shadows.[3] In the young Arsen'ev's world, the remembered colors were the monochromatic, apocalyptic, penitential, or ferrous. They feature shocking whites and blacks; lenten pinks, mauves, and lilacs; blazing blues and golds; and every shade of enshackling gray. Indeed, the pervasive colors of samsara—not nature in its full array of life and splendor—are the only constant in the terrains Arsen'ev recollects from his youth.

COMING HOME

It is a telling comment that whenever Arsen'ev moves in from the vast backgrounds of nature to focus on the family estate, he renders his home and its inhabitants as still more regressed. Arsen'ev recalls Kamenka Farm (compare the Russian word, *kamen'*, or "stone") and other family estates as museumlike—shadowed and almost godforsaken. At home, to a lively lad, gray clapboard and gloomy corridors make the house seem "stifled, tedious, and somnolent" (34, 100). Portraits of tsars and ancestors with "curly perukes" and "snub noses," are complemented by the samsaric network of "manacled" windowpanes in which the light of the sun and moon "burn blue and ruby spots" on walls, ceilings, and floors (100, 102, 147).

Not without irony, Arsen'ev recalls that "some life is going on" (9) at Kamenka farm, for most of the people there are lethargic or asleep. Revealingly, though, several members of Arsen'ev's family do sense their shackled lot. His father is "happily idle" and seeks "emancipation from the burdens and liabilities of life" (13). Such a description brings to mind Lorenzo, the enlightened boatman in *The Gentleman from San Francisco*. Arsen'ev's father is only "horribly" (25) (regressively) free. Details such as his gray stubby chin and his braided hair denote a being that has "craved ruination" (46) and a "rounded" life in chain.

Arsen'ev's father also recalls other earlier characters in Bunin. Like the unhappy officer in *The Elagin Affair*, he exalts ego by banging doors and striding heavily on floors, and by being warmly passionate one moment but coldly indifferent the next. Like Grandfather Petr in *Dry Valley*, Arsen'ev's father dramatizes his decay by drinking "clotted" liquids, such as fizzing "acid water with soda" (14, 77). Finally, like Petr's son, Arcadii, Arsen'ev's father evades suffering in "self-defense" (88) and does little other than let the estate slip through his hands, play the guitar, pine for the past, and consign everything to the devil.

Arsen'ev's mother is more "enlightened" and aware of shackling and fate. She senses that "her love for everyone and everything" (15, 40) is bringing her to grief. More tellingly, the unhappy woman realizes that "the world is a place of partings, illnesses, sorrows, unfulfillable dreams, unrealizable hopes . . . unshared feelings—and death" (40). Like her spouse, however, she does not act decisively upon what she discerns. Instead, she dramatizes her chained state by wearing clothes with gray hoods and a "multitude of flounces" (89). She progresses from "sorrow incarnate" to a "huge white ghost" and ultimately to an "eyeless skull and gray bones" in a nameless grave. Arsen'ev had always been devoted to his mother, but his recording of her regression also reveals that loving and losing her has been, perhaps, the "bitterest love" of his life (15, 43).

Masters and men in Arsen'ev's recollections uniformly lack the prospect for enlightenment, since they have withdrawn totally from reality or they negotiate it in spurious ways. The squires are round, thickset, and half-mad. They wheeze with asthma and live in "lonely hostility, shutting themselves up in fortresses." Their large and cropped heads house eyes that are gray with unwholesome "yellowish whites" and "golden brown spots." Their "peaked" caps" and "old wedding rings on their small dark hands" (113) betray slavery to chain—and not even a glimmer of recognition that liberation is possible or desirable.

The folk are even further down the regressive line. They literally thirst for "self-destruction" and yearn to be "vagabonds and idiots" as they revel in "waste and decay" (13, 41, 62, 84). Furthermore, if either lord or peasants even suspect their sorry state, they, like Arsen'ev's parents, do nothing to offset it. The healthiest among these folk bear a deceptive resemblance to the peasants in Tolstoi's *Anna Karenina* in that they, too, charm the young "master" with their toil; but Arsen'ev's peasants are not in sync with the universe; rather, they are in rebirth. They produce the effect of "chain" gangs: bent backs are speckled with sweat; heads are pockmarked and wrapped in cloth; torsos are a riotous aggregate of contours and curves. Peasant women are buck-toothed, pregnant, and encumbered with "pot-bellied babies" (35). Together with the men, they walk with "rocking strides . . . swinging their scythes" (123, 124).

If the more robust peasants of Arsen'ev's past stride toward rebirth, their sicklier brethren are like lepers who watch helplessly, as their own minds and bodies rot.[4] Some, hovering on the brink of another "round" of life, are "cave dwellers" (17, 119). Others have lapsed into "everlasting sleep" (25). They have been "reborn" as animals, devils, or ghosts. As did the mobs in *The Village* and in *The Gentleman from San Francisco,* these folk flock together, "exuding a smelly warmness" (33). Individual peasants appear as "bandy-legged devils" (16) and "bent . . . goblins with gray curls" (25).

In short, samsara and chain are the print and background in the fabric of Arsen'ev's early recollections.

ARSEN'EV AS CHILD

The "manacled" environment of Arsen'ev's home life underscores his own regressed childhood, adolescence, and youth—a period beginning in the early 1870s and ending with the death of his love, Lika, approximately twenty-four years later. To the extent that Arsen'ev's story is a confessional tale, he portrays his immature years with shame and remorse. He recalls his childhood remembrances as ego incarnate, an "I" apart from the "All." He is a "timid and tender soul who has not yet quite awakened to life, and who dreams his dream of life, alien to everybody and everything" (9). Possessed by his own secret dreams and hopes, the hypersensitive Arsen'ev is easily overwhelmed by existence. Love and loss touch him; but so does a sense that life is futile, aimless, and absurd. Arsen'ev's child wonders about the people, places, and things of his daily world, but, unlike his mature self, the child is unnerved by the regression that his senses report to him.

Being so sensitive, the child is sometimes a victim of circumstances. Very early in his life, the "extremely steep stony slope" (24) that he descends in a visit to church serves as a metaphor for the sudden decline of his family and its fortunes, as well as for that of "patriarchal" Russia. Not unlike the young Khrushchevs in *Dry Valley,* Arsen'ev's child also recognizes hints of the regressed state of his ancestral abode. He grasps that much of the land is gone, the household is small, and the remaining servants are few. "I already knew that we were poor," he writes, "that our last belongings would soon be under the gavel . . . and that Russia . . . was sinking before our eyes with such miraculous rapidity" (62).

Encountering misery on many fronts, the child is unsupported and unguided by those nearest him. When the child asks questions about life and death, family and folk divert his attention from truth and expose him to their own shackled state. His father influences his "inchoate tastes," his mother "fills his soul with torment" (14), and the folk admit him to a "criminal friendship" (18), which makes him feel anxious and ashamed.

Far worse for the child, however, is his tutor, Baskakov, who resembles Balashkin, Kuz'ma's obnoxious mentor in *The Village.* These tutors absolutely model regression, and each causes lifelong harm to his charge. Baskakov, as recalled by the unsuspecting Arsen'ev, falls somewhere between a devil and a primordial animal or crustacean. He is bent, hook-nosed, and dark-faced, "like a demon." His eyes are like those of "a crayfish," and the lapels of his coat "float and flap about" like the wings of a prehistoric bird (30, 32).

Baskakov, a "half-crazy vagabond" (35) without known blood ties, is an individual at war with the world. He is that "dreadful species of Russian" who is gifted and highborn but who "creates misery by his own will . . . with almost savage cheerfulness" (30). His display of hatred for humankind resembles Gervas'ka's in *Dry Valley*. Baskakov inflicts discomfort by his caustic silence, sardonic smiles, or angry mumbling, and, as if unable to disguise his regression in his gait, he walks "swinging evenly and rapidly on his thin, crooked legs" (45).

Baskakov infects the highly impressionable Arsen'ev with his inner sickness. He mesmerizes the child with his mercurial temperament, his bizarre history, and his "savage and secluded existence" (31). Also, by immersing the child in "passions and dreams" (31), Baskakov intensifies the child's isolation. He confuses the child by representing things as exclusively good or bad, black or white. Stemming primarily from this association with his tutor, the child's worldview lacks a golden mean and is fragmented into the "most contradictory images and ideas" (31).

A Yearning Self

Arsen'ev's family and folk develop in his child self an inordinate love for samsaric items that symbolize craving, eros, and death. The child savors foods that connect imaginatively to regression, such as onions that are "gray and grainy," cucumbers that are "hairy and pimply," and beverages in bottles with "fine, wiry nets" that he "stretches this way and that" (18, 25, 40). The child also has an immoderate attraction for things with an erotic allure. A plant intrigues him with its "crimson Virgin's flower and sticky brown stem," and a leather riding crop is cherished as an "elastic, flexible thing" that is "fingered . . . with voluptuousness and bliss" (12, 21).

Indeed, the child has a keen but vague sense that sex pervades everything. For instance, he is magnetized by straining bodies and straddling legs. The earth commingles soft furrows, drenched and dewy fields, and "extremely thick and fresh fir trees" (78). Early on, also, the child is seized by ill-defined longings that he would like to act out but does not yet know how. Like young Mitia's desires, the child's yearnings are "languorous but insolvable" (35) since he cannot as yet identify the "who or what" that moves him to such "incredible love and tenderness" (9, 35).

Closely akin to his attraction to sexual things is the child's strong fascination with objects of death. Phallic knives and (circular) sabers and scythes arouse him to "voluptuous joy" (33). When the child watches how his father draws the "white blade" of a hunting knife "from its sheath," and "rubs it idly with the flap of his jacket," the lad longs to "kiss it, press it to his heart . . . and to thrust it in up to the hilt" (33). It is a key irony, a paradox in *Arsen'ev*, that the child is destructive even of what he professes to love. For example, using a scythe, he kills a defenseless bird. After this, he perfunctorily begs God and the world for forgiveness, but he secretly revels in a new sense of power and pleasure that derive from his act.

This taking of life, together with the child's preference for regressed people, places, and things, moves him steadily into samsara. By age seven, when the child looks into an "oval" mirror, he is both flattered and frightened by a reflected self with all of its regressive flaws. The two-dimensional image staring back at him is tall and thin, with fading patches of sunburn and "curly" hair bleached by the sun. In a moment of insight, the child grasps that "change, perhaps for the worse" (29), has entered his life.

Other Worlds

If Arsen'ev's child complains that he is a "stranger" in a "primeval void" (34, 54), it is partially because regressive phenomena often rouse images and ideas that darken existence. The child finds that real life—so "simple and meager" in itself—can be energized by ego. Then it becomes "transfigured" into "dreams" and "soothing illusions" that are "bright," "poetic," and "unearthly" (15, 22, 23, 40, 45). No one encourages the child to "think things out to the end" (147), so he daily seeks surroundings that are "warm and snug" and yearns for "new, unfamiliar . . . and invented life" (10, 16, 40, 47, 55). In short, cravings of every sort remake what his real situation can provide.

The child believes, for instance, that the sun, moon, and stars summon him to other worlds. Made heady, in part by eating hallucinatory plants, he even longs to join God and the angels in heaven. Such musings "fill his body and soul with desire and even . . . absolute power, to rise in the air and fly anywhere" (17). The child's imagination also "runs riot" (35) when, accompanied by his parents, he makes a "first" voyage to a "forbidden land called 'town,'" and when he discovers fairy tales, saints' lives, maps, pictures, and stories of adventure and romance (e.g., *Don Quixote, Robinson Crusoe,* and Gogol's stories). This first visit to town, however, underscores his lengthening ties to chain. When he enters the previously "forbidden" town, he is assaulted by a collage of circles and squares. Billboards, plazas, and "sun-warmed iron roofs" surround a prison with a "hermetically closed" gate and "many small windows . . . each with its own iron grating" (11–12, 59, 90). He passes close enough to see one of the prisoners at a window, an individual in a "gray blouse and cap," who has an expression of "sorrow, blunt resignation, deepest longing . . . as well as of some passionate and somber dream." To the quixotic child, however, the unhappy man is not a warning about attempting to live beyond bounds; rather, the captive vaguely suggests the stuff of make-believe, a "fairy-tale" hero (12, 13).

On a broad scale, fairy tales and other fiction cause him great harm. What he reads and hears from his mother, Baskakov, and others does not enrich his mental facilities so much as it disorients his being and insulates him from family and friends. He begins to "wander" like a "sleepwalker, seeing nobody and nothing" (35). The child is not totally unaware of what is happening. He grasps that such narratives enkindle dreams that are "sweet, half-crazy, and tormenting"; that they are "poison . . . nonsense, an intoxicating vision, and something totally absurd and unreal"; and, that they are the stuff of "poets" who are cut off from life, "intoxicated . . . and under the spell of some irrational creature" (37, 45); yet the child avidly internalizes these tales of escape.

When he is reading, the child easily "loses himself" in "screaming colors" and passions. "Dream, spell, variety, and confusion" overwhelm him as "something floating and changing" in the distance (31, 37). The "dots" (36) of Polynesian islands, together with the iron gates of castles and towers, excite the child's fancy, and accounts of martyred saints bring him to "morbid ecstasy" (45, 69). The latter arouse in him simulated cravings for "suffering, self-exhaustion, and self-mortification" (45). In imitation, for hours on end, the child wears a hair shirt, writhes on the ground, and refuses all but water and black bread. In short, masochism and illusion feed, but do not nourish, his already hypersensitive personality.

Literary and pulp fiction also cause the child to revel in tales of extremes of human behavior. He takes as much delight in stories that are "bitter, biting . . . and bear witness . . . to human meanness and cruelty" as in love tales that "extol heroic and exalted things . . . the fine and noble passions of the human soul" (32). Even in good literature, however, the child is fascinated by fictional images of samsara; for example, in Pushkin's *Ruslan and Liudmilla,* he fixates on "footprints," "curved shore," "breaking waves," "golden chains," a shackled "learned cat," and "circling, continuous movements" (37, 38).[5]

Mesmerized by rounds of stories and tales and craving fiction to mold his "vital substance" (38), Arsen'ev's child is seized by "youthful longings for distant wanderings, by passionate dreams of things remote and beautiful, and by a secret music of the soul" (126). Having only an illusion of freedom, though, the child already shackles himself, almost inescapably, in the manacles of "invented life."

ARSEN'EV AS ADOLESCENT

As adolescence emerges, so does an intensified need for escape. The reality of leaving home to pursue formal education oppresses Arsen'ev's heretofore untrammeled spirit. As a child, he had experienced the descent down a steep slope as a metaphor for the decline of his family's fortunes and those of "patriarchal" Russia; now, as an adolescent, he links his sense of imminent confinement to a new image—a sentry box and tollgate that are marked by a "striped" bar and "clinking chains" and that are manned by a soldier with "bushy gray whiskers" from the "time of Nicholas I" (58).

His adolescent distress is both national and personal. He laments that the "soul of old Russia" is becoming a "legend, a thing of the past," and that his homeland is reverting to its Mongol heritage, to "rebirth" as a razed vassal state. Blizzards are "Asiatic" in force and trees look like "hollow, storm-battered skeletons" (56, 57, 58, 77). Ravens, which his father tells him live for centuries, augur doom.

A much more personal distress flows from the fact that the adolescent feels boxed in by his impending entry into school. For all his love of reading about exotic people, places, and things, the young gentleman secretly abhors the thought of formal education. He believes that, by going to school, he is moving from "complete freedom" to "slavery" and "jail" (49, 54, 66). Won't he forget his old life? Won't his new one be a dreadful and absurd experience of submission to stern teachers? Won't he experience terrible homesickness for his family, Baskakov, and the household folk?

In fact, when Arsen'ev leaves the estate to take his entrance exams, he and his family act as though he is about to be executed. He zealously crosses himself, and his legs go weak from fear. His tearful mother rushes to hug and kiss him. The town and school intensify his samsaric woe. The building, located alongside a prison and a monastery, has chainlike windowpanes and brass door handles that glitter in the sun. His descriptions of the people near and in the school suggest a rebirth that exceeds that of the folk of the estate. The police chief wears a "silver belt" and looks like a "boar's carcass." Women are decked out as "exotic birds." The headmaster looks like a "hyena." Teachers have "gold-buttoned tailcoats . . . with crane tails" (49, 66, 67). The combined impressions accentuate the adolescent's "perpetual sense of loneliness" and imprisonment, that his head is "close-cropped" and that he is "wasting" his time and talents amidst surroundings that are "coarse and painful to a sensitive young soul" (65, 66).

The new student senses death in these regressed surroundings. He fears anew for the passing of the gentry class, the downfall of his family's way of life, and the sudden and/or violent deaths of family and friends, masters and men. Separations, such as being confined at school, make the adolescent feel that every illness is an "unconsummated death . . . a kind of nonexistence . . . a crazy journey into certain realms of the beyond . . . and a descent into hell" (42).

As an adolescent, and unlike his later, mature self, Arsen'ev is dismayed by death. Later he would say, "Whence was my great perplexity? What is it—this needless and horrible thing that had happened in the world?" (35), but death is now the adolescent's greatest nemesis. It is a force that is evil and powerful, random and dark. Death "blocks the earth like a cloud," robs life of "interest, legitimacy and meaning," and infects "everyone and everything with weariness and grief" (28). Death is also "incongruously hideous." In its wake it leaves an aggregate collage of crushed and skewed bodies; of "dainty doll-like corpses with long, black eyelashes"; of lips ringed "with bulging purplish blackness"; and of "silver brocade" and "sinisterly splendid golden coverings" (36, 43–47, 73, 104–105, 120). To the adolescent Arsen'ev, death raises uncomfortable notions of God. On one hand, the Almighty is a Being who rules the earth, creates beauty, sends guardian angels, and endows the adolescent with an immortal soul. On the other hand, God is a Being linked to death and hell—to "aggregates" of "loathsome figures, faces, beasts, and plants moving tremulously in flaming waves" (45). In religion, mortification, punishment, and "Old Testament darkness" (76) outweigh resurrection, renewal, and joy. In personal accounts, the adolescent has grasped that God is silent, remote, and menacing, even regressed—a figure defined by angles, lines, and curves. As an "All-Seeing Eye," God peers out from a "triangle, oblong, cruel, and enigmatic." Even in anthropomorphic conceptualizations, God is represented by a jumble of circles and lines. The Deity dwells amidst "rotund closed cupolas, and "stony blue-gray clouds"; this same Deity has "outstretched arms" that extend perpendicularly from under "undulating robes" (41, 111).

Holy days and feast days affect the adolescent adversely. At Christmas there will be "crude rejoicing" and "endless drinking" by persons enshrouded in caftans and cloaks (43, 65). Each Easter vigil evokes fears that the holy night could be the last one and that the Last Judgment could well be at hand.

Away from home, disaffected by God and ritual, Arsen'ev's adolescent feels compelled to fortify himself against further losses. Strangely, funerals and wakes stir in him "fond feelings for self" (111). Also, repressing the fact that his family has entered upon hard times, he takes solace in his social lineage: the presumed "superiority of his nobility" (24). Laboring to distance himself from his poverty-stricken circumstances in town and dependent on the mercy of strangers, the student withdraws into his earlier "secret pride" (24). He continues to act as if he and his family are pillars of the church—people who sit ahead of others and pray "well, masterfully, and decorously" (24). Since he is a "gentleman's son" (60), he thinks that he must regard everyone and everything with contempt.

This self-induced disdain for others is unsupportable, however. Such an attitude intensifies the samsaric nature of his environs: "Dot" drizzles fall on "dusty iron roofs," and "black trellised sheds," and, speckled crows, "humpbacked and taut, portend no good" (60, 70). His self-inflation further reduces people to regressive states. He scorns a fellow boarder whom he sees as a "caged cub" filled with "animal mistrust" (60). He is repelled by the "poor, lower-middle-class surroundings" (59) of the home of Rostovtsev, his merchant landlord.

Rostovtsev recalls other types in Bunin. Like Tikhon in *The Village*, Rostovtsev is taciturn, controlling, and pragmatic. He wears gray and shroud-like clothes, observes strict schedules and rules, and has a gloomy grin and a beard that is "shot through with silvery hairs" (60, 61). The daily fare at the Rostovstevs' is gray, circular, and speckled (e.g., pickled watermelon rind, buckwheat pudding, and "gray, shaggy, trout") (61). Upstaging the Gentleman from San Francisco, Rostovtsev has *two* daughters firmly situated in samsara. The girls show "rounded necks" and spend their days "cracking bobbins" and making chainlike lace (61, 71).

It is the adolescent's failure to accept his situation that causes some of his own fixations and his accelerated entry into regressed life. Unaware of harming himself, he flaunts his "sharp outward change," his burgeoning freshness and youth, and the "blossoming out of his entire being" (93). He thinks himself above passersby; he rebels against his teachers, reminding them that he is no longer a boy but a "self-willed whippersnapper" (94).

Arsen'ev's prowess is, however, only wishful thinking. In actuality, he is becoming increasingly linear, dotted, and dark. His torso elongates and is only partially concealed in formless clothes and high boots; his face takes form: "more clearly outlined . . . coated . . . with sunburn . . . and covered with golden down" (95). Since he continues to be solitary, passive, and even morose, his uneventful life bores him. There is an unmitigated parade of sameness: "the same going to school, the same sad and reluctant evenings . . . the same unfailing dreams, the same counting of days until Christmas" (66). School is a particularly unsavory barrage of unpleasant impressions. Crowds are "aggregates" of "uniforms, decorations, and three-cornered hats." He is stifled by the "hot and uncanny proximity of huge bodies which press upon him from all sides," and he is benumbed by the sights of flares and "purple flames," the smells of rivers and tanneries, and the sounds of marches, trumpets, and bands (67–68). In the "motley crowds" that flow in human "streams" and converge in "stinking, noisy rooms" (87), he loses the last shreds of identity. Circuses, funerals, and wakes are all that is left to interest him (24, 67, 87).

Most grievously, the adolescent projects his "pride" (61) on everyone he meets. He feels that the entire town "chokes on its own [sense of] wealth and importance" (61). Close inspection, however, reveals to the reader that this pride is only feigned. It springs from nostalgia and a chauvinistic desire to overlook the political and spiritual shortcomings of Russia. Such pervasive denial, though, accelerates large-scale decline. For instance, when Arsen'ev's father, Rostovtsev, and others assert that Russia is "wealthier, stronger, more righteous, and more glorious than any other country in the world," they do so through clenched teeth and with hearts that are frozen by terror. They can do nothing to prevent the imminent demise of their country—an incapacity that deeply distresses the youngster. The situation resembles theater as self resorts to "showiness and roles" (62) to perpetuate its own survival.

For example, when Arsen'ev's father visits him at school, the man lodges at a so-called Nobleman's Hotel so that he can play the part of a *grand seigneur* and have his son parade as a "little gentleman to whom everybody smiles and bows" (72); but the ruse is both transparent and tragic. The hotel has a curved staircase and glowing "dot" lamps; these, together with the presence of a prince in a "huge fur wrap" and with "cold, vulture eyes" (73), expose the fallen condition of the Russian gentry and the samsaric nature of their pretense. Moreover, although Arsen'ev's father and friends are conscious of the "falsity of their acting" (72), they continue to feign the "exaggeratedly gentlemanlike manners, suspiciously insolent exactingness, and voices low because of vodka rather than breeding" (72, 73) that the adolescent has rejected in the townspeople.

My Brother, the Socialist

The subtle warnings about the pervasiveness of regression and chain that Arsen'ev's adolescent notes during his years at school become painfully explicit with the arrest and exile of his brother, Georgy. Georgy is a university graduate, but his shining eyes, darkly flushed cheeks, and gold medal for academic diligence hint at progress in samsara, not enlightenment. Specifically, Georgy is infected by the "biblical leprosy" (82) of socialism. He looks to "socialism" in his life in much the same way that his younger brother (and other characters in Bunin) uses daydreams. Specifically, Georgy uses socialism as an ideological ploy to distract himself from the challenges of everyday life and to give ego a "lie" it can withdraw into (84). Georgy's fantasy world consists of "fictitious emotions" (84), sham community, and frenzied activity. Georgy enthralls Arsen'ev with his own dreams of "self-intoxication" and "unfettered freedom." He craves "merry idleness," a samsaric swirl of circles, meetings, dreams, songs, speeches, and plans—all of which will, of course, be clandestine and seditious but marked by camaraderie. The rebellious Georgy personifies aspects of the dissolute, national self. That is, it has long been true that, under the guise of "revolt, holy-foolery, wandering, ritual orgies, and self-immolations," Russians have sought "always to shun inconspicuous, unhurried, and unobtrusive life . . . to be ridiculously severed from reality . . . to be unwilling to submit to it in the slightest degree . . . to find 'rejuvenation' in something young and joyous . . . [and to savor] a certain sweet fermentation, a release from reason, and from the bonds and rules of everyday life" (83–84). The adolescent Arsen'ev expresses conflicting emotions at the sights of his brother's literally shackled state. For instance, he can correctly read Georgy's inner decay and fanciful isolation from his world. Even before leaving his home, Georgy shows a "peculiar prison pallor" (86).

Dressed in a gray suit and his father's raccoon coat, he is "caged" in "misery and chains" (86), bereft of freedom, happiness, and community. When Georgy departs the estate, he leaves only a "sorrowful residue" (87) in the minds of his family; yet Arsen'ev seems not to have learned anything from Georgy's tragedy, except to pity him—and himself. His brother's departure gives a moment of insight into the inevitable parting of everyone from this earth. There is a momentary ray of enlightenment when Arsen'ev realizes that, notwithstanding his own exile at the prison-school, he has been spared his brother's fate. He is physically and spiritually free. He is seized by a love of life and feels "sweet rapture" (92) at the "iconographic beauty" of his land. He makes the connection that reality demands "life and joy"; he graps the cyclic immutability by which "everything passes and repeats itself" (92). Momentarily, despite Georgy's loss of freedom, Arsen'ev's adolescent is at peace with the world.

Misguided Steps, False Progress

Like almost every character in Bunin who experiences liberation—or a glimpse of it, the adolescent's delight in existence is short-lived. Just when the paroled but still metaphysically shackled Georgy returns to the estate to continue his sorry life, the adolescent takes "lordly license" (94) to discontinue school and to return home. Not surprisingly, this action is attended by chaos, not "freedom" (92). For instance, as he heads for home, freezing winds tear at his "uplifted collar" and splatter his face with snow. Reminiscent of the young Mitia in his return to the country, the adolescent Arsen'ev finds comfort in the "snug, warm coziness" of the train car and in the "swinging, lulling motion" of the ride. During the journey, he delights in chain-induced sights, sounds, and smells. For instance, Arsen'ev sees his "fur coat" dangling on a peg in front of him. He gazes upon the train's "quickly spinning wheels" and "the diamonds of frosted windowpanes." He hears "the banging of [the train's] doors," "the clatter of its little hammers in the blazing stove," and the "bubbling, boiling noise of its engine." He also attunes his ear to the "hollow sound" of snow-covered conductors with "red reeking lanterns in their hands," the "loud solemn bassos" of porters who "drawl with stern and threatening sorrow," and the "desperate cry of the engine," which, like the *Atlantis* in *The Gentleman*, hurls itself "somewhere into the impenetrable darkness." Such samsaric markings, fascinating the youth, move him down chain. He is roused to "pant for joy" and to "jump up with purely animal briskness" (98–100).

Once home, Arsen'ev's adolescent embarks on a "strange way of life" (131). Like young Mitia, he sleeps days and is awake nights. He also resumes his isolated, "intellectual" pursuits. Fairy tales, saints' lives, and stories of romance and adventure rekindle his imagination, but he also delves into the more literary works he has read in school, such as *The Odyssey* and the writings of Walter Scott. He sates himself, also, with Russian and European fiction of the late eighteenth and early nineteenth centuries. From Europe, the adolescent reads Schiller's *Wilhelm Tell* and *Don Carlos*, Goethe's *Faust*, and Byron's *Childe Harold;* from Russia, he reads *Eugene Onegin*, *A Hero of Our Time*, *Rudin,* and *Fathers and Sons,* as well as the verse of Derzhavin, Pushkin, and Zhukovskii. In his state of mind, these writings are deleterious because he savors only the images and ideas that are rigid, stratified, and "patriarchal." From antiquated classical and romantic schools, he chooses the "caustic, complaining, Gothic, dying, disenchanted, and shameless" (117). The indiscriminate young reader does not value poetry for its intrinsic beauty or wisdom, but for "vignettes" (101) or aggregates of lyres, urns, helmets, and wreaths. He even selects books for such external trappings as the type, gray paper, and binding.

Since the adolescent does not read critically, egocentric heroes "insinuate themselves" into his being. He readily internalizes the "feelings and destinies" of "Hamlets, Don Carloses, Childe Harolds, Onegins, Pechorins, Rudins, and Bazarovs" (116). Through reading, therefore, the adolescent regresses into a "perfect" world, one that, being exalted and deathless, rouses unparalleled flights of fancy. Eros, escape, and hysteria intoxicate him. Reading Pushkin and others, the adolescent "lives through first youthful dreams and enthusiastic transports of the spirit." Fancying that life itself will be "voluptuous and miraculous," he waxes eloquent over "remote, happy lands," and "longs to sing, to shout, to laugh, and to weep" (102, 105). Consumed thus by irreality and chaos—which he mistakes for exalted freedom—he is imprisoned in craving and desire.

Arsen'ev as Youth: The Lure of Love

Aroused, the adolescent seeks to bank the fires of his yearnings in "love," in writing, and in "wandering" through Russia. His attempts at all three are unsuccessful, though, since he misperceives life exclusively in terms of self. For example, in encounters with members of the opposite sex, Arsen'ev, like young Mitia, relates to women only in the aggregate—that is, in "dense maidenly throngs" (71) or shardlike parts. He gives undue attention to "every tiny shoe . . . every white cape . . . and every youthful breast" (78). He is also drawn to gentry and peasant lasses who are in various stages of regression. Metaphorically, the objects of Arsen'ev's love are a nameless assembly line. The few details that are given remind a reader of Mitia's Katia and Elagin's Sosnovskaia. The women and girls who catch Arsen'ev's eye have "flying hair," "consumptive eyes," and "long frost-silvered eyelashes" (80, 123, 207). They wear "flowing peignoirs," "floating skirts," and "curly pigtails tied with large white bows" (123, 129, 130, 207).

Self as Author

As was also the case with Katia and Sosnovskaia, the adolescent's damsels appear amidst samsaric surroundings. If they do not step out on dance floors with "glistening powder" and under the "pearly light of chandeliers," they beckon alongside "elongated leaves" and gushing fountains that "bedew" flower beds with "cool watery vapor" (66, 81, 128). They usually "fade from view" within sight of funeral trains that feature "powerful, stuttering jerks of pipes," and a "drive shaft, long and smooth like a white ribbon of steel" (195, 196).

These loves further recall Katia and Sosnovskaia in that, as "women-girls" (81) who know "what's what" (80) in the world, they advance the unrealistic youngster to new rounds of life. For his part, Arsen'ev anticipates encounters with women either as an animal lying in wait and catching the "scent" (69) of his prey, or as a figure bordering on rebirth, with his hair "*en brosse*" (80), his ears "ablaze," and his hands alternately "hot" and "ice-cold."

For all his inflamed sensibilities, though, Arsen'ev engages the opposite sex only superficially. The adolescent savors only the "taste" and "feelings" of love (66, 102); he is as unclear about females and selfless affection as he is about most things in life. For instance, when Arsen'ev meets young girls at a ball, he yearns only "for that something that lay inside [their] fur coats, galoshes, and hoods" (78). Love quickly loses its "light, mysterious, and beautiful" character and becomes "something virile and physical." It is associated with "the discordant cawing of rooks . . . in impetuous and agonizing ecstasy" and with the crossing of "a fatal and long-coveted line . . . the uncanny threshold of some sinful paradise" (80, 113). Arsen'ev is enthralled by "that peculiar and terrible something which lurks in the lips of a laughing woman, in the childlike intonation of a woman's voice, in the roundness of a woman's shoulders, in the slimness of a woman's waist, even in that inexpressible something of a woman's ankle" (81).

Attempted trysts are unfulfilling. They aggravate sadness and longing. There is no communion, only awkwardness or attempts at dominance. For example, one neighbor lass, Lisa, rebukes Arsen'ev as a "mere boy" who "makes a mess of things" (130); but when another neighbor, Annchen, sits on his knees, Arsen'ev feels only the "blissful weight of a woman's body" (115). When self is finally aroused—only *after* Annchen leaves him—he then "weeps so fiercely and abundantly . . . [filled] with poignancy of the sweetest love for the world, for life, for physical and moral human beauty . . . and for the tormentingly amorous happiness of life" (115–16).

Much like his literary predecessor, Mitia, Arsen'ev begins to see Annchen's image in everything he feels, reads, and thinks. Soon, though, Annchen fades to a chimera. In Arsen'ev's mind, she "loses living shape" and is thought of and felt "only poetically." The adolescent, meanwhile, drowns in "a yearning for love in general, for some universal, lovely, womanly image . . . [for] images from the poems of Pushkin, Lermontov, and Byron" (122). Though he is a nobleman's son, Arsen'ev's chosen role is a lovelorn paramour who fantasizes via such banal romantic props as his bed, a twilight garden, and excerpts from turgid verse. The poetry Arsen'ev uses as scores of romantics, including Mitia, have done. The very lyrics are incantations to preserve the ideality of the beloved. Arsen'ev recites Lermontov, begging, contradictorily, for Morpheus to give the solace of sleep; yet the youth revels in his regressed dreams of "an unknown woman . . . who captivates him forever . . . on shores washed by rumbling waves" (127).

When Arsen'ev finally does have sexual relations, the triumph for his body is a tragedy for his soul. The first object of his desire is a peasant girl by the name of Ton'ka. Local villagers call her "the jackdaw" and the "savage," and Arsen'ev himself notes that she looks like an "Indian," with her dark complexion, a "coarse jet of lank hair" and "dark, nut-colored, narrow-slitted eyes." He is roused to "sweet and uneasy yearning" by all that is samsaric about her, such as her "flat, bluish lips," her "dark silvery earrings," and "the slope of her dark youthful neck" (141–44).

In the actual liaison their mutual regression is apparent. Ton'ka resembles a cavewoman, scantily clad and illumined by the multicolored flames from a stove as "fantastic as a black cave" (121). After "squatting" beside his love, "full of inside tremors," Arsen'ev forces himself upon her. Afterwards, he is revisited by the same moral ambivalence that had accompanied his childish killing of the defenseless bird. A sense of "utter depravity" seizes him; as if caught in a samsaric swirl, he "can no longer feel the ground beneath." His dread is momentarily counterbalanced by "exultant, victorious triumph" and "masculine pride" (142, 143). But what price this victory?

He is "rent asunder" by new yearnings for Ton'ka, by the "cruelest jealousy" at the sight of her husband, and by the mixed signals of admiration and indifference that he receives from his "love" (143–44). He both loves and loathes Ton'ka with an intensity that "makes him quiver all over" (143). Indeed, it is only Ton'ka's sudden dismissal from the estate that averts tragedy; for "thoughts of death gladly come to Arsen'ev's mind" (145) as he plans to end Ton'ka's life and also his own.

Nothing in his encounter with Ton'ka leads to enlightenment. If anything, his vague yearnings grow apace while he, oblivious to the samsara implicit in the "glossy willow branches that arch downward toward the silvery mirror of the water" and the rain that causes "countless nails to rise up on its surface" (146), wanders aimlessly into a new season.

The Lure of Writing

The adolescent's absorption into fiction and love triggers a longing to express himself in writing. Arsen'ev's literary motivation is no more authentic than Kuz'ma Krasov's pretensions to authorship in *The Village*. His desire to write evolves by "accident" (93), as the only course in a life of quickly shrinking alternatives. Arsen'ev is ill equipped either for civil service or for the management of the estate; the "poetry of his soul and life," together with his paternal inheritance of "waywardness and sentimentality" (94), augurs badly for him.

Not surprisingly, the adolescent's first attempts at authorship are "inane" (102). He loves the *idea* of being a writer, but shaping objects of beauty does not interest him. All he wants is to be a "second Pushkin or Lermontov," or maybe even to have the "sad beautiful eyes" and "untimely death . . . of a Nadson" (95, 122). He now lays claim to all sorts of entitlements: "wealth, luxury, and freedoms of every sort." He even declares his intention to travel and to join with "fellow dreamers who share his ardor and tastes" (116–18, 165).

The post-adolescent Arsen'ev mistakenly assumes that he has entered upon "full-fledged adult life" (116) and has a mature knowledge of the world. He takes literary fame for granted and enjoys an "exalted state of mind" (117) as his birthright.

In truth, though, Arsen'ev's attempts to write trace a circular path. As the reader well knows, neither Arsen'ev's tutor nor scant years at school have prepared him for the discipline of art. Mere aggregates of historical and cultural trivia constitute his learning; and the disjointedness that follows from his ill-disciplined life and study shows even when he attempts to write his own autobiography. Arsen'ev is prone to self-pity and is quick to blame others for his own inadequacy. Dissolute as ever, the youth takes no steps to remedy his deficiencies. He continues to regard Pushkin and Lermontov as his fellow travelers and to allow his inner life to remain "blissfully tipsy" on the stuff of "sensations" and "hazy dreams. He cannot relinquish the "confusing," "intense," and "tormentingly amorous" (117, 118, 120).

More objectively, Arsen'ev's dreams of becoming a writer collide with the regressed, circular, and Scythian realities that afflicted him from early on. For instance, his brother sees him as "a congenital idiot" (262); his father calls him a "raw sprig of nobility" and chides him for the "nonsense in his head." The father also forces the youth to wear Georgy's "gray" suit and to sell frames from family icons to a woman "of terrible Eastern visage, hook-nosed, bewhiskered, with bulging eyes, and covered in . . . signet rings" (117, 122, 214).

The youth's accumulating experiences also drag him down. For instance, when he visits an inn owned by the writer Nazarov, he encounters a totally samsaric environment. There are bedbugs, windows and mirrors clouded by steam, and icons that "rise up like black tombs" and that cast spidery shadows on the walls. The people there are pockmarked, with "long upper lips," "Suzdalian noses," and loose-fitting shirts with high collars. Furthermore, when Arsen'ev attempts to write verse—only in the evenings and on the brink of "irresistible sleepiness"—he does so in the company of his own shadow (a regressed self?) and night moths that descend into the "flames of sputtering candles" (130), their charred remains falling like dust on his desk. Incongruously, Arsen'ev's youth continues to yearn for a bright future in one-horse towns, as well as in his "cheap iron" bed, and facing a family icon with a "crude iron frame" that depicts three angels with "wild Eastern brown-sooty faces staring through rounded holes" (119, 154, 198, 241).

Given the decay pervading Arsen'ev's surroundings, it is not surprising that when the youth actually puts pen to paper, he expresses emotions ranging from quiet sadness to "growing agitation . . . and total despair" (236). Although he wishes to compose stories that are "sublime, uplifting . . . and selfless," he routinely draws pictures that show the "poetic nature of ruin" and that are notoriously diminished, circular, and harsh. One sketch features a "Tolstoian": "rather fat" and with "milky face . . . and a protruding round belly." The character also wears a gold pince-nez, a flowing gray shirt, and a "lamb's wool" cap and collar. A second story depicts a dead child with a "swarthy high brow," a "little porcelain face," and "something lilac around his swollen closed eyelids and triangular mouth" (242). Indeed, given the regression infecting Arsen'ev's writing, it is not surprising that he gives up writing altogether and settles for a job ordering pencils, paper, and quills for others.

The Lure of Wandering

Arsen'ev cannot realize his dreams as a writer, but as he himself admits, he is a restless "wanderer" (261) who is always casting about. At home, the youth roams the rooms of the manor, decries autumnal boredom and decay, and, like his increasingly morose father, rides, hunts, and meanders anew. The samsaric images that surround him—like the "sinister omen" of "smoky and leaden" clouds and the "mournful veil" of a "ringed" moon with a "misty, miserable and slightly tilted face" (159)—seem to disturb him more than formerly.

Arsen'ev's youth lacks stability, focus, and a life plan. He is baffled because his life is "horrible nonsense." His mental images are "chaotic" and "vague," his ideas are "fruitless" and "excruciatingly arbitrary," and his memories are "so weighty and horrible" that he prays for salvation from them" (159, 161, 236, 262, 281). His musings continue to stem from fiction, from "confusion and naïveté" (159). What he craves is the happy and full life that he believes—wrongly—that Pushkin, Lermontov, and Tolstoi had. He wants to live in the palace of Bakhchisarai, or in the company of Tolstoi's children, or with the characters of *The Cossacks* and *War and Peace*.

Arsen'ev thinks "mostly about himself" and yearns "for freedom from something . . . and striving to somewhere" (134, 155). Under this vaguely defined influence, the youth embarks on a journey unlike any travel undertaken by a Bunin character discussed thus far. This excursion will stretch out over "whole years of wandering and homelessness, of reckless and unruly existence . . . fruitless and without meaning" (161).

From its onset, Arsen'ev's jaunting about forges a chain of harmful events. To him distance and speed outweigh either purpose or destination. Once, having no idea where the train was headed, he writes, "I felt that it was magnificent, this lack of knowledge" (240). By his "wanderings," Arsen'ev escapes the responsibilities of life. What is really a whimsical, festive allure affects him as "freedom, space . . . the dream of some joy . . . a holiday" (260). Such sojourns also rapidly accelerate his move down chain. Traveling by sleigh, for example, he is weighed down by "shaggy" (160) snow and his father's "heavy raccoon coat." Galloping on horseback and hypnotized by the "rhythmic motions," he feels "within himself someone bold, ancient . . . [wearing] a bearskin coat" (210).

On his longer trips, Arsen'ev roams from city to city, job to job. Because he is half-conscious of pursuing a goal, these jaunts are even more destructive than his purposeless short ones. Trains "rock him crazily" as they rush into raging storms and darkness. They loom up like "fiery dragons," marked by "brightened squares of windows" and "cast-iron wheels that spin faster and faster" (161, 162, 195, 196, 249). Passengers "dance with wild abandon to the rhythm of the wheels," and engineers have clothes that "shine like iron," eyes that are "expressively Negroid," and eyelids that "seem purposely painted . . . like actors" (199, 249).

Arsen'ev cannot even recognize the samsara implicit in this mode of travel. To him the "hell" (199) arising from trains is wonderfully suited to his escapist needs. In fact, at this point in his life, it is the train—not literature or the estate—that allows the youth to pursue "sensations and dreams" and to find "everlasting and lofty joy" in "paltry" people, places, and things (162). Trains give the youth "a pleasant homey sense of human life" and provide the "very acme of bliss." Where else could one delight in "all the warmth and coziness of wealth . . . barricaded" against the snowy plains, telegraph wires, and other vicissitudes of modern life (161)?

Traveling by train to Kharkov, Orel, and the Crimea, Arsen'ev follows self-referential (and self-destructive) patterns of behavior. He acts in the frenetic belief that he is journeying south to "fairy-tale lands" and that he is realizing "dreams" (161, 195, 199), although every stop "makes him giddy" with new impressions and encounters, and everything is "deliciously new"— more "springlike and agreeable" (163).

Wandering through Russia, he actually turns his back on his native roots and past. He also plunges into a timeless present filled with regressed people, places, and things. Arsen'ev moves through "dusty arches," "circular yards," and "dark seas of earth." He meets women selling "bagels, seeds, and gray bread" and men "rotating their hands in perfect half-circles" as they sprinkle seeds on the earth (164, 192, 196, 197). From a window of a cellar lodging, Arsen'ev is intrigued by "legs passing to and fro along the street" (165); and stopping in Sevastopol, he sees a "Tatar" boy tending "gray" sheep on the "bare gray loaves" of hilltops (177). In Vitebsk, he comes across young Jewish men with "languid antelope glances" and forelocks "resembling the tubular, curling horns of a ram" (250).

When opportunities for enlightenment do come along, Arsen'ev rejects them, even saying that he has "no use for wisdom" (182). Consistent with this attitude, the youth takes only passing note of what could be "liberating" phenomena—such as how the "remote past" (177) arises from the "boundless springtime expanse of southern Russia" (177, 179), or how daybreak issues forth from the "dark, moist nocturnal womb of night" (176), or how *The Igor Tale* and the resonance of church bells reflect the enduring beauty of the national soul.

Arsen'ev's youth is equally obtuse about realities that suggest enshacklement. For instance, he misses the implications of the "iron balcony" of his hotel room, the "metallic foliage" of trees, or the "sadly mysterious, nebulously colored ring" of frost encircling the moon (182, 208, 209, 226, 233). He sees, but does not reflect upon, how the night and the "fathomless dark abyss" of the sea live a "painful life that is senseless and hostile" (177). Like Tikhon in *The Village,* he does not ponder the menacing ambience of cemeteries, with their "yawning graves," and "skeletons rising forth . . . toothy and bony." Nor does he see the significance of an "enormous angel . . . his clothes flapping behind in strips, his naked girlish legs bent at the knee, and his long chalky feet streaming behind" (208). Inevitably, Arsen'ev's wandering youth has neither time nor desire to take into account his deepening decline. A trip to the barber's may give him a "beautifully shaped and fragrant head," but nothing can conceal his "gypsy tan," and the "weather-beaten leanness" of his torso and face (181, 192, 199).

Similarly, the youthful Arsen'ev does not learn from the mistakes of shackled colleagues and associates. For instance, when he arrives in Kharkov, he is appalled to see and hear that revolutionary circles are made up of primitive individuals. The revolutionaries he meets strike him as "oxen" and "troglodytes" with twisted arms, bulging eyes, and "big potlike skulls" (170, 171). One even rolls pellets of bread into balls. They are also egressive exemplars: intolerant and rigid, "completely detached" (167) from their nation, and consumed with "their own affairs, interests, happenings, celebrities, their own morals, their own rules of family life and friendship, and their own attitude toward Russia: the negation of her past and present and the dream of her future" (167). Simply put, the revolutionaries whom Arsen'ev meets on his travels are the modern-day "humiliated and injured" who believe that "all salvation" lies in anger and "upheaval" (168).

Although Arsen'ev's youth is received by such circles with emotions ranging from distrust to disgust, he is sharp enough to see through the "falsity" of their "storms" (169), their "hopes" for the future, and their "prattling" (170) on Russian history, literature, and life. Their angst is one he can recognize. They want a "composite" (170) (aggregate) folk rooted in theory, not life. Ironically, though, the youth cannot see that the shortcomings of Georgy and his comrade socialists parallel his own. Swept up in their whirlwind activities and sham camaraderie, he can, in fact, distract his being totally from writing, enlightenment, and other liberating tasks. In a timeless, time-consuming way, he indulges in "festivals of new impressions": "tea drinking, smoking, and debating . . . in meetings, soirees, and private parties" (168, 192).

Seeking still another diversion, the youth also delights in the world of libraries, bookstalls, and concerts. These interests, too, increase his torpor and the unconscious embrace of "manacled" life. For instance, Arsen'ev "circles around" book stalls "hungry as a wolf" (234), tormented by a "vague and vain desire" to compare himself with famous people. In this state of mental paralysis, he also wishes "to write something that [he himself] is unable to understand, has neither daring to undertake nor skill to cope with, and is all the time putting off" (172). Similarly, when he hears a piano concert, he immediately desires "the greatest of all illusions . . . the divine possibility of becoming all-blissful, all-powerful, and all-knowing" (173). Such a yearning quickly gives way, though, to a vision of the pianist as a madman prisoner dressed in a "gray" shirt and confined to a narrow cell with a "grated" window.

Even when Arsen'ev momentarily stills his "nomadic passions," he cultivates another enshackling situation. For example, seeking work in the editorial offices of a journal in Orel, he enters a "long gray house" with deeply recessed corridors and low dirty rooms. Here he sees writers and workers who have buck teeth, consumptive spots, and "tightly curled" or "cropped lead-colored hair." One columnist appears to be half-child, half-animal. He is as "small and frail as a ten-year-old" but has "thick dull-gray hair . . . like a porcupine" and is wearing a "long pleated coat of rabbit fur." He is joined by a copy editor with "an olive-green face . . . and ash-gray lips" and by an editorial writer who moves with "simian agility," though half of his right hand is missing (227–28).

The machinery of the place underscores samsaric influence. As was the case with the machines in *The Village* and the engines of the *Atlantis* in *The Gentleman,* the printing presses in *Arsen'ev* dramatize the activity of Chain. "Dark leaden boards" move to and fro; "grates" go up and down. The machines monopolize the space, and shatter peace with their "rumbling." Everything is covered with dirty, greasy papers and with print that looks like "grains of shiny black caviar" (183, 228).

Arsen'ev's youth receives his new surroundings as passively as he has responded to all the other regressed people, places, and things in his life. A sense of *deja vu* dully pervades his thoughts and deeds, including his "love" for a fellow worker, Lika, and the other women he meets there.

Love (Again)

Arsen'ev's love for Lika and her companions at the editorial office in Orel recalls his adolescent amours with the peasant girls at home. At first, Lika claims only a very small part of Arsen'ev's affection, since he, "of course, is in love with everybody and everything" in the chained world of "female society" that surrounds him. Lika seems only to be part of a general flurry— an aggregate of "beads . . . embroidered frocks . . . rounded arms and plump elongated knees" (184).

As Lika and Arsen'ev begin to pair off, they ignore warnings of disaster. The two meet on cliffs, precipices, and dilapidated balconies. They profess or fantasize about love under "enormous semicircular windows," alongside "graying" houses, and against gray skies, burning suns, and moons like the "white mask of a corpse" (194, 200, 202, 235, 270). Lika and Arsen'ev drift along even when the sights are harsh and sounds and smells distasteful. For instance, the pair is impervious to gatherings in which dogs pant and bark; "gray" roosters crow with "husky and helplessly blissful voices"; schoolboys bombard them with "clatter, shouts, and raucous laughter"; or people "stomp their feet and bang empty tin mugs" to "thunderous cavorting music" (94, 200, 204).

Lika and Arsen'ev are also privy to the enduring samsara arising from the unhappy unions of other couples. Arsen'ev, for instance, is "momentarily dumbfounded" by marital "absurdity," when a widowed coworker, Avilova, shows him the portrait of her late husband, "a consumptive . . . hirsute man in glasses and with wide, bony shoulders, who stares out discontentedly from the frame" (193).

The inadequacy of Arsen'ev's relationship with Lika brings to mind the liaisons of Mitia and Katia and of Elagin and Sosnovskaia. Arsen'ev and Lika begin their life together as "intoxicated and senselessly gay," but they soon slip into "inertia and somnambulism" (184) and finally into boredom, separation, and grief. Again as was the case with the other fictional couples, both Lika and Arsen'ev are guilty of inflicting pain and suffering on each other. For instance, Lika bears the karmic legacy of family regression. Her mother is dead, and her father has allowed her to be "completely free" (207). The father is a man marked by "swollen eyes," "enormous gray beard," and a "robe of patterned Turkish silk." The regressed ambience of Lika's paternal home is heightened by her sister's looking like a "fiery-eyed Tatar beauty" and her brother's being "gloomy, swarthy, with eyes that are small, dark, and the color of pale malachite." Even the family's servants have "thin pigment-spotted hands" (201, 287).

Lika also mirrors the chained images and actions of her literary predecessors, Katia and Sosnovskaia. She wears dresses with "smart flounces" (200), and she often "disappears" into the darkness. Contentious and fickle, she keeps Arsen'ev unsettled with her theatrics. For instance, she raises the youth's spirits by "puckering her face" (204) and singing songs of love. If she is not stretching her hands towards Arsen'ev or placing them on her chest, she is dashing off "foolish" notes of love, or enveloping him with aggregates: hands, eyes, and skirts. Lika, however, can also dash her lover's ardor to shards by darting from his sight or holding him to monotonous routines. What is even more painful to the youth are the occasions when Lika writes him letters of farewell, or treats him like a child or like a novelty who merely distracts her from her real life.

For his part, Arsen'ev "passionately yearns for love" (193), but his outlook is as circumscribed by self as Lika's. Not unlike Mitia's attachment for Katia, Arsen'ev's devotion to Lika is illusory, a figment of his imagination. With him, love, like his idealization of writing, springs solely from the *idea* of love rather than from its realization. Arsen'ev is captivated by Lika's "smells, dresses, perfumes, and housecoat," and "the charm of her eyes, face, laugh, and voice" (203, 204, 226). He has no understanding, however, of who she is as a person. In the realm of role playing, Arsen'ev easily competes with Lika in being "excessively theatrical" (245). Generally, Arsen'ev's unreal outbreaks stem either from his family's delusions of grandeur or from works of fiction. Arsen'ev and Lika are matched for insincerity, though neither recognizes this or understands the reasons why.

For example, when Arsen'ev first meets Lika, he not only claims to reside at the Nobleman's Hotel, but he also runs up impressive bills that he cannot pay. When her father asks the youth who he is, he—"with pride"—replies with "nonsense" from Goethe (that contains ironic truth at that time): "I do not know myself, and may God spare me that I ever do" (205). Similarly, galloping through the steppe at night, Arsen'ev recalls the "poetic ecstasies . . . of ancient tomes"—for example, Zhukovskii's ballad *Svetlana* (210) and the "poetic dreams of life" (205) as found in such works as *The Cossacks* or such characters as Pierre Bezukhov, Anatoly Kuragin, and Ivan Ilyich.

Given his love of love, Arsen'ev looks upon Lika with "shameless excitement" (200, 201). There is something amoral about the way he desires possession and dominance instead of intimacy and risk. Arsen'ev rushes to answer any summons by Lika, just as he becomes insanely jealous whenever she looks at regressed lovers other than himself, as, for example, when she shows her affection for an officer "with an elongated, dull-swarthy face . . . and in a frock coat reaching below his knees" (194).

"Love" drives Arsen'ev to "insane feelings." If he is not rushing off in sleighs or riding horses in "wild ecstasy," he "staggers" as if "the ground has opened up beneath him," or he "falls into a deep sleep . . . [unable to] stay on his feet, much less think through anything" (201, 202, 219, 235). For him, doing or dying seem to be obverse ideals: either he will take possession of Lika in her aggregates, or he will end the affair in murder and suicide. "I mentally repeated only one thing," he writes. "Either she gives herself (those batiste skirts, the rustling of her fleeing feet) . . . back to me tonight, or neither of us shall live!" (202).

The lovelorn Arsen'ev is far more unsettled than young Mitia. Arsen'ev does not reflect upon the regression inherent in his affair with Lika, but he is well aware of wrongdoing. At times, racing through "rustling stubble" and "glassy grain" (201), he also admits to the self-forged qualities of his affection, as well as to the imperious demand of his nature for emotional attachment. "I had invented a love in which I already believed completely," he says. "And the one feeling that prevailed over all others . . . was that I had made some kind of particularly lucky acquisition" (195).

Strangely, though, Arsen'ev does not obsess over Lika when the two are separated for long periods of time. Once she is out of his sight, the "dream" of Lika fades from the youth's consciousness (196). He reevaluates his previous threats of murder and suicide as "ridiculous" (202) and becomes immediately susceptible to the "attributes" of any woman close at hand. For instance, in Lika's absence, the youth experiences "musical happiness" and "acute loving pain" for Avilova. He is particularly attracted to her lacy dress and lambskin coat, as well as to her "portiered face" and the "tender tops of her breasts" (227, 229, 235). He confesses to difficulty restraining himself "from suddenly kissing that close naked body, her curled fragrant hair" (235).

"Wild feelings and ideas" burn in Arsen'ev also whenever he encounters his landlady, Nikulina, amidst such menacing stimuli as the "measured beat of the alarm clock," the "slamming of shutters" with "iron kingpins" and "metal blades," and the presence of photo portraits of her late husband, "white faced" and lying in a coffin (209).

Given Lika's and Arsen'ev's understanding of love and life, it should not be surprising that when the couple reunites after periods of separation, their relationship resumes its downward spiral. For instance, Arsen'ev rushes to meet his love on a train, a "dark and shaggy locomotive . . . breathing heavily and exuding an awesome triangle of dull-red flame." When it is at full speed, the train "screams, squeals, and whines." Its windows look like "gray diamonds," and, its cars shake so violently that "everything falls and collapses." These assaults on equilibrium and the senses leave the couple nonplussed. Arsen'ev "feels queasy . . . from internal shaking." Lika, now marked only as "she," has a "hot, unseeing face" and a fur coat over her shoulders

(210). The sheer violence of the trip destroys the possibility of their rebuilding intimacy.

Furthermore, although Arsen'ev pretends to a "new and terrifying intimacy" (211) with his "love," the two almost work consciously to increase the gap between them. Lika seeks always to be "inaccessible" (211) to her lover. She is always "out there" (211), as far from his mind, soul, and heart as possible. For example, she loves to whirl about on ice skates in the highly regressed world of ice ponds surrounded by "martial music, lilac gaslight, and flying black figures" (211). She is "relentlessly indifferent" to Arsen'ev's "poetically savage joy" of life. She refuses to share his love for the charm of the ancestral estate, the romantic verse of Fet, and such binding images as roads "stretched tight like lilac bands . . . and blinding golden ribbons (214, 215).

Lika's antics drive Arsen'ev to "anguish, jealousy, and insult" (211), but, in Bunin's terms, deprivations such as Arsen'ev's could offer a chance for enlightenment. Arsen'ev does, in fact, have lucid moments in which he realizes that he is "demeaning himself for Lika's sake." He glimpses the truth that he is being rent apart by the "eternal schism between dreams and reality, and by the eternal unrealizability of the fullness and integrity of love" (211, 212, 241). Since he senses that communion of mind and spirit is rare, he begins to question his present life and to worry about his future as a "petty provincial bureaucrat" (272).

Arsen'ev is still too enthralled by Lika to sense the manacled threat that she represents. He is still captivated by the physicality of Lika's "frozen freshness" and the tears that "cause her lips to swell up at once" (211, 212). The youth, ever a creator of moods and associations, is also mesmerized by Lika's chain-tinged wardrobe: her "gray outfit, gray squirrel cap, and gray stockings" (211, 212). Lika's "gray coat" he greets "ever more joyfully and warmly"; the "heavy material" of her "gray skirt . . . torments him with desire all by itself"; and her "dear gray boots" are for him "the most touching of all" (212, 219). Arsen'ev is even unconscious of the regressed images in the poetry he reads to her, in which "silvery serpents" crawl across drifts of "shining sands" (214).

Most revealing, Arsen'ev does not notice that Lika's poses, infatuations, and dalliances with other men intensify the samsara- and shardlike aggregates that constitute his own relationship with her. He can, for instance, look blankly at Lika's being "curled up" on a sofa. He derides her love for the theater, even mocking such characters as Chatskii and Hamlet—personages whom the youth had identified with as an adolescent. Also, Arsen'ev's heart pounds with an animal-like agitation whenever he hears the "swish" of Lika's skirt and legs as she "gets lost . . . in the gyrating crowd" or when she frolics in "protracted twirl" with the "unnaturally tall officer with black sideburns, an elongated, dull, and swarthy face, and unmoving dark eyes" (213, 215, 221).

By this time, the growth of animosity between Lika and Arsen'ev is the only momentum in the relationship. They engage in mutual recrimination. Lika berates her lover for his egocentric stance. "You think only of yourself," she tells him. "You want everything your way . . . to separate me from everyone the way you separate yourself" (213). Arsen'ev's responses to the situation are twofold: first, to reduce Lika to a child, his to love alone, so that, when she is "simple, reticent, helpless, and meek" (213), the youth's "soul grows faint from rapturously selfless tenderness toward her" (213, 215). Second, he becomes a modern-day Underground Man, who—"alien and alone . . . nervous and tense" (219, 221, 251)—regards life with malice and contempt but who also demands love and respect from all. When rebuffed by Lika for either of these strategies, Arsen'ev "treats people even more cruelly and arrogantly." He succumbs to a "destructive loneliness . . . that mounts to a kind of ecstasy." He is "gladdened by his alienation," and he envies "men of action"—that is, "anyone with ready-made cares and worries . . . with simple, direct and definite duties." More poignantly, Arsen'ev's youth "plays the part of an alienated, unkind observer, who secretly revels in his alienation and malevolence, and who keenly hones his impressionability, insight, perspicacity toward every human inadequacy" (213, 219, 226, 230, 251).

Although Arsen'ev is not able to "shackle" Lika to his side, "he will also not let her go" (227). Arsen'ev's controlling behavior brings the relationship to an impasse. The youth rides an emotional roller coaster, as wild as the "dives and bumps" (235) that his sleigh takes in negotiating the roads he travels. The mood swings operate like this: When no one pursues Lika, when nothing threatens the "harmony" (220) between the two, Arsen'ev radiates stability and joy; otherwise, he falls into "cold enmity," into melancholy and despair. "What a mass of amazing contradictions!" Lika tells him (219, 221).

Lika continues to seek independence, and life for Arsen'ev becomes as "narrow" and "gray" (226, 235) as his surroundings. The decline of each is unabated. Arsen'ev sees himself as a "tall, mute devil" or as a ghost, "pitifully thin in his gossamer nightshirt" (227, 235). Looking at the moon, Arsen'ev tilts his head back until it "hurts"; and "circles of youthful flush" darken his cheeks. Fast-paced trains now make him feel as "though beaten by wet laundry" (240). At balls and other gatherings, he not only "gets tangled up in the uniforms" of others, but he also appears "thinner" (221), since he must wear the tails of Avilova's dead husband, whose regressed portrait had looked so warily upon the couple. Even worse, wishing to destroy his "enemies" (213), Arsen'ev has the metaphorically cannibalistic wish to "gobble up" a regressed police officer—"a strong forty-year-old animal . . . fleshy and broad-shouldered . . . his fat back . . . and his calves encased in shiny, firmly bulging boots" (218).

Lika's decay is just as rapid. When Arsen'ev comes to her in the Crimea, she appears ghostlike: thinner and "deathly pale." The wind whips her hat, hiding all her facial features, except her "squinting eyes." Fortunately unable to lift the hat's veil, she kisses Arsen'ev through its chainlike lace. Immediately, Lika identifies Arsen'ev as the source of her woe. "What have you done to me, what have you done to me!" she exclaims (253). Yet, just as the wind prevents Lika from seeing physically, so does the whipping force of self keep her from discerning her plight spiritually. Lika and Arsen'ev keep a tryst; but, not unlike Arsen'ev's liaison with Ton'ka, their lovemaking only melds aggregates. Arsen'ev embraces Lika's legs, kissing them through her skirt. He strokes her "cool, bare shoulders," and her "shining plaited braids." He drinks in her "warm breath," the scent of her hair, and the "hot and cool parts" of her body (262, 265, 283). There is, however, no union of souls. What coming together there is is enacted among fettered spirits attuned to the error of the couple's ways, if only because these spirits made similar mistakes in other rounds of life. A rook "bawls worriedly, like a drunk," and, as the portrait of Avilova's dead husband had seemed to do, "strange figures stare down from . . . the chalky white ceiling" (254).

Though Lika joins Arsen'ev in his wandering, their travels do nothing for their relationship. They briefly visit Arsen'ev's family and the ancestral abode and then travel—again by train—to take jobs, this time in Kharkov. On the train, Lika shades her eyes from the sun, which casts "hot stripes over her face" (255). In passing, she misses the warning implicit in "silvery green burial mounds" (255) because she is asleep, with a pillow hiding her head, a shawl covering her body, and her legs being drawn up under her.

In Kharkov samsara is more evident than ever. For instance, the beauty of Ukrainian summer days is foreshortened by the "luminous links of a train" (264). It is also marred by big-bosomed women with water yokes on their strong shoulders, a landlord with a "round-cropped head of gray hair," and a servant girl with a "touch of Tatar" in her features, together with her "slanting eyes" and "ankles as thin as a thoroughbred mare's" (256, 257, 261).

Lika and Arsen'ev do not reflect upon such manacled warnings; rather, they become increasingly erratic and unstable. Each seeks to bind the other yet desires to be "free and preeminent in everything" (269). Arsen'ev begins to insist that Lika "live only for him and through him" (272). He wishes to know all of her "secrets" and to imprison her inside a remote palace or hut for his pleasure alone; yet, for himself, he listens—"sweetly, sadly and enviously" (263)—to songs of Cossacks who crave the road, not women. He is repelled by the "eternal inseparability" (268) consequent on marriage, children, and a home. Wanderlust seizes him, and he finds it more and more difficult to stay at home with his love. For instance, Arsen'ev believes that he is "completely happy" (266) whenever he departs from Lika, even though he encounters further decline. As the youth journeys amidst dusty paths, gray skies, and thick stubble, he sees Ukrainian women who "chirp" and have "almond" and "hawklike" eyes, and an adolescent in a "light gray coat," who appears "unusually plump" and "very handsome in a Persian sort of way" (265, 266, 276, 277, 281).

Additionally, regressed women from all social classes stir Arsen'ev's fancy. For instance, peasant women appear as triangles and circles. Arsen'ev is "blissfully tortured" by "strangely bright yellow eyes," pronounced hips and breasts, and limbs that are "akimbo" and lips that are "wide apart" (278). A well-dressed young lady also piques Arsen'ev's interest, if only because her inner decay speaks to his own. The woman is "palely powdered to a leaden pallor." Her broad cheekbones, wide hips, and firm breasts make it almost impossible for Arsen'ev to resist grabbing her.

In Kharkhov, Lika initially acquiesces to Arsen'ev's fantasy world. "Looking up" into her lover's face, she affirms her own desire for "self-renunciation" (269), as well as Arsen'ev's right to his own feelings and actions. She quickly loses patience, though, because her lover's interests are so one-sided. "You call all my dreams vulgar," she berates him. "You deprive me of everything and deny yourself nothing" (280). Lika becomes painfully aware of Arsen'ev's roving eye and is hostile to his other loves. She is horrified at his plans to sequester her in a palace or "harem" (262) and to wander anew because, in his eyes, she has "deteriorated" and become a "commonplace housewife" who dismisses the "young filly" servant girl (275). Arsen'ev seems to regard Lika as a spirit who, like "air" (265), can no longer fill the yawning gap in his life. "Nothing is enough for me now," Arsen'ev tells her (265), but Lika holds more tightly to her love and tells Arsen'ev that she will release him only if she interferes with his calling as a writer. This avocation has become spurious and is taking a backseat to his recently assumed positions of statistician and curator of government documents; yet she hopes that such a threat (or promise) will speak to a youthful idealism and have staying power. No tangible effect is produced, however.

Lika's and Arsen'ev's conversations become increasingly ponderous and strained. They cite Goethe and Turgenev and prattle on about love, art, and immortality; but they studiously avoid all mention of their feelings or distress. In their dialogue, however, the couple inadvertently come upon an element of truth—their possession by a doppelgänger self. Arsen'ev tells Lika: "Immortals create; mortals produce copies of themselves." Almost immediately, he adds: "We are dependent on the creatures of our own making" (270). He is also deeply chagrined to read Lika's protest against her lack of freedom in a passage she has underlined in Tolstoi's *Family Happiness*. "All my thoughts . . . and feelings are not mine, but his" (271).

Not surprisingly, Lika and Arsen'ev move each other to death. For instance, although Lika insists that her love has, with time, become "more steadfast, gentler, and nicer" (272), his brother, Nikolai, affirms that Arsen'ev "has placed a cross over himself" (268). Indeed, in samsaric terms, the youth seems to have died. Arsen'ev ambles amidst "waiting" tombs and smells the "graveyard odor of decaying leaves." He seeks solace and solitude in the "crypt" of his office, in the "fortresslike thickness of its vaults and walls" (273, 274). Arsen'ev also attempts new trysts alongside "long cheap coffins," the latest objects of his fancy being regressed peasant women who "choke with laughter" and who "skitter away goatlike" after kissing him "with wild delight" (279).

Lika also faces an unhappy end. In a crucial scene, despite Arsen'ev's objections, she prepares for a masquerade by choosing a black mask and "something black, thin, and long" (280). For hours on end, Lika lies on a sofa, fetuslike, "her feet tucked beneath her" (281). When she finds the courage to leave Arsen'ev forever, she leaves only a note, berating him for her "disillusioned love" and his wish for a "new, completely free life" (282, 283).

Somewhat like Mitia's and Elagin's reaction to the loss of their "loves," Arsen'ev responds to Lika's departure with apathy, anger, and thoughts of shooting himself. Apparently crushed by Lika's "stony cruelty" (287), Arsen'ev seemingly rushes toward his end. As he gulps down vodka, his face becomes icy and taut; he feels the earth collapsing under his feet, and he is horrified by the dotlike rain and "thick white haze" (283) that abounds. As if speaking to his conscience, an icon of the Mother of God, painted on an old board like "cast bronze," looks at him sternly, "her large, black eyes outlined by a dark band" (283).

At this point, Arsen'ev has not yet learned anything from his experience. He continues to delude himself that he is as "free as a bird" and that "man is created for happiness, like a bird in flight" (284). In reality, though, he only has new encounters with regression. For instance, in his travels, the youth accompanies "repulsive" people whose faces are blue with cold and whose bodies are "muffled and girded with shawls." He sees "gray and harsh frozen days," "frozen cobblestone roadways," and "endless walls of third-class wagons . . . heavy and large" (284, 285).

Arsen'ev also encounters death everywhere he goes. Even his family estate is now a "grave" marked by aging parents—his father is "thinner, smaller . . . terribly wizened, and completely gray." His sister is "decaying" and the "decrepit" house and garden match the porches turned "blue-gray" from age (284, 285). Unable to experience compassion or love, Arsen'ev once again chooses the road. His life as a wanderer continues, and enlightenment is not yet possible or desirable.

AN "OPEN" ENDING

The conclusion of the adult Arsen'ev's story contains elements of both tragedy and triumph. On the negative side, Lika dies of pneumonia—and possibly of the torments of love. Arsen'ev records his regret that he has not known or understood his father, a man who belonged to a "very specific age and generation" and who had been able to take to heart the "the sorrow and youth" bedeviling his son. His father had had "rare spiritual openness and secrecy," a tragicomic and bittersweet wisdom achieved only by people who negotiate craving and grasp that "everything in life passes no matter what we do, and that tears are of no use" (286, 287).

In marked contrast to almost everyone in his story, though, and notwithstanding his own unhappy beginnings and the years he has frittered away, the adult Arsen'ev does not end his tale in bitterness and despair. Rather, he hallows the lives of long-departed family and friends. In so doing, Arsen'ev not only safeguards loved ones from the ravages of time and space but also experiences new joy and peace that they live, resurrected in his mind and heart. For instance, the adult Arsen'ev often sees Lika in his dreams. At times, she appears to him as regressed: indistinct, thin, and apparently in mourning; at other times, the Lika who appears is ageless, looking exactly as she did when they were both young. Revealingly, in these belated dreams, there is no trace of struggle and bitterness in his feelings. Arsen'ev responds to Lika's image with "surges of joy and love," a sense of a "physical closeness" that he claims he feels for no one else, but that, in truth, he has felt for various people and things ever since his childhood, adolescence, and youth.

CONCLUSION

In *The Life of Arsen'ev*, Bunin extends the message of the Khrushchev siblings in *Dry Valley*. Here he sketches a vast portrait of gentry decline but ends the work with his speaker affirming love and life, not bitterness and death. The adult Arsen'ev emerges as a true disciple of Gautama. He is the one character in all of Bunin's writings to whom the author could point with admiration and pride, for he was the prototype of what Bunin himself struggled to be.

Conclusion

Émigré readers and reviewers were so delighted with Bunin's *The Life of Arsen'ev* that they wanted a sequel. They wanted to see how the young Arsen'ev progressed to his mature enlightened self against the backdrop of war, revolution, and exile. In truth, Bunin had planned to expand *Arsen'ev* with portraits of the "present" and of "living beings," but he did not do so for several reasons. As he complained to friends, he could not find a suitable form for his content. He also found it difficult to write about people, places, and things that still existed. Finally, when Bunin finished "Lika," the fifth book of *Arsen'ev,* in 1939, he was sixty-nine years old and would soon face yet another struggle for survival in the Second World War. In short, whatever inclination Bunin may have had to continue *Arsen'ev* was lost amidst more pressing concerns.

Neither age nor war, however, stopped Bunin from probing issues of chain, rebirth, and enlightenment and writing about them. What he turned his back on was the long narrative. Never again would he attempt works like *The Village, Dry Valley, The Gentleman from San Francisco, Mitya's Love, The Elagin Affair,* and *The Life of Arsen'ev.* Never again would he portray such "types" as lord, peasant, entrepreneur, youth, officer, actress, and author in such pervasive and self-sustaining ways.

It should be noted, though, that amid all the suffering and pain Bunin had endured in life, the cycle of long narratives from *The Village* to *The Life of Arsen'ev* was, for him, a singular source of comfort and delight. These works had ensured his presence on the literary scene; they had established him as a "modern" writer who was rooted more in the twentieth century than in the nineteenth; they had underscored his belief in Buddhistic tenets. For example, Bunin agreed with Guatama that self and craving bore the fruits of suffering and pain in the world, and that humankind could either succumb to regression, rebirth, and chain, or find liberation in memory, enlightenment, and Nirvana.

Of greater importance to Bunin personally was that his long works allowed him to transcend the tags of "realist," "modern," "liberal," and "conservative" that critics had applied to him throughout his literary career. He could now appropriate unequivocally the one "label" that he had cherished in life—that of a disciple of Gautama, whose apostolate was the world and whose writing was a poem to truth.

In 1901, Bunin concluded his sketch "Silence," with these lines: "To my friend, with whom I have experienced so much on my way . . . I dedicate these lines. And I send my regards to all our friends who have shared their feelings, wanderings, and dreams" (2:240). This expression of collegial regard is as relevant to readers at the end of twentieth century as it was to those at its beginning. To all, Bunin extended an enduring invitation to join with him as a disciple of the Buddha in life.

Notes

PREFACE

1. A. Wachtel, "The Great Unread," *American Scholar* 63, no. 1 (Winter 1994): 151.
2. See Mark Scott's introductory article in Ivan Bunin, *Wolves and Other Stories* (Santa Barbara: Capra Press, 1989), 7.
3. Iu. Mal'tsev, *Ivan Bunin, 1870–1953* (Moscow: Posev, 1994), 7. For instance, the only study of Bunin in emigration, V. Lavrov's *Kholodnaia osen'. Ivan Bunin v emigratsii, 1920–1953. Roman-khronika*, (Moscow: Molodaia Gvardiia, 1989), is little more than a collage of dates, details, and citations. It fails to provide a coherent view of Bunin's life and writings and has been rejected by scholars in Russia. See, for instance, A. Baboreko, "Osenniaia kliukva," *Novyi mir*, no. 1 (1990): 263–68.
4. J. Woodward, *Ivan Bunin: A Study of His Fiction* (Chapel Hill: University of North Carolina Press, 1980), ix.

CHAPTER ONE

1. K-skii, "O novoi povesti I. A. Bunina," *Odesskii listok*, 12 March 1910, 3, as quoted in A. Ninov, "K avtobiografii I. Bunina," *Novyi mir*, no. 10 (1965): 224.
2. I. Bunin, "Avtobiograficheskaia zametka," in *Sobranie sochinenii v deviati tomakh* (Moscow: Khudozhestvennaia Literatura, 1965), 9:264–65. Unless otherwise stated, all references to Bunin's works in this study are to volume and page number from this edition.
3. During Bunin's lifetime, writers and critics sporadically noted or implied both his fascination with the East and, in particular, his attraction to Buddhism. For instance, as early as 1908, V. Aleksandrovich noted that "life [in Bunin] is closely tied to Nirvana . . . and nonexistence." See Iu. Aleksandrovich, *Posle Chekhova. Ocherk molodoi literatury poslednego desiatiletiia, 1898–1908* (Moscow: Obshchestvennaia Pol'za, 1908), 52. A. Blok and M. Gor'kii also noted Bunin's love of Eastern philosophy and culture. See A. Blok, "O lirike," *Zolotoe runo*, no. 6 (1907): 41–46, and Gor'kii's letter to I. Zhiga,

written on 15 August 1929, in M. Gor'kii, *Sobranie sochinenii v tridtsati tomakh* (Moscow: Khudozhestvennaia Literatura, 1956), 30:146–47.

Within the past twenty or so years, critics have commented more frequently upon Buddhistic strains in Bunin's fiction, but they have avoided in-depth discussions of the topic. For Russian scholars who discern the influence of Buddhism on Bunin's fiction, see, for example, O. Slivitskaia, "Bunin i vostok (K postanovke voprosa)," *Izvestiia Voronezhskogo gosudarstvennogo pedagogicheskogo instituta* 114 (1971): 87–96; O. Soloukhina, "O nravstvenno-filosofskikh vzgliadakh Bunina," *Russkaia literatura*, no. 4 (1984): 47–59; S. Antonov, "Ot pervogo litsa. Ivan Bunin. 'Zhizn' Arsen'eva'," *Novyi mir*, no. 2 (1973): 243–64; and Iu. Mal'tsev, *Ivan Bunin, 1870–1953* (Moscow: Posev, 1994), 8–9. For Western scholars, see J. Woodward, "Eros and Nirvana in the Art of Ivan Bunin," *Modern Language Review*, no. 65 (1970): 576–86, and "Structure and Subjectivity in the Early 'Philosophical' Tales of Bunin," *Canadian Slavic Studies*, no. 4 (1971): 510–13. Also see J. Connolly, "Desire and Renunciation: Buddhist Elements in the Prose of Ivan Bunin," *Canadian-American Slavic Studies*, no. 1 (1981): 11–20, and M. Artz, "A Biblical Motif in Ivan Bunin's Stories Written between 1916 and 1925," *Dutch Contributions to the Tenth International Congress of Slavists* (Amsterdam: Rodopi, 1988), 1–18.

4. See Bunin's interview with *Odesskii listok* on 2 March 1910, V. Shcherbina et al., eds. *Literaturnoe nasledstvo. Ivan Bunin. Kniga pervaia* (Moscow: Nauka, 1973), 362. Also see Bez podpisi, "Moskovskaia khronika. Intsident na bankete," *Rech'*, 18 October 1913, 5.

5. G. McVay, *Esenin. A Life* (Ann Arbor: Ardis, 1976), 36.

6. See, for instance, N. Rubakin, *Sredi knig* (Moscow: Nauka, 1913), 265–66. Sample titles include I. Minaev, *Buddhism* (1887), *Buddhist Catechisis* (1902), and *The Life and Teaching of Siddartha Gotama, Called the Buddha* (1911). For more on the reception of Eastern philosophy and religion in *fin de siècle* Russia, see Slivitskaia, "Bunin i vostok," 87–96.

7. *A Record of Buddhistic Kingdoms* was translated into French in 1836 and into English by 1869, 1884, and 1886. The edition that Bunin knew was the 1886 one by James Leege, which was republished by Paragon and Dover Publications in 1965. Also see Bunin's story "City of the King of Kings" (1924), and Shcherbina, *Kniga vtoraia*, 97 and 116.

8. *The Sutta-Nipata* appeared in Russia in at least four separate editions between the years 1898 and 1905. It should also be noted that despite the widespread popularity of Buddhism in Russia circa 1900, not everyone approved its message. Gor'kii, for instance, took issue with the passivity and idleness he believed the Buddha offered as the path to salvation. "[As regards] Buddhistic teaching," he wrote to A.P. Surguchev on 26 January 1912, "I have read the *Sutta-Nipata* and the *Buddhistic Suttras* . . . and I do not like them. Obviously, one has to be a Hindu, live in a hot and humid climate,

and sense dissolution so that this yellow tedium can be understood. Run from the East—it's time we did." See Gor'kii, vol. 29 (1955), 221.

9. Rubakin, *Sredi knig*, 266. Additionally, Tolstoi edited P. Burlanzhe's scholarly work *The Life and Teachings of Siddartha Gotama, called the Buddha, i.e., the Most Perfect One*, published, after Tolstoi's death, in 1911. He also wrote the introduction and first two chapters of a book by V. G. Chertkov, entitled *From the Life of Siddartha, called the Buddha, i.e., the Holy One*, that was also published after the great writer's passing, in 1916. See Slivitskaia, "Bunin i vostok," 88.

10. See Bunin's letter to M. B. Karamzina written on 20 July 1938, in Shcherbina, *Kniga pervaia*, 670.

11. I. Odoevtseva, "Na beregakh Seny," *Russkii al'manakh* (Paris: n.p., 1981), 406.

12. See Bunin's letter to Gor'kii, dated 11 April 1911, in B. Mikhailovskii, ed., *Gor'kovskie chteniia, 1958–59* (Moscow: Izdatel'stvo "Akademii Nauk," 1961), 59–60. For more detailed accounts of Bunin's visits to Ceylon, see his stories "In the Land of the Ancestors" (1911), "Third Class" (1921), "City of the King of Kings" (1924), and "The Waters are Many" (1925–1926).

13. M. Grin, *Ustami Buninykh* (Frankfurt/Main: Posev, 1977), 1:101–2.

14. G. Kuznetsova, *Grasskii dnevnik* (Washington, D.C.: Victor Kamkin, 1967), 275.

15. See Bunin's interview with the newspaper *Footlights and Life*, on 13 February 1912, in Shcherbina, *Kniga pervaia*, 375.

16. G. Alekseev, "Zhivye vstrechi," *Vremia*, 22 August 1921, 2.

17. O. Mikhailov, *I. A. Bunin. Zhizn' i tvorchestvo* (Tula: Priorskoe Knizhnoe Izdatel'stvo, 1987), 230–31.

18. In Bunin's story "The Compatriot" (1916), the character Zotov notes what he considers the striking similarities between Russian and Buddhist monasteries and between the lacquered statuettes of the Buddha and the polished cups and basins sold at Russian fairs. See 4:402–3.

19. More specifically, the "chain of causation" usually contains twelve links, each link being both a cause and effect of the link following or preceding it: ignorance > predisposition > consciousness > name-form > the six senses > contact > craving > grasping > becoming > birth > old age and death > ignorance.

Bunin wrote in *The Liberation of Tolstoy:* "The Buddha could not help but know that the world was home to sickness, suffering, old age, and death. But why was he so shocked when he saw such things . . . ? Because he saw them with the eyes of an Adam, and because the endless chain of previous existences suddenly formed a circle, the last link joined to the first. Hence Guatama's particular feeling for the 'Unity of Life'" (9:124).

20. Mal'tsev, *Ivan Bunin*, 8. Bunin's colleagues and friends often saw him as a victim of regression. For instance, Valentin Kataev, himself no

stranger to Buddhism, showed the 1919 Bunin as having entered rebirth. In his view, Bunin was now a "new incarnation . . . a lean, sinewy wolf . . . or an old goat with gaunt bony flanks . . . a haggard, tormented face . . . and the eyes of a Buddha." Such regression went beyond appearances. Kataev recalled that when a detachment of armed soldiers had sought to enter Bunin's home, Bunin "bared his strong, sharp yellowish teeth" and threatened to "bite the throat" of anyone who crossed his threshold. See V. Kataev, *Sviatoi kolodets. Trava zabveniia* (Moscow: Sovetskii Pisatel', 1967), 207, 209, and 218.

21. "Anything abstract," Bunin's wife recalled, "Bunin's mind could not accept." See Muromtseva-Bunina, *Zhizn' Bunina, 1870–1906* (Paris: n.p., 1958), 31. Also see N. Berberova, *Kursiv moi. Avtobiografiia v dvukh tomakh* (New York: Russica Publishers, 1983), 1:293.

22. See Bunin's diary excerpt of 12 February 1911, in Grin, *Ustami Buninykh*, 1:96.

23. Critics have called attention to the "feminine" qualities of Bunin's writing. N. Meshkov, for instance, astutely noted that "Bunin never sings of a definite woman, but rather of an Eternally Feminine beginning." See N. Meshkov, "Poeziia Ivana Bunina (K 25-tiletiia poeticheskoi deiatel'nosti)," *Put'*, no. 12 (1912): 33. Also see G. Mesniaev, "Tvorcheskii put' I.A. Bunina (K desiatiletiiu konchinu)," *Vozrozhdenie*, no. 143 (1963): 62, and Gor'kii's letter to Bunin written circa 20 November 1904, in Mikhailovskii, *Gor'kovskie chteniia*, 35.

24. Bunin had little use for conventional notions of time and space. "All my life," he wrote in "Night," "I have sought to overcome and destroy space, time, and form" (5:305).

25. See Bunin's diary excerpt written on 20 August 1917, in N. Smirnov-Sokol'skii, "Posledniaia nakhodka," *Novyi mir*, no. 10 (1956): 218. Two days later he added: "Learning is remembering—Socrates." See 217.

26. Similarly, Bunin's narrator in "The Dreams of Chang" writes: "If [the dog] Chang loves and senses his [dead] Captain, if he sees him with the eyes of memory, with that divine attitude which no one understands, then it means that the Captain is still with him in that world which is without beginning or end, and which is inaccessible by death" (4:385).

27. Shcherbina, *Kniga pervaia*, 382. Bunin reiterated such an affirmation in his story "Night" (5:300–1).

28. Shcherbina, *Kniga pervaia*, 384–85, and Malt'sev, *Ivan Bunin*, 8.

29. A. Baboreko, "I. A. Bunin na Kapri (Po neopublikovannym materialam)," in *V bol'shoi sem'e* (Smolensk: Smolenskoe Knizhnoe Izdatel'stvo, 1960), 238–53. Also see Kuznetsova, *Grasskii dnevnik*, 105.

30. Shcherbina, *Kniga pervaia*, 87.

31. In 1928 Bunin similarly exclaimed to Kuznetsova about medieval church bells in Provence: "How strange to think that five hundred years ago,

these bells rang exactly the same way they do now . . . and that then as now, their ringing was such a noble defense against everything, even against death itself. Why don't people understand this!" See Kuznetsova, *Grasskii dnevnik*, 91.

32. Baboreko, "I. A. Bunin na Kapri," 241.

33. A. Sedykh, "I.A. Bunin," *Dalekie, blizkie* (New York: Izdatel'stvo "Novogo Russkogo Slova," 1962), 196.

34. See Bunin's diary excerpt, written on 15 February 1911, in Grin, *Ustami Buninykh*, 1:97, and his letter to Iulii Bunin, dated 18 February 1911, in A. Baboreko, "Neopublikovannye pis'ma I. A. Bunina," *Vesna prishla* (Smolensk: Smolenskoe Knizhnoe Izdatel'stvo, 1959), 236. Years later, Bunin not only claimed physical kinship with the tropical natives that he had met in his travels but also asserted that in another life he had actually lived with them in "paradise." He wrote in his story "Night": "It is quite probable that my ancestors dwelt . . . in the tropics of India. . . . So when I see coconut palms bent along the ocean shore, or dark-brown, naked people in warm tropical waters, how can I not recall what I once felt when I was my dark-brown, naked ancestor?" (5:301).

35. Mal't'sev, *Ivan Bunin*, 8. Bunin also quotes from Tolstoi: "Truly, we existed before this life, although we have lost the consciousness of this existence" (9:129).

36. I. Bunin, "Otryvok," *Rossiia*, 24 December 1927, 2.

37. Kataev, *Sviatoi kolodets*, 177.

38. See Bunin's diary excerpt, written on 20 August 1923, in Grin, *Ustami Buniaykh*, 2:116.

39. See Kuznetsova's diary excerpt, written on 22 November 1932, in Kuznetsova, *Grasskii dnevnik*, 278.

40. See Bunin's diary excerpt, dated 22 January 1922, in Grin, *Ustami Buninykh*, 2:75.

41. See Bunin's diary excerpt, written on 20 August 1923, in ibid., 2:117.

42. See Bunin's diary excerpt, written on 13 February 1911, in ibid., 1:96–97.

43. See Kuznetsova's diary excerpt, written on 3 June 1933, in Kuznetsova, *Grasskii dnevnik*, 291.

44. See I. Baboreko, *I. A. Bunin. Materialy dlia biografii s 1870 po 1917* (Moscow: Khudozhestvennaia Literatura, 1983), 241.

45. See Kuznetsova's diary entry written on 11 February 1933, in Kuznetsova, *Grasskii dnevnik*, 279.

46. Baboreko, "I. A. Bunin na Kapri," 240. Bunin's hero similarly exclaims in the story "Silence" (1901): "What great happiness to live, to exist in the world, to breathe, and to see the sky, the water, and the sun!" (2:239).

47. V. K., "Da zdrastvuet zhizn'! (Beseda s I.A. Buninym)," *Vechernye izvestiia*, 4 May 1913, 3. The reviewer felt compelled to add: "Bunin's eyes

began to burn. His face grew lively. Earlier, Bunin had been calm, no, more accurately, he had been stern [*strogii*]. Now he had become completely transformed, having grown younger before my eyes."

48. Shcherbina, *Kniga pervaia,* 386.

49. See Bunin's interview with the *Odessa News* on 8 September 1911, in Shcherbina, *Kniga pervaia,* 369.

50. O. Slivitskaia, "O kontseptsii cheloveka v tvorchestve I. A. Bunina. Rasskaz 'Kazimir Stanislavich,'" *Russkaia literatura XX veka (dooktiabr'skii period)* (Kaluga: Tul'skii Pedagogicheskii Institut, 1970), 156. Bunin similarly wrote in his diary on 4 August 1917: "If a person does not lose his capacity to wait for happiness—then he is happy. For happiness exists!" See N. Smirnov-Sokol'skii, "Posledniaia nakhodka," *Novyi mir,* no. 10 (1956): 218.

51. Bunin accepted later advancements in age with even greater dignity. "Today is Ivan Alekseevich's birthday," Kuznetsova wrote in her diary on 23 October 1930, "He is sixty years old. A completely ordinary day. . . . Vera Nikolaevna [Muromtseva-Bunina] says that, in earlier years, he would go out of his mind in the days right before his birthday . . . but this time, he is quiet and very cordial. . . . He has not even changed his clothes, but goes about in the same old striped robe with its tattered belt." See Kuznetsova, *Grasskii dnevnik,* 180–81.

52. Several critics noted the "reborn" quality of Bunin's thought and art. One wrote in 1913: "To his descriptions of sunsets and falls, of old gardens and quiet estates, Bunin brings something invigorating, the enlightening presentiment of the coming day. . . . He replaces sad thoughts of dying leaves with the joyous premonition of first flowers. . . . He speaks constantly of the 'eternal beauty of existence,' that winter storms are a forerunner of spring." See V. L'vov-Rogachevskii, "Poema zapusteniia," *Snova nakanune. Sbornik kriticheskikh statei i zametok* (Moscow: Knigoizdatel'stvo "Pisateli," 1913), 10. Three years later, another critic was moved to write: "A new Bunin is born, peaceful, and in love with life." See M. Levidov, "I. A. Bunin," *Novyi zhurnal dlia vsekh,* nos. 4–6 (1916): 45, and M. Olgin, "Bunin," *A Guide to Russian Literature (1820–1917)* (New York: Harcourt, Brace and Howe, 1920), 251.

53. M. Aldanov, "O Bunine," *Novyi zhurnal* 35 (1953): 130.

54. He similarly told Kuznetsova on 10 September 1930: "I have been so pliant in life that several people have died in me. . . ." Kuznetsova, *Grasskii dnevnik,* 171.

55. Bunin often traveled this Path of Egression; that is, he was an ego consumed by what he himself called a *"mania grandiosa"* for glory and fame. Indeed, years before Bunin became formally acquainted with Buddhism, he had grasped that ego and craving were causing his pain and that he would do well to give up both. He wrote to a friend in 1891: "We do not value life.

We are never satisfied with what we have; we want more than there is.... That is why we are unhappy." Several years later, Bunin formulated his problem even more precisely: "I am a great egoist," he wrote to Tolstoi in 1896. "And I have often told myself that it would be better to rid myself of such a burden." Bunin's friends and colleagues also often attested to his healthy ego. For instance, Nina Berberova recalls that in his years in exile, Bunin reacted to his world with "savage egocentricism." A. Baboreko, *I. A. Bunin. Materialy,* 54; and "Neopublikovannye pis'ma," 221. Also see T. Bonami, *Khudozhestvennaia proza I.A. Bunina (1887–1904)* (Vladimir: Vladimirskoe Knizhnoe Izdatel'stvo, 1962), 13, and Berberova, *Kursiv moi,* 305.

56. Bunin often equated Tolstoi to the Buddha. For instance, he wrote in an article on 20 November 1919: "Some people now often say: Tolstoi did a great deal of harm by destroying the prestige of the government and the state, and by castigating the upper levels of Russian society and Russian rulers. But they forget that Tolstoi, almost throughout his entire life, was like all the great teachers of humankind in that he spoke not for a specific moment in time. And, they also forget that in rebuking him, they also rebuke ... the Buddha." B. Lipin, "Bunin v 'Iuzhnom slove,'" *Zvezda,* no. 9 (1993): 138.

57. G. Struve, "The Art of Ivan Bunin," *Slavonic and East European Review* 2 (1932–33): 427.

58. In a letter written on 15 May 1957, Bunin's wife, Vera Muromtseva-Bunina, confessed to a friend: "The feelings of the Englishman in 'The Brothers' are autobiographical." A. Baboreko, "Poeziia i pravda Bunina," *Pod"em,* no. 1 (1980): 136.

59. *Zolar's Encyclopedia of Omens, Signs and Superstitions* (New York: Prentice Hall, 1989), 321.

60. In the aforementioned letter to Baboreko, Muromtseva-Bunina wrote: "We spent half a month on Ceylon. Bunin almost got sick there. He could not bear to see the rickshaw drivers with their lips bloodied by betel." Baboreko, *I. A. Bunin. Materialy,* 164.

CHAPTER TWO

1. As quoted in E. Chirikov, "Pri svete zdravogo smysli," *Sovremennyi mir,* no. 2 (1916): 89.

2. I. Popov, "I. A. Bunin i narodnichestvo," *Stolichnaia molva,* 29 October 1912, 3.

3. E. Koltonovskaia, "Intelligent i derevnia," *Kriticheskie etiudy* (St. Petersburg, 1912), vol. 1, 274.

4. See Bunin's diary excerpt, written on 14 May 1911, in M. Grin, *Ustami Buninykh* (Frankfurt/Main: Posev, 1977) 105.

5. N. P., "Nashi besedy. U I.A. Bunina," *Odesskii listok*, 1 March 1912, 3.

6. A. Baboreko, "I. A. Bunin na Kapri (Po neopublikovannym materialam)," in *V bol'shoi sem'e* (Smolensk: Smolenskoe Knizhnoe Izdatel'stvo, 1960), 251.

7. K-skii, "O novoi povesti I. A Bunina," *Odesskii listok*, 12 March 1910, 3, as quoted in A. Ninov, "K avtobiografii I. Bunina," *Novyi mir*, no. 10 (1965): 224.

8. For all the debate on *The Village* during Bunin's life and since, only a handful of critics discerned that the work was more than social exposé and that it was the dynamic of ego and rebirth that drove the work. For instance, lost in the critical din were more perceptive comments that Bunin was focusing on the Slavic id, or that he was indicting Russia as a (regressed) "kingdom of Hottentots and gorillas," as an "Asia in which people walk on all fours"; or that his village was the most recent in a series of "historical ruins . . . peopled by ghosts and entering the great circle of devastation and death." See E. Koltonovskaia, "Ivan Bunin. 'Derevnia,'" *Vestnik Evropy*, no. 2 (1911): 396; L. Voitlovskii, "Ivan Bunin. K 25-tiletnemu iubileiu," *Kievskaia mysl'*, 30 October 1912, 2; and Gor'kii, *Ivan Vol'nov*, (Moscow, 1952), 17:324.

9. I. Bunin, *Derevnia*, in *Sobranie sochinenii v deviati tomakh* (Moscow: Khudozhestvennaia Literatura, 1965), 3:13. Subsequent references to *The Village* in this chapter are to page numbers from this edition and volume.

10. A. Amfiteaterov, "Literaturnye vpechatleniia. 'Derevnia,'" *Sovremennik*, no. 2 (1911): 287.

11. In the citizens of Durnovka, gender boundaries often seemed obscured. A flour merchant has a womanish face and small feet, "plump and repulsive like a housekeeper's" (77), and a peasant woman smokes a pipe, "just like a man" (100).

12. Furthermore, when the narrator of *The Village* depicts an individual peasant face, he takes care to imply the regressed skewedness and animality that rule the person's life. The handyman Yegorka, for instance, has a more convex, puppetlike visage. He has "a wedge-shaped head . . . an indented forehead, a face like a lopsided egg, bulging fisheyes, and white lids with lashes like a calf's." Yegorka's lids seem "to be stretched over the eyes as if there weren't enough skin. If the lad closed his eyes, he'd probably open his mouth, and if he closed his mouth, he'd have to open his eyes wide" (26).

CHAPTER THREE

1. E. Koltonovskaia, "Kto my? Ivan Bunin. Sukhodol," *Rech'*, 14 May 1912, 2.

2. A. Amfiteatrov, "Literaturnye vpechatleniia. 'Derevnia,'" *Sovremennik*, no. 2 (1911): 285.

3. N. Korobka, "Literaturnoe obozrenie. 'Dvorianskie gnezda' v izobrazhenii sovremennoi belletristiki," *Zaprosy zhizni*, no. 21 (1912): 1263–64.

4. P. Grigor'ev, "Ivan Bunin. Sukhodol," *Sovremennik*, no. 3 (1913): 342.

5. V. Muromtseva-Bunina, *Zhizn' Bunina, 1870–1906* (Paris: n.p., 1958), 122.

6. I. A. Bunin, *Sukhodol*, in *Sobranie sochinenii v deviati tomakh* (Moscow: Khudozhestvennaia Literatura, 1965), 3:137. Subsequent references to *Dry Valley* (*Sukhodol*) in this chapter are to vol. 3 and page numbers from this edition.

7. E. Koltonovskaia, "Bunin kak khudozhnik-pisatel'," *Vestnik Evropy*, no. 5 (1914): 338, 339; Korobka, "Literaturnoe obozrenie," 1267.

8. Compare Bunin's remark on the Buddha: "And in his heart, Guatama decided to leave his wife and son, to free himself from the 'silk nets' of the earth, and to escape his home and the world" (9:49).

9. Gleb Struve, for instance, cites Natal'ia for her "romantic loveliness." See G. Struve, "The Art of Ivan Bunin," *Slavonic and East European Review* 2 (1932–33): 427.

10. Compare Molodaia's "angled" head when she is raped by Tikhon in *The Village*.

CHAPTER FOUR

1. See, for instance, Bunin's letter to N. Cheremnov, written on 15 October 1914, as quoted in V. Afanas'ev, "Ot 'Derevni' k 'Gospodinu iz San-Frantsisko' (Proza I. A. Bunina 1910–14 gg.)," *Uchenye zapiski Moskovskogo gosudarstvennogo pedagogicheskogo instituta*, no. 222 (1964): 137. Also see I. Bunin, "Iz predisloviia k frantsuzskomu izdaniiu 'Gospodina iz San-Frantsisko,'" in I. Bunin, *Sobranie sochenii v odinadtsati tomakh*, vol. 1 (Berlin: Petropoulis, 1936), 78.

2. I. Gazer, "Pis'ma L. Andreevna i I. Bunina," *Voprosy literatury*, no. 7 (1969): 192.

3. Ibid.

4. V. Zenzinov, "Ivan Alekseevich Bunin," *Novyi zhurnal*, no. 3 (1942): 303.

5. See B. Mikhailovskii, ed., *Gor'kovskie chteniia, 1958–59* (Moscow: Izdatel'stvo Akademii Nauk, 1961), 67.

6. I. Bunin, "Proiskhodenie moikh rasskazov," *Literatura i zhizn'*, 5 August 1960, 4.

7. Ad. B., "Slovo. Sbornik piatyi," *Letopis'*, no. 1 (1916): 418.

8. I. A. Bunin, *Gospodin iz San-Frantsisko*, in *Sobranie sochinenii v deviati tomakh* (Moscow: Khudozhestvennaia Literatura, 1965), 4:308. Subsequent references in this chapter to Bunin's works are to volume and page number from this edition.

CHAPTER FIVE

1. A. Baboreko, "Iunosheskii roman I. A. Bunina (Po neopublikovannym pis'mam)," *Literaturnyi Smolensk. Al'manakh*, no. 15 (Smolensk: Smolenskoe Knizhnoe Izdatel'stvo, 1956), 285.

2. See Bunin's letter to Pashchenko, written on 13 March 1892, in A. Baboreko, "Pis'ma I.A. Bunina," 315; and on 27 February 1895, in "Neopublikovannye pis'ma I.A. Bunina," *Vesna prishla* (Smolensk, 1959), 228.

3. See Bunin's letter to Pashchenko, written on 13 August 1891, in Baboreko, "Pis'ma I.A. Bunina," 304.

4. I. Bunin, *Mitina liubov'*, in *Sobranie sochinenii v deviati tomakh* (Moscow: Khudozhestvennaia literatura, 1965), 5:219. Subsequent references to *Mitia's Love* in this chapter are to page numbers from this edition and volume.

5. *Othello*, 5.2.383.

CHAPTER SIX

1. V. Afanas'ev, *I.A. Bunin. Ocherk tvorchestva* (Moscow: Prosveshchenie, 1966), 303.

2. A. Chekhov, *Sobranie sochnenii v dvednadtsati tomakh* (Moscow: Khudozhestvennaia Literatura, 1963), 11:511.

3. E. Plevako, "Delo Barteneva," *Sudebnye rechi izvestnykh russkikh iuristov* (Moscow: Izdatel'stvo Iuridicheskoi Literatury, 1956), 325–46.

4. See Bez podpisi, "Smert' ubiitsy Marii Visnovskoi," and "Sud'ba ubitsy Visnovskoi," *Vozrozhdenie*, 15 December 1932, 3, and 21 December 1932, 3.

5. Two Bunin scholars, James Woodward and Julian Connolly, have shed light on the Buddhist mythos of *The Elagin Affair*. For instance, Woodward claims that Elagin and Sosnovskaia are "exceptional natures," but he calls them "degenerates," in the primary meaning of this word. That is, Elagin and Sosnovskaia willfully defy "their ancestral qualities"—the chain of their family and social backgrounds—and attempt liberation through love. It is through love, Woodward contends, that both Elagin and Sosnovskaia attain enlightenment and transcend the limits imposed by personality, physical existence, and death.

More correctly, Connolly theorizes that Sosnovskaia and Elagin do love life and its pleasures but that they also yearn to break free of self and desire. More judiciously than Woodward, perhaps, Connolly leaves open the question of Sosnovskaia's fate—her salvation or damnation—though he, like Woodward, interprets Elagin's indifference at the tale's end as evidence of Nirvana.

Although Woodward and Connolly correctly relate *The Elagin Affair* to the Buddhist mythos in Bunin's works, there is insufficient evidence for them to interpret the couple as enlightened. As will be shown, *both* Elagin and Sosnovskaia remain shackled to self and fail to achieve the Nirvana they desire. See J. Woodward, "Eros and Nirvana in the Art of Ivan Bunin," *Modern Language Review,* no. 65 (1970): 577, and J. Connolly, "Desire and Renunciation: Buddhist Elements in the Prose of Ivan Bunin," *Canadian-American Slavic Studies,* no. 1 (1981): 18–19.

6. I. A. Bunin, *Delo korneta Elagina,* in *Sobranie sochinenii v deviati tomakh* (Moscow: Khudozhestvennaia literatura, 1965), 5:260. Subsequent references to *The Elagin Affair* in this chapter are to page numbers from this edition and volume.

CHAPTER SEVEN

1. It should be mentioned here that Arsen'ev also draws spiritual strength from aspects of the Judeo-Christian tradition. For instance, he is deeply touched by the tradition of Adam and Abraham, by the prayer of the Church to "honor the memory of all who have died since time began," and by monuments of faith such as ancient cathedrals towering over "decaying towns" and heralding the coming of the "Heavenly City." (I. Bunin, *Zhizn' Arsene'va,* in *Sobranie sochinenii v deviati tomakh* [Moscow: Khudozhestvennaia literatura, 1965], 6:8. Subsequent references to *The Life of Arsen'ev* in this chapter are to page numbers from this edition and volume.) He also professes belief in a Supreme Being, who, he believes, rules the earth with a firm but gentle hand and who is a bearer of justice and retribution, as well as a source of ecstasy and peace.

Such avowals are peripheral, however, to Arsen'ev's worldview. They do not inform his passage to Enlightenment, his youthful struggle with craving and self, his belief in memory and rebirth, and, finally, the chain and regression that he sees as pervading both his present and his many pasts. Indeed, as will be seen, Arsen'ev's Judeo-Christian beliefs actually impede his path to awareness.

2. The adult Arsen'ev also mentions the Acropolis, Balbek, and Thebes, together with the Gothic cathedrals and organs of Europe, and the church of Saint Sophia in Constantinople (35–36).

3. Compare skies that are "stone cloudy," have "large iridescent halos," and are like an "underwater vacillating abyss"; and stars that appear "silvery" and "glitter like azure diamonds" (120).

4. For instance, they wear nailed boots, cone-shaped hats, corduroy knickers and jackets, and gray blouses and caps. They have long and "incredibly lean bodies" and are covered with thick yellow stubble. Necks are

201

like "cracked cork," lips are "corroded to real wounds," fingers are "rigid and black," and feet, hands, and faces are "dried, burnt, and peeled off by the sun" (18, 25, 33).

    5. Compare the child's delight in the "silver ring" and "wandering waves" of Lermontov's verse, as well as in the "steep bank," "the ring affixed to the ceiling," and the "silver" Dnieper, goblets, and heels in Gogol's *The Terrible Vengeance* (38–39, 126). Later on, as a youth, Arsen'ev again is fascinated by images from Gogol's notebook, such as "silvery sand" and a "squeaky windmill flapping its wings" (266).

Index

Aksakov, Sergei, attempt to recapture his past by, 155
Aldanov, Marc, 18
Alekseev, Georgy, 6
Alenka (*Mitia's Love*) as Mitia's ruin, 122–24
anatman (no-self) doctrine, 7
anitya (impermanence of all things) doctrine, 7
Arsen'ev, Aleksei (*The Life of Arsen'ev*): adolescence of, 166–87; Buddhistic beliefs of, 158, 159; as Bunin's alter ego, 155, 157; in chain, 171, 177; childhood of, 160, 163–66; desire to dominate Lika of, 181, 184; detachment from existence of, 156; dream world in childhood of, 165–66; Elagin (*The Elagin Affair*) compared to, 180; exile of, 158; family estate of, 160–63, 166; love for, 180–87; maturity and peace of, 156; memory interpreted by, 157–58, 159–60; Mitia (*Mitia's Love*) compared to, 173–74, 180; parents of, 161–62, 163, 170, 188; pride of, 168–70; reading of, 171–72; regression recognized by, 158–59, 161; *samsara* for, 164–66, 177, 180, 187; schooling of, 167–69, 175; as seeking enlightenment, 156, 160, 171, 178, 201n.1; sexual longings of, 164, 172–74, 182; as surviving suffering, 158–59; tutoring by Baskakov of, 163–64; wandering for, 176–80, 185, 186–87; writing for, 174–76
Atlantis (*The Gentleman from San Francisco*): crew of, 88–89; destruction of, 100; signs of doom on, 89–90; as symbol, 85–86, 89
"Azra," 110

Bal'mont, Konstantin, translation of *The Life of Buddha* by, 4

Bartenev, Alexander, 127–29
Bibikov, Arsenii Nikolaevich, Vara Paschenko as leaving Bunin to marry, 102
Book of Revelation: Bunin haunted by, 81; to set theme of *The Gentleman from San Francisco*, 82
Buddha. *See* Guatama, Siddartha (Buddha)
Buddhism: Bunin's motifs from, 4, 18–22, 157, 200n.5; Bunin's references to, 6–11; "Four Noble Truths" of, 8; sources for Bunin of, 4–6; *Sutta-Nipata* discourses on, 4–5
Bunin, Ivan: abstraction not accepted by, 194n.21; affair with Vivara Vladimirovna Pashchenko of, 102–3; aging for, 196n.51; as Buddhist disciple, 3–32, 189, 191–92n.3; at Capri, 79–80; death for, 18; ego of, 196–97n.55; enacting rather than living life for, 127–54; enlightenment from past for, 16–18; "estate" fiction of, 54–78, 156; exile from Russia and emigration to France of, 3, 102, 155, 191n.3; goal of, 78; happiness for, 196n.50; identification of author with protagonist for, 155–88; key beliefs from Buddhism of, 6–7, 157; key concepts from Buddhism of, 7–9; kinship with natives of, 195n.34; labels of, 3; marriage of, 103; Nobel Prize for Literature to, 3; past as refuge for, 10–15, 155–56; pessimism about Russian gentry of, 53, 54–55, 160–61, 188; rebirth in youth for, 102–26; "reborn" quality in art of, 196n.52; Saint Francis as hero of, 83; seen as regressive, 193–94n.20; space, time, and form for, 194n.24; transcendence of literary tags of, 189–90; travels of, 5, 80, 193n.12, 197n.60; views on ego and enlightenment of, 79–101; views on

Index

village and peasants of, 33–53, 162, 201n.5; "village" literature and, 33–34; vision of new society of, 79; wish for long life of, 15. Works: "Anonymous Notes," 11; "Autobiographical Note," 3; "The Book of My Life," 8, 11, 17; "The Brothers," 18, 19, 22–32, 80–81; "The Call," 80; "City of the King of Kings,"192n.7; "The Compatriot," 21; "The Dreams of Chang," 21, 194n.26; *Dry Valley*, 3, 11, 54–78, 129–31, 163, 164; *The Elagin Affair*, 3, 19, 127–54, 200n.5; "Gautami," 18–20; *The Gentleman from San Francisco*, 3, 9, 79–101; "The Goddess of Reason," 12; *The Liberation of Tolstoy*, 5, 10, 17–19, 193n.19; *The Life of Arsen'ev*, 3, 155–88, 189; *Mitia's Love*, 3, 102–26, 128; "Night," 10, 16–20, 195n.34; "The Night of Renunciation," 20, 21; "On the Night Sea," 18; "The Rose of Jericho," 11; "The Scarabs," 12–13, 16; *Shadow of a Bird,* 80; "Silence," 190, 195n.46; "Small World Landowners," 80; "The Son," 19; "The Unhurried Spring," 13–14; *The Village,* 3, 33–53, 56, 75, 163, 198n.8; "The Waters Are Many," 14–15

Capri: Bunin's visits to, 79–80; funeral parade on, 98; Gentleman's dashed hopes on (*The Gentleman from San Francisco*), 93–97
Ceylon islanders in "The Brothers": bodily decay of, 27; culpability for their sins of, 26–27
chain: attempts to escape bondage to, 64; breaking free of, 8; as Bunin's chief obstacle, 10; characters succumbing to, 32, 153; Gautama's view of existence as subject to, 7, 21; keepers of, 24–25; regression of captives of, 22, 165; as salvific, 11–12; set in motion by *karma,* 8; symbols of, 68, 84, 100; twelve links in, 193n.19
Connolly, Julian, 200–201n.5
counsel for the defense (*The Elagin Affair*): method of, 132; as narrator's ally, 131

De Musset, Alfred, 144–45
Devil: image in *The Gentleman from San Francisco* of, 100; monk Iushka (*Dry Valley*) as, 70, 72; owl seen by Mitia (*Mitia's Love*) as, 115
dharma (sacred law), Bunin's admiration of, 6
Dmitrievich, Nikolai (Grandfather Petr, *Dry Valley*), as Bunin's grandfather, 55
Dmitrievna, Ol'ga (partial model for Aunt Tonia, *Dry Valley*), as Bunin's great aunt, 55

Eden, 13–14
Eightfold Path of Right, 9
Elagin (*The Elagin Affair*): arrangement of death scene by, 138–39, 153; Arsen'ev's father (*The Life of Arsen'ev*) compared to, 161; background of, 140; body of, 133–34; confession of, 133, 138, 141; defense of, 133; desire to leave Sosnovskaia of, 149; hallmarks of regression in, 133–34, 139, 148, 150, 153; *karma* of, 141, 152; letter of, 148; Mitia (*Mitia's Love*) compared to, 140, 146, 148, 149; narrator as "defender" of, 131; past of, 139–42; reaction to love of, 140; return to Sosnovskaia of, 150; sexual maturation of, 140–41; signs of change in, 148–49; testimonies of, 129, 146; town's view of, 132, 150–51; uninvolvement with trial of, 138; as wolf, 137, 139
Englishman in "The Brothers": as autobiographical, 197n.58; ego of, 21–32; as keeper of chain, 24–25; on Path of Return, 25; potential for *Nirvana* of, 24, 25–26; retreat from life of, 26; as succumbing to *samsara* and chain, 32
enlightenment. *See Nirvana* (enlightenment)
Esenin, Sergei, views of sin of, 4
estate fiction, Bunin and, 54–78, 160
Europeans of Ceylon in "The Brothers," 25–27

Fa-Hien, *A Record of Buddhistic Kingdoms,* 4

Gautami, Princess, move to *Nirvana* of, 20
Gentleman from San Francisco: attempt to regain control by, 95–96; body of, 86, 93, 96; call to enlightenment of, 90, 92–93, 97; compared to Tikhan Krasov, 82, 86;

Index

death of, 96–98; as doomed, 83; flirtations of, 88; as model of modern man, 82–83, 91, 94; sailing to rebirth of, 86; wisdom quest of, 83–84

Georgy (*The Life of Arsen'ev*): arrest and exile of, 170; return to estate of, 171

Gervas'ka (*Dry Valley*): body of, 70; encounter with Grandfather Petr of, 68; hatred for humankind of, 164; threat to Arkadii of, 69

Gor'kii, Maksim: attempt to recapture his past by, 155; Buddha viewed as too passive and idle for salvation by, 192–93n.8; letter to Bunin of, 81

Guatama, Siddartha (Buddha): background of, 6–7, 20; citations in "The Brothers" of, 24; death at age eighty of, 7; guidelines for seekers of truth from, 15, 83; realities as in flux for, 7; warnings about earthly love by, 29, 88, 105

Gunther, Konrad, 81

Ich-Erzählung, 56, 129

Iushka (*Dry Valley*): rape of Natal'ia by, 70, 75; ruin of clan by, 70

Kamenka Farm (*The Life of Arsen'ev*), 161–63

Karataev, Platon, 37

karma (past deeds resulting in present state of individuals): Bunin's belief in, 7–8; capitulation to bad, 21; cyclic nature of, 8; family, 107, 141, 152, 159, 180; form in rebirth determined by one's, 8; Krasov history (*The Village*) steeped in bad, 34, 38; unconscious victims of, 60, 68

Katia (*Mitia's Love*): abducted to past, 108–9; as acceding to family *karma*, 107; demand for her freedom of, 105, 106; doomed love of, 106–7; as heroine, 104, 105; letters from, 116, 124; love of the theater of, 106; Mitia's creation of idealized, 109, 111, 114; Mitia's obsession with, 119–22; move toward regression and death of, 107–8, 120; passage into abstraction of, 116; rejection of Mitia by, 124–25; samsaric loop evoked by, 106, 110, 111; Sosnovskaia (*The Elagin Affair*) compared to, 142–43

khanavada (flashes), existence as, 14

Khrushchev, Arkadii (*Dry Valley*): Arsen'ev's father (*The Life of Arsen'ev*) compared to, 161–62; as unconscious victim of *karma*, 68

Khrushchev, Aunt Tonia (*Dry Valley*): as nun, 72, 74; regression and pain of, 71–72, 76; relationship of Iushka and, 70, 72; relationship of Voitkevich and, 71; romantic love as driving force of, 71

Khrushchev, Uncle Petr (*Dry Valley*): body of, 69; death of, 69, 76; love of Natal'ia for, 72–74, 76; as model of gentry, 69; as unconscious victim of *karma*, 68

Khrushchev siblings (*Dry Valley*): adolescent voice of, 60–62, 64; adult voice of, 62–63; amends for wrongs made by, 62; child voice of, 58–60, 163; desire for enlightenment of, 57–59, 61, 77; narrator in *The Elagin Affair* compared to, 129; peasants brought into clan by, 62; search of past by, 56–63, 76–77

Kirillich, Grandfather Petr (*Dry Valley*): Arsen'ev's father (*The Life of Arsen'ev*) compared to, 161; attempt to regain control by, 67; death of, 67–68; as despotic tyrant, 66; diminished estate of, 65–66; regression and decline of, 66

Krasinski, Zygmunt, 144, 145

Krasov, Kuz'ma (*The Village*): circuitry of *samsara* for, 48; disintegration of, 44, 48, 51; as dreamer, 34–35; as failed writer, 47; tutoring by Balashkin of, 46, 163; unfulfillment of enlightenment for, 45–46

Krasov, Tikhon (*The Village*): as archetypal modern man of ego, 36–37; background of, 35; beliefs of, 35–36; circuitry of *samsara* for, 43–44; comparison of Gentleman from San Francisco to, 82, 86; disintegration of, 43, 51; enlightenment frustrated for, 36–37, 40, 42–43; as entrepreneur, 34; introspection about material gain of, 36; journey to past of, 37–39; look to the future and to Orthodoxy of, 39; rape of Molodaia (Youngbride) by, 40–41; return to the present of, 39–40; surroundings of, 41–42; treatment of women by, 40–41

Index

Kuznetsova, Galina, diary entries about Bunin of, 6, 15

Lika (*The Life of Arsen'ev*): animosity between Arsen'ev and, 184; Arsen'ev left by, 187; Arsen'ev's desire for dominance of, 181, 184; body of, 181, 185; lack of intimacy with Arsen'ev of, 182–83; regression of, 180; threat of, 183, 186; wandering of, 185

Mann, Thomas, 81

Mara (Tempter and Lord of Passion and Pleasure), 7, 19; renunciation of, 20; vows of characters to, 29

memory: of ancient and medieval culture, 12–13; Bunin's past born of, 10–12, 156; of family and clan, 11–12, 57–58, 64; misuse of, 73, 75, 103; of primordial existence, 13–14; as releasing creative "female" in Bunin, 15; transforming magic of, 16–17

Mercurius of Smolensk, 60, 64

Mitia (*Mitia's Love*): Arsen'ev (*The Life of Arsen'ev*) compared to, 173–74, 180; attendants to chain surrounding, 122–24; body of, 105, 123, 124; death of, 125; doomed love of, 106–7; Elagin (*The Elagin Affair*) compared to, 146, 148, 149; entry to rebirth of, 120, 122; fantasy world of, 109–11, 116; journey to past of, 112–14, 123; Katia as projection of his mind for, 105, 114; missed occasions for enlightenment of, 103, 114, 119, 123; as model of breed of men, 103; move toward death and rebirth of, 116, 121, 124, 126; nature for, 113–14, 117; obsession with Katia of, 119–22; as Othello, 106, 108, 110; pitfalls of romantic love ignored by, 105, 113, 126; as protector of Katia, 106, 112; realization of change in Katia by, 107–9; samsaric family of, 119, 125; visit to country home of, 110–12; warnings to, 109–10

"modern" music and theater, 50

Mohammed as reborn for, 20

Muromtseva-Bunina, Vera (wife of Bunin): Bunin's mind described by, 194n.21; description of Bunin's aunt Varvara by, 55; diary entry of, 5–6; marriage to Bunin of, 103

Naples, decay in (*The Gentleman from San Francisco*), 91–92

narrator, role of: in "The Brothers," 22–24, 26–28; in *Dry Valley*. See Khrushchev siblings (*Dry Valley*); in *The Elagin Affair*, 128–33, 135–42, 146, 150–51, 153; in *The Gentleman from San Francisco*, 82, 85, 89, 92, 94, 100; in *The Life of Arsen'ev*, 155, 158; in *Mitia's Love*, 106; in *The Village*, 34–36, 48–50

Natal'ia (*Dry Valley*): body of, 61, 63, 64, 74, 76; bondage to chain of, 64; exile of, 72, 73; as guide, 58, 63, 64–65; misuse of memories of, 73, 75; as nun, 74; passing of Russian gentry told through, 56; rape of, 70, 75; return from exile of, 74–76; romantic love as driving force of, 71–74, 76

Nikolaevich, Aleksei (Arkadii, *Dry Valley*), as Bunin's father, 55

Nikolaevich, Nikolai (Uncle Petr, *Dry Valley*), as Bunin's uncle, 55

Nikolaevna, Varvara (partial model for Aunt Tonia, as Bunin's aunt, 55

Nirvana (enlightenment): Buddhist teachings about, 9; Bunin's theories about, 19; Bunin's visions of, 13–15; failure of most of Bunin's characters to attain, 21, 45, 57, 73, 86, 95, 144, 153, 156; potential of Englishman ("The Brothers") for, 24, 25–26; pretenders to, 128; Tolstoi's ideas on, 5

noblemen, Russian. See Russian gentry

Parasha (*Mitia's Love*), 114–16

Pashchenko, Varvara Vladimirovna, as Bunin's first love, 102–3

passengers to Capri, missed enlightenment of (*The Gentleman from San Francisco*), 98–100

paticca-samuppada (chain of causation). See chain

peasants: Bunin's view of, 33–34, 162, 201n.5; regression of, 34, 49–50, 53, 61, 162, 198n.12; similarities for Bunin of noblemen and, 55

Petrovna, Nastasia (*The Village*), 40

Index

prosecuting attorney (*The Elagin Affair*): irrelevant charges of, 141–42; method of, 137–38

Proust, Marcel, adult "I" to recreate early years by, 155

Pusheshnikov, Nikolai (Bunin's nephew), Bunin's joy in life described to, 15

Put' Vozrata (Path of Return): Bunin's use of, 11–13; characters blocked on, 42; defined, 10; Englishman ("The Brothers") on, 25; geniuses and saints who traveled, 20; Gentleman and family (*The Gentleman from San Francisco*) on, 93; Khrushchev siblings (*Dry Valley*) on, 58; Mitia (*Mitia's Love*) on, 112; psychic bonds with people encountered along, 16

Put' Vystupleniia (Path of Egression), 10, 19; abandoning, 156; Bunin on, 196–97n.55; characters' struggles along, 105; European masters of Ceylon on, 22; geniuses and saints who traveled, 20

readers as jurors in *The Elagin Affair*, 131, 132, 146

rebirth: animals in, 49, 61, 90; Bunin viewed as entering, 194n.20; Bunin's acceptance of Buddhist idea of, 11, 157; characters' regressions toward, 47, 49–50, 62, 74, 86, 111, 116, 125, 143, 149, 162–63; Englishman's ("The Brothers") view of, 26; *karma* as determining one's form in, 8; physical and spiritual movement into, 120; positive, 157, 159

regression: Bunin seen as victim of, 193–94n.20; of captives of chain, 22, 162; gentry viewed by Bunin as victims of, 55, 60–61, 161, 162; peasants viewed by Bunin as victims of, 34, 49–50, 53, 61, 162, 198n.12; royalty as victims of, 87; signs of, 123, 133; transcending, 156, 157–59

rickshaw driver in "The Brothers": bad *karma* of, 28, 29–30; death of, 31; dilemma of father and, 28–30; fate of, juxtaposed to Englishman's, 26; liberation of, 30–31; loss of bridge of, 29–30; march to *samsara* of, 28

Rostovtsev (*The Life of Arsen'ev*): Arsen'ev repelled by, 168; compared to other characters, 169

Russian gentry: Bunin's pessimism about, 53, 54–55, 160–61, 188; *samsara* of, 170; similarities for Bunin of peasants and, 55; social and economic change following Emancipation for, 54; as victims of regression, 55, 60–61, 161, 162

samsara (circular return to existence): arcs, circles, links, and spheres as images of, 23, 43, 52, 84, 90, 93, 95, 115, 143; characters on verge of, 23, 85, 174; defined, 7; entry into, 30, 32, 153, 165, 170; *karma* as binding humans to, 8; menace of, 160, 185; passage of Katia (*Mitia's Love*) to, 108; rickshaw driver's ("The Brothers") march to, 28; of Russian gentry, 170; as salvific, 11–12; wedding (*The Village*) symbolic of, 51–52; World War I as bringing Russia to brink of, 79

samouchka (self-taught person), 46

sobornost, Bunin's belief in, 15–16

Solomon as reborn for, 20

Solov'ev, Vladimir, Buddhist beliefs of, 4

Son'ka (*Mitia's Love*), tormenting of Mitia by, 118–19

Sosnovskaia (*The Elagin Affair*): autopsy results for, 136; as corpse, 133–36; desire for death of, 143, 145–47, 149–50; differences between Elagin and, 142; ego of, 142, 147, 152; fate of, 200–201n.5; flaws of, 136; hedonism of, 151; journal of, 143–45, 148, 151; Katia (*Mitia's Love*) compared to, 142–43; melding of bondage and liberation in, 134; murder by Elagin of, 132–33, 151, 153; past of, 142–46; posthumous voice in notes left by, 135–36; regression of, 143, 150; roleplaying death by, 152; suspension between lives of, 136

Struve, Gleb, 22

suffering: cause of, 8; cessation of, 9; Noble Truth of, 8; path that leads to cessation of, 9; survivor of, 158–59

summary text, *The Life of Arsen'ev* as, 155

Todestanz (dance of death), 147–48

Tolstoi, Aleksi: attempt to recapture his past by, 155; gentry chronicles of, 54

207

Index

Tolstoi, Leo: attempt to recapture his past by, 155; Buddhistic thought of, 5, 193n.9, 195n.35; existential horror in works of, 96; letter from Bunin about ego to, 197n.55; as modern saint to Bunin, 20, 197n.56; peasants in works of, 162
Ton'ka (*The Life of Arsen'ev*), 174

"village" literature, Bunin and, 33–34

village, Russian debate over lot of, 33
villagers of Durnovka (*The Village*), 48–52
Visnovska, Maria, 127–29

Woodward, James, 200–201n.5

Zaitsev, Boris, 6
Zotov, rebellion against Buddhist teachings of, 21, 193n.18